The American Churches in World War I

THE
AMERICAN CHURCHES
IN
WORLD WAR I

John F. Piper, Jr.

OHIO UNIVERSITY PRESS
ATHENS, OHIO
LONDON

Library of Congress Cataloging in Publication Data

Piper, John F., 1936–
  The American churches in World War I.

  Bibliography: p.
  Includes index.
  1. World War, 1914–1918—Religious aspects. I. Title.
D639.R4P57   1985   940.4'78   85-4864
ISBN 0-8214-0801-1

55,757

To my beloved wife and children

Margaret Rose
John and Kelly

Table of Contents

Acknowledgments

The publication of this book gives me the opportunity to thank the many people who have advised, encouraged, and supported me during the years of research and writing. Their gifts have been immense. I have offered them private expressions of my gratitude and rejoice that I may now offer them public ones as well.

My study of the role of the American churches in World War I began during my graduate work at Duke University, under the careful direction of Richard L. Watson, Jr., of the Department of History, and Waldo Beach of the Department of Religion. Since then I have sought and received advice and counsel from them and from a number of students of the Church in America, including H. Shelton Smith and Stuart C. Henry of Duke; Edwin S. Gaustad of the University of California, Riverside; Robert T. Handy of Union Theological Seminary, New York; James H. Smylie of Union Theological Seminary, Virginia; Robert Trisco of Catholic University of America; William R. Hutchison of Harvard University; and Martin E. Marty of the University of Chicago. I offer a special word of thanks to Professor Marty who read an early draft of my manuscript, made many suggestions for its improvement, and then added personal words of encouragement.

Colleagues and deans at Mount Holyoke and Lycoming colleges have been very supportive. I have been privileged to work in departments with congenial colleagues who have broad academic and intellectual interests. I recall with affection J. Paul Williams of Mount Holyoke and Loring B. Priest of Lycoming, both deceased, who guided me in my early teaching career and made many suggestions for my research. I also thank Robert F. Berkey, Tadanori Yamashita, Robert H. Ewing, Robert H. Larson, and Richard J. Morris. My research received support from Dean Meribeth Cameron and two Faculty Grants from Mount Holyoke, and from Deans James Jose and Shirley Van Marter and two Faculty Development Grants and a sabbatical from Lycoming.

This book would not have been possible without the cooperation and interest of the many librarians and archivists who have generously permitted me to use their facilities and the manuscript collections in their care. I thank Emerson Ford, Librarian of Duke University; Robert F. Beach, Librarian of Union Theological Seminary, New York; Kenneth S. Gapp, Librarian, James S. Irvine, Assistant, and Marsha Tuttle, Archivist, of the Speer Library of Princeton Theological Seminary; Mary J. Carpenter, Archivist of the Case Memorial Library of The Hartford Seminary Foundation; M. Dorothy Woodruff, Research Librarian of the Board of Missions of The Methodist Church, New York; Victor Gondos, Jr., Chief, and John Taylor, Archivist, of the Army and Air Corps Branch of the National Archives and Records Service, Washington, D.C.; A. Ray Appelquist, Executive Secretary of The General Commission on Chaplains and Armed Forces Personnel, Washington, D.C.; Robert Trisco, Department of Archives and Manuscripts of Catholic University of America; David C. Mearns, Chief of the Manuscript Division of the Library of Congress; William F. Manning, C.S.P., Rector of St. Paul's College, Washington, D.C.; Bishop Loras T. Lane of the Diocese of Rockford; Wilbur C. Parry, Associate General Secretary for Executive Operations, and Constant H. Jacquet, Jr., Librarian of the Bureau of Research and Survey, of the National Council of the Churches of Christ in the U.S.A., New York; and Susan Beidler, Reference Librarian of Lycoming College. I also thank Eric M. North for permission to use the Papers of Frank Mason North and Margaret B. Speer for permission to quote from the Papers of Robert E. Speer. I am particularly grateful to A.C. Cunninghame, Librarian of the Seeley Historical Library of Cambridge University, England, for the generous treatment I received as a visiting scholar.

A number of persons have shared their time, talents, and friendship during the completion of this project. Reinhold Niebuhr, Samuel McCrea Cavert, Benson Y. Landis, and Eric M. North graciously granted interviews. Julie Hensley, Frances Eakin, Judy Chaplin, June Wagner, and Madlyn Wonderlich added their talents to the preparation of the various drafts of the manuscript. Clement Alexandre, Bob and Thelma Jopling, Philip Johnson, and Tom Rhodes gave encouragement and friendship. My parents and other members of my family have offered constant interest and love. I thank the members of the DuBoistown and Nisbet United Methodist churches for allowing me to borrow time from them, and for their enthusiastic support.

Versions of various parts of this book were first published in several journals. I thank William B. Miller of the *Journal of Presbyterian History*, Eugene B. Gallagher, S.J., of the *Records of the American Catholic Historical Society of Philadelphia*, and Robert P. Scharlemann of the

Journal of the American Academy of Religion, for permission to use some of these materials.

This book is dedicated to those who have formed my closest community. I offer it to them with love.

Introduction

This book is the story of the ministry of the Christian churches of the United States in World War I. It focuses on those religious organizations and churches which worked to create a cooperative and national ministry. It embraces Protestants and Roman Catholics alike.

This story marks three new departures in historical study relating to the Great War. First, attention to religion and the Christian churches introduces a largely neglected element into that study. Historians have written on military and political matters, including the preparedness campaign before the war, the battles during it, and Woodrow Wilson's role at the Versailles Peace Conference and his struggles to win entry to the League of Nations that followed it. They have assessed and reassessed progressivism and have argued that the war transformed but did not kill the search for social change that characterized the pre-war years. They have concluded that the war marks a turning point in American life, but they have reached this conclusion with little reference to religion or the work of the Christian churches.[1]

Second, the study of the Christian churches in the war opens a subject long closed, even for church historians. Most historians of the churches in the era of the Great War have worked around the war itself. They often interpret it as a turning point, not because of what happened during it, but because it seems to separate distinct developments. Some have concentrated on the Protestant Social Gospel in the years before the war and on its decline in the 1920s; others have focused on the variety of relatively independent Catholic social action movements in the pre-war period, and on their centralization under the authority of the Hierarchy after the war. When church historians do refer to the wartime ministry of the churches, they typically rely on information gleaned from two highly outdated sources: Ray Abrams' *Preachers Present Arms* (1933) and Michael Williams' *American Catholics in the War* (1921).[2] Not only were these works written at a time when manuscript collections and memoirs were not yet available, but

1

also they reflect certain religious and cultural biases that strongly influenced their interpretations.

Abrams is the fountainhead of most of the analysis there is of the churches' involvement in the war, a participation he characterized as a surrender of the imperatives of the Gospel or as a sellout. His argument included all Christians, although it was most extensive in its evaluation of Protestants. He maintained that the Protestant churches adopted the views of the government on the war to the point of abandoning a ministry or message distinctly their own. The war revealed to him three basic social facts about the relation of the churches to society. First, it showed an intimate connection between institutionalized religion and capitalism, and since religion was a vital part of the acquisitive society, "it was inevitable that, during the war, the churches should have conformed in their judgment and should have been controlled by the will of the vested interests." Second, it made clear a close bond between Christianity and nationalism. The actions of the churches proved "what has long been suspected, that Christianity has been becoming increasingly nationalistic, while the god of Nationalism is more powerful in his ability to command obedience and devotion unto death than is Jehovah himself." Third, it disclosed that the clergy were not, by virtue of their calling, protected against war psychology and the mob mind. Christians, "while claiming to be motivated by the teachings of Jesus and superior humanitarian desires, did not in general demonstrate any different code of ethics or type of behavior from the unbelievers."[3]

He substantiated these arguments with considerable evidence, and no one can justify the ease and enthusiasm with which some clergymen damned the Hun or draped themselves in the American flag. However, he approached his subject with a strong pacifist bias and a determination to show that not only the war but all those who shared in it were morally wrong. The singlemindedness of his work helped him establish his point and also led him to misunderstand much of the churches' ministry. The discovery of acculturation in the churches' wartime work was like finding sand on a beach. Christians, clergy and laity alike, who regarded national norms and wartime goals as their own could be expected to support them, perhaps even extravagantly. Long ago de Tocqueville recognized that Christianity and civil liberty, religion and democracy, were intertwined in America in a unique way that could easily lead to confusion of values. What Abrams missed was the work and testimony of those who accepted the war but who agonized over their roles, who sought a national wartime ministry that would lift up the Gospel, and who also gradually came to realize that the struggle had changed life for them and their institutions. More correctly, he did not so much miss them (for some of them are mentioned in his account) as he failed to grasp the significance of what they said and did. His argument led him to debunk and discredit and prevented him from understanding those Protestants who found themselves in search of new forms of ministry for a society at war.

Michael Williams wove together narrative and documents in an unrelieved paean to Catholic response to the war. His account fell just short of hagiography and was largely a celebration of the degree to which the church accommodated itself to the nation and its needs. While he did focus on the theme of loyalty to the nation, he also placed some emphasis on the special nature of the Catholic wartime ministry and on its national scope. Certain factors help explain his treatment, including his participation in the Church's war effort and the uneasy awareness shared by many Catholics that some of their fellow Americans were suspicious of their loyalty at the outset of the conflict. Although his line of vision came from a source different from the one used by Abrams, those lines intersect at the point of general failure to see in the sources the unique national character of the wartime ministries and the much larger and more important significance of the war for the life and ministry of the churches.

The third new departure is the focus on the ecumenical and national character of the wartime ministry of the churches. Abrams and Williams each told part of the story, but Abrams slanted it with his bias and Williams remained within the limited context of his own Church. The distinctive wartime ministry belonged to the Federal Council of the Churches of Christ in America and the National Catholic War Council. The leaders of these groups, including Frank Mason North, Robert E. Speer, and William Adams Brown for the Federal Council, and James Cardinal Gibbons, Father John J. Burke, C.S.P., and Bishop Peter J. Muldoon for the National Council, saw the need for national ministry during the war and also perceived that the ministry needed an ecumenical perspective. The Roman Catholics stressed the national character of their ministry and Protestants the ecumenical nature of theirs, but on occasion the two groups worked together to create a fuller ecumenism. In the process of working to achieve these goals each group realized the war had introduced into American life new factors which required new structures and forms of ministry for the future.

The Federal Council of Churches was the major Protestant form of the ecumenical movement in the World War I era. Founded in 1908, it was an effort to establish church cooperation on more solid ground than earlier federative attempts. Preceding ventures, like the Evangelical Alliance, were decided upon largely by interested individuals whose official ties to denominations were often tenuous. The Federal Council was constituted by the denominations themselves and therefore had access to the very centers of Protestant ecclesiastical power. Its membership included representatives of most of the major bodies—Methodist, Lutheran, Congregational, Baptist, Presbyterian, Episcopal, Reformed, Quaker, Moravian, Mennonite, and other points of view. The only large denominations not holding membership in 1916 were the Southern Baptist Convention, the Evangelical Lutheran Church, General Conference, The Evangelical Lutheran Church, Synodical Conference, the Mennonite Church, and the Unitarian Churches. On the eve of the war the constituents of the Council had a combined total of 103,113 ministers and 17,742,509 communicants, over two-thirds of all Protestants in both categories.[4]

Direct entree to such a substantial percentage of the Protestants was useful but it did not mean that the Council suddenly became the spokesman or the program planner for them. It has not even become this in its modern form as the National Council of Churches. What it did was slowly and surely to articulate a social policy called "The Social Creed of the Churches," and a series of programs that led many of its member churches into new, broader, and more cooperative forms of ministry. By 1916, Frank Mason North, Chairman of its Executive Committee, could affirm that the period of experimentation was over. The Council might need further refinement, but there was no doubt "that the fellowship of great churches in America expresses in some large measure the mind of our common Lord. . . . "[5] The truly great opportunity of the Council and the years of real growth in cooperative Protestantism came during the war. The tasks of the churches in the warring nation were simply too immense for any one denomination; moreover, division in the chaplaincy, in industrial communities, and in dealing with government officials was quickly discovered to be detrimental to any effective ministry. As one historian of the Council said, it emerged from the war "perhaps the most influential organization in American Protestantism, or indeed in the entire American religious scene."[6] The wartime service was coordinated and performed in large part by a specially organized General War-Time Commission of the Churches.

The situation of the Roman Catholic Church at the start of the war was quite different. It was as separated as the Protestants were united. This is true despite the enduring myth, doubtless in large measure a residue of nativism, that the Catholic Church has always been a monolithic structure, firmly united. The American Catholic Church did not even gain canonical legitimacy as an independent unit of the Roman Church until 1908. Prior to that time it was a mission under the primary jurisdiction of the Congregation for the Propagation of the Faith in Rome; after that it had full and equal status with the older European branches of the Church. By wartime it was still a very young national Church.

The Church had, in fact, just come through one of the most remarkable and difficult periods in its history. Many of the immigrants that came to America between 1880 and 1910 were Roman Catholics from southern and eastern Europe. They added greatly to the size of the Church and also to its problems. They established ethnic communities, often as isolated from one another as from the rest of American society. They needed priests who could speak their languages, and they needed programs to help them relate to and learn the ways of their new home. Few of them had the educational backgrounds or the economic resources to enter quickly into the mainstream of American life. The Church worked at meeting some of these specific needs, including support of a labor movement, the Knights of Labor, and of Americanization programs. However, it poured most of its energy in the three decades before the war into the more basic organizational tasks of establishing parishes, dioceses, schools, and other institutions so that its ministry could reach its new members.

The leader of the Church was Cardinal Gibbons of Baltimore, but his national authority, like that of his fellow cardinals, was largely persuasive. The real power to establish plans and carry them out lay with the more than one hundred bishops of the country. They had not met in a Plenary Council since 1884, and their separate programs in no way constituted a national one. In addition to these many spheres of independent power there were a number of social service groups, many run by laymen, loosely organized in the American Federation of Catholic Societies. John Tracy Ellis points out that prior to the war there was no "national clearing house for general Catholic affairs among the churchmen themselves. The only approximation to such, the annual meeting of the archbishops of the country which had been a feature of the life of the American Church since 1890, was entirely inadequate in the present circumstances."[7] Myths to the contrary, a major feature of the Church before the war was its division and lack of a cohesive, national organization. The Church had a social policy, but it lacked a national agency to present that policy or related programs to its people or to the nation at large.

The war was the catalyst that united the Hierarchy. It brought them together for concerted action and led them to develop a national organization. In a post-war national meeting they undertook direction of Catholic social activities in America. As one leading church historian has said, "it was not until after World War I that the Roman Catholic Church in America began to exhibit the full marks of maturity as an indigenous expression of the Roman Catholic faith."[8] The agency of the Hierarchy for its national wartime ministry was the National Catholic War Council.

The varieties of ministry of the Federal Council and the National Council obviously did not constitute the full response of the American churches to World War I. Many denominations and Catholic dioceses had programs of their own or gave a special emphasis to the nationally suggested one. In some cases these groups had their own war commissions, as for example the National War Council of the Methodist Episcopal Church and the National Service Commission of the Congregational Churches. In addition, countless local churches and parishes had war committees. Moreover, there were a large number of agencies not directly church controlled, but certainly church encouraged and supported, not the least of which were the Young Men's Christian Association, the Young Women's Christian Association, and the Knights of Columbus. Some of these groups figure in the present story, but by no means is it inclusive of the full range of their war work. These limitations suggest that this book concentrates on the ministry of the churches which was most fully national and ecumenical.

1. See, for example, Arthur S. Link, ed., *The Impact of World War I* (New York, Evanston, and London: Harper and Row, 1969), p. 6; Charles Hirschfeld, "The Transformation of American Life," in Jack J. Roth, ed., *World War I: A Turning Point in Modern History* (New York: Alfred A. Knopf, 1967), pp. 63–81; Allen F. Davis, "Welfare, Reform and World War I," *American Quarterly* 19 (Fall, 1967), p. 533; and William E. Leuchtenburg, "The New Deal and the Analogue of War," in John Braeman, Robert H. Bremner, and Everett Walters, eds., *Change and Continuity in Twentieth-Century America* (Columbus: Ohio State University Press, 1964), pp. 81-143.

2. Ray H. Abrams, *Preachers Present Arms* (New York: Round Table Press, Inc., 1933. Reprinted with some of his more recent articles by Herald Press, 1969); and Michael Williams, *American Catholics and the War* (New

York: The Macmillan Company, 1921). Recent general studies that adopt Abrams' view include Winthrop S. Hudson, *Religion in America* (New York: Charles Scribner's Sons, 1965); Sydney E. Ahlstrom, *A Religious History of the American People* (New Haven and London: Yale University Press, 1972); and Dorothy Dohen, *Nationalism and American Catholicism* (New York: Sheed and Ward, 1967).

3. Abrams, *Preachers Present Arms*, pp. 244-47.

4. Henry K. Carroll, ed., *Federal Council Year Book* (New York: Missionary Education Movement of the United States and Canada, 1917), pp. 109, 214.

5. Charles S. Macfarland, ed., *The Churches of Christ in Council* ("Library of Christian Cooperation," vol. 1 New York: Missionary Education Movement, 1917), p. 149

6. John A. Hutchison, *We Are Not Divided* (New York: Round Table Press, Inc., 1941), p. 175.

7. John Tracy Ellis, *American Catholicism* (Chicago: The University of Chicago Press, 1956), p. 138.

8. Hudson, *Religion in America*, p. 392.

I

The Churches Face the War

The United States entered the First World War on Good Friday, 1917. The war was already in its third year and had devolved into a desperate and highly debilitating struggle in the trenches. The Allies and the Central Powers were stalemated all along the Western Front, and American entry promised some change in the situation. It definitely assured a new degree of commitment by the American people. Debates over neutrality and preparedness had drawn considerable public attention, but had not united the nation. The incumbent Wilson had won the election of 1916 by promising "continued peace, prosperity, and progressive democracy," and with slogans such as "He kept us out of war." Signs in the first months of 1917 indicated that he could not keep the promises, particularly the peace. Germany renewed unrestricted submarine warfare, the President responded by breaking diplomatic ties with the German government, and the Zimmermann Note became public knowledge. Few people were surprised at the declaration of war in early April. It marked the beginning of total involvement.

Churchmen in general were not different from their fellow citizens, either in their knowledge of the European conflict or in their less than full attention to it, prior to that fateful Good Friday. Church leaders, however, were charged as official spokesmen to interpret their faith and the position of their churches in relation to national affairs. Catholic and Protestant leaders, notably members of the Roman Catholic Hierarchy and of the Federal Council of Churches, had concurred with official government policy favoring neutrality and the maintenance of peace. The leading members of the Hierarchy had supported the policy partly because it kept the United States out of the war and partly because it helped further their hopes for peace in Europe.[1] The Federal Council had worked since 1914 through its Commission on Peace and

8

Arbitration for various arbitration plans. In December, 1916, it changed the name of the group to the Commission on International Justice and Goodwill. This indicated a decreasing commitment to mediation, but did not in any way lessen Council support for the nation's determination to remain at peace.

Awareness of the war and even statements in support of specific policies were not the same as preparedness, and neither the nation nor its citizens were really prepared when war finally came. No large army existed and there were few places to train one, to say nothing of the totally inadequate number of officers. The government spent the summer erecting camps and training officers and the fall developing an army. Soldiers serving under the stars and stripes did not get into the front lines in France in large numbers until the spring of 1918. Moreover, armed intervention provided little if any indication in the early months that it could achieve the goal of world peace more surely than further attempts at arbitration. The goals of the war in terms of specific plans for peace were incomplete when Congress declared war. The League to Enforce Peace had developed a plan for a league of nations, but no one had charted the road from fighting to the establishment of a new world order. When Pope Benedict XV made his dramatic peace proposals in August, 1917, most of the Allied leaders, including Wilson, found themselves unwilling to support the appeal.[2] The relative absence of military preparations and political plans suggested a similar deficiency in the moral and religious areas of life.

The moral rationale of the people as they faced the war is virtually impossible to untangle. At the very least, genuine ambiguity existed in terms of moral values. Numerous political and religious figures were alert to this and knew that the war could well place tremendous strains on many accepted attitudes and values. President Wilson saw this as clearly as anyone else. A few weeks or so before his call for war he shared some of his deepest fears about it with a newspaperman. Entry into the struggle could mean "that we should lose our heads along with the rest and stop weighing right and wrong," and that "the spirit of ruthless brutality will enter into the very fibre of our national life, infecting Congress, the courts, the policeman on the beat, the man in the street."[3] He told Georgia Democrat William C. Adamson that war relaxed legal and moral restraints and was often accompanied by exploitation and profiteering.[4] To Congress he said: "It is a fearful thing to lead this great peaceful people into war, into the most terrible and disastrous of all wars, civilization itself seeming to be in the balance."[5]

Leading churchmen shared his anxiety over the potential destruction of the people's values. Frank Mason North, President of the Federal Council, declared that the time had come for the churches "to consecrate their resources of courage, of sacrifice, of service, of prayer, to the uses of the nation as it steadies itself for the travail and triumph of war." Responsible Christian action required that the churches "will resist with all their power the sordid influences of selfishness and materialism which war so surely fosters and will strive, with the Divine power, to keep pure the springs of motive and to renew from day to day the moral and spiritual vitality of the nation without which the victory of its arms would be the defeat of its ideals."[6] Robert E. Speer, prominent Presbyterian mission executive, said that he had heard people propose that the church should sacrifice certain aspects of its ministry in the interest of single-minded devotion of all of its energies to winning the war. He urged instead that the true response of the Christian and the churches in such a situation was to extend their ministry. "Let us not yield," he counselled, "to any influences that would make us smaller men today than we were five years ago, nor yield to any ideals or pressures that would contract our vision or narrow the field or strangle the forces of our ministry."[7]

Those who were concerned about the ability of the churches to offer religious and moral guidance to the nation and about the direction of their ministry in wartime found answers to their questions in the summer of 1917. The churches faced the war that summer, along with every other organization and institution in America. It was the summer of mobilization. President Wilson initiated it with his call for everyone to grasp the size of the task of fighting a war, and to understand "how many kinds and elements of capacity and service and self-sacrifice it involves."[8]

Protestant mobilization varied tremendously, both in numbers and motivations. Over two hundred separate Protestant denominations existed when the war began. In addition, Protestants ran inter-denominational and non-denominational agencies, like the Federal Council, the Young Men's Christian Association, the Young Women's Christian Association, the American Bible Society, the American Sunday School Union, the Home Missions Council, and the Salvation Army. Many denominations and all of these agencies created wartime committees or commissions. More than forty of them emerged during the war.[9] Numerous as they were, they did not encompass the entire scope of wartime religious organizations created for war work since they did not include the multitude of community and local church war councils. They also did not embrace those individuals, preachers and publicists, who joined the task apart from official or organizational channels.

During that first summer Protestants took three reasonably clear and distinct positions concerning Christian ministry and participation in the war. Some claimed the pacifist position, which repudiated all participation in war, and rejected the war as evil. Others chose the militant position, which celebrated war as a weapon of righteousness, and accepted the war as a holy crusade. Still others argued for a middle ground position, which focused on ministry and sought to develop a wartime ministry without damning either war or the enemy.

Traditional peace churches, like the Society of Friends, the Mennonites, and the Church of the Brethren stood by their heritages, although most of them contained some non-pacifists. They worked for peace and supplied a large proportion of the conscientious objectors. The American Friends' Service Committee and the Fellowship of Reconciliation engaged in reconstruction projects while the war raged. John Haynes Holmes, Rufus Jones, and Norman Thomas were among the most outspoken advocates for pacifism and humane treatment of the men who opposed the war.[10] They represented an important if small minority and their voices were unfortunately occasionally muted by a disagreeing press and the government censor.

Advocates of the militant position were much more vocal than those supportive of pacifism and were almost totally unrestrained, either by Christian conscience or the censor. Described in detail by Abrams, these persons preached a holy war, praised the nation beyond all reason, and sang hymns of hate. The most prominent militants included Billy Sunday, Newell Dwight Hillis, Charles Eaton, and Lyman Abbott.[11] They condemned the German people, recited atrocity stories, and indicted Germany as solely responsible for the war. Evangelist Sunday put his view very plainly: "I tell you it is Bill against Woodrow, Germany against America, Hell against Heaven . . . Either you are loyal or you are not, you are either a patriot or a black-hearted traitor . . . All this talk about not fighting the German people is a lot of bunk. They say that we are fighting for an ideal. Well, if we are we will have to knock down the German people to get it over."[12] Dr. Hillis, pastor of Plymouth Congregational Church of Brooklyn and famous raconteur of atrocities, merged the same attitude with a sophisticated plan. The German people were clearly at fault and something had to be done to prevent a repeat performance. Sterilization offered a massive but fully effective solution. He supported the call for a conference of surgeons "to consider the sterilization of 10,000,000 German soldiers and the segregation of the women, that when this generation of Germans goes, civilized cities, states and races may be rid of this awful cancer that must be cut clean out of the body of society."[13]

Most of the denominations and agencies shared neither the pacifist nor the militant opinion. Their official statements and those of their spokesmen show that a large middle ground existed between the other more or less extreme positions. They held this middle in the name of traditional Christian imperatives such as loving one's enemies, ministering through Word and sacraments to all men in need, sustaining social and economic justice, and maintaining an international outlook. Their primary motivation was to carry on and fulfil the Christian ministry. Of course, that was the stated goal of all Christians concerned for ministry in the war, including pacifists and militants. Those who occupied the middle believed, however, that the advocates of pacifism and militancy were so consumed by their messages that they slighted the full ministry. Without question the strain of wartime psychology placed some limits on the precision with which the churches and their members stated and practiced the imperatives, but many recognized the challenge and engaged in the struggle.

Some denominations interpreted their ministry in terms of service to the men in the armed forces through chaplains and various kinds of camp work at home and abroad, and the names of their national wartime bodies were quite specific: the National Lutheran Commission for Soldiers' and Sailors' Welfare; and the Lutheran Church Board for Army and Navy, U.S.A., of the Synod of Missouri, Ohio, and other States. The majority of the denominations that established wartime organizations adopted a more extensive set of purposes. They were primarily concerned for an adequate chaplaincy, but they also sought to respond to various social dislocations. The Congregational Churches charged its National Service Commission "to give early and diligent attention to the duties arising from the war, especially reenforcing the work of the chaplains and the Y.M.C.A.; aiding churches near training camps to meet the demand upon them; cooperating with the Government Food Administration; promoting patriotic responses to the nation's needs; serving the welfare of the young men being sent to war; and furnishing the churches all possible help in their study of the world problems, in the solution of which they must share."[14] The National War Council of the Methodist Episcopal Church, in addition to recruiting chaplains, worked on ministries in war industries and urban areas unsettled by population shifts. The National Service Commission of the Presbyterian Church in the U.S.A., organized in

May, 1917, created twelve committees to sort out and perform its work. The War Service Commission of the Reformed Church in America, the War Commission of the Episcopal Church, and other denominational bodies shared similar broad interpretations of ministry.

The Young Men's Christian Association was chief among the Protestant agencies that made their primary concern the men under arms. General Secretary John R. Mott telegraphed the President the day of the war declaration offering him the services of his organization. Four days later, again at the instigation of Mott, a Conference on Army Work convened at Garden City, New York. Leaders of the International Committee and of state and local Associations met and resolved to undertake "in a comprehensive and united way, to promote the physical, mental and social and spiritual welfare of the one million and more men of the military and naval forces of the United States . . . ." The Conference further decided to operate a large financial campaign, to work with men in industry, to serve prisoners-of-war and aliens, to promote citizenship studies, and "to strengthen the hands of the Chaplain's Corps and to serve the Churches." The representatives created the National War Work Council as the agency to fulfil these goals.[15]

The Association carried out its program through "Y" Secretaries, some of whom were ordained clergy, but most of whom were not. Their ministry concentrated on social and recreational programs. They did not, unless ordained, deal with the sacramental aspects of their faith. At the outset of the war there were pitifully few chaplains. Mott and others in the Association "regarded the secretaryship as sufficiently broad to include most of the functions of the chaplaincy."[16] Many church leaders vigorously disagreed. The Association was a major arm of Protestant America, but did not represent the churches directly and did not see ministry the same way many of the churches did. In fact, Y.M.C.A. church relations during the war were generally poor.[17] The Association had an important ministry during the war, but the nature of that ministry, far from fulfilling the churches' ministry, helped them see the need for additional organization to provide a fuller ministry.

The Federal Council became the churches cooperating and uniting for that ministry, and it developed by far the most comprehensive Protestant one. Chaplains and their needs came first, for they carried the Word and sacraments to the men under arms. It also authorized its commissions to add to their work ministries related directly to the war and it constituted a new commission to coordinate these ministries and to initiate new ones. The Council raised funds to support this work and issued frequent statements defining it. These statements established the middle ground view of the war. The Council was at the heart of the struggle to hold that ground in the face of arguments from both pacifists and militants.

Early in 1917, Charles S. Macfarland, General Secretary of the Council, sensing that the war might cross the Atlantic, acted to extend cooperative programs and create new ones. Council headquarters was in New York City, but he felt the chaplains' work would be better located in the nations's capital, so he organized the General Committee on Army and Navy Chaplains there. This was the first step taken by the united Protestant churches to prepare for wartime ministry.

Shortly after the declaration of war Macfarland called a special meeting to convene in Washington in May. The invitation went not only to the Council and denominational officials directly involved, but also to a host of Protestant mission and social work agencies with which cooperation would be essential. The purposes of the meeting were: "For prayer and conference; To prepare a suitable message for the hour; To plan and provide for works of mercy; To plan and provide for the moral and religious welfare of the army and navy; to formulate Christian duties relative to conserving the economic, social, moral and spiritual forces of the nation."[18] When the delegates assembled at Calvary Baptist Church on May 8, they constituted the most representative group ever brought together by the Council, and perhaps the most representative group of American Protestants ever to gather.

The Special Meeting and its message were fundamental to the war work of the Council. A number of prominent Protestants, including North, Speer, Mott, James I. Vance, Chairman of the Council Executive Committee, and Henry Churchill King, President of Oberlin College, gave platform addresses that set the tone for the meeting. The delegates were organized into several committees, charged to formulate a united wartime policy and to discuss and define cooperative wartime ministries.

Vance led the delegates in worship. He prayed for a three-fold vision. The vision of the crucified Christ would inspire sacrifice; the vision of the compassionate Christ would lead to ministry to a suffering world; the vision of the revealing Christ would demand humility and penitence. And he prayed for love, "love to him and love to one another, for love for our enemies, that these days of strife may not engender either permanent or temporary hatred, that we may never hate people, but that we may ever hate sin, injustice, unbrotherliness, and ill will . . ."[19] North charged the meeting with its tasks. He called on the churches to maintain in the best possible way the moral and spiritual quality of the nation and its people. "We are here today," he said, "not to stimulate our patriotism, nor to assert our loyalty, but to accept our responsibility, to define our task, and to determine our program."[20] President King reminded the churches that they could not neglect their call to serve men just because they abhorred war. To stand aloof from the opportunities of service presented by the war was itself abhorrent. Aware of the danger that the nation could approximate the error it was fighting and fall prey to militarism and materialism, he warned: "We want no Kaiserdom in America. And if there is to be no Kaiserdom in America, it will be the responsibility of the church above all to make sure that that is so. The church is bound here to bear no uncertain testimony, bound scrupulously to guard our Protestant inheritance of freedom of conscience, freedom of thought, freedom of speech, freedom of investigation."[21]

The delegates received a number of committee reports and adopted the one by the Committee on Message as the wartime policy of the churches. King served as Chairman of this Committee: William Adams Brown, Roosevelt Professor of Systematic Theology at Union Theological Seminary in New York City, wrote the first draft of its report, which he called "a personal confession of faith."[22] The message consisted of two sections: "Our Spirit and Purpose"; "Our Practical Duties."

The initial section carefully juxtaposed the commitment of the churches to Jesus Christ as Lord and their obligation to the nation. It established the basis of the wartime ministry.

> After long patience, and with a solemn sense of responsibility, the government of the United States has been forced to recognize that a state of war exists between this country and Germany, and the President has called upon all the people for their loyal support and their wholehearted allegiance. As American citizens, members of the Christian churches gathered in Federal Council, we are here to pledge both support and allegiance in unstinted measure.
>
> We are Christians as well as citizens. Upon us therefore rests a double responsibility. We owe it to our country to maintain intact and to transmit unimpaired to our descendants our heritage of freedom and democracy. Above and beyond this, we must be loyal to our divine Lord, who gave his life that the world might be redeemed, and whose loving purpose embraces every man and every nation.[23]

The message set forth the Council's version of the war. War was evil; nevertheless, it had come despite every effort to prevent it. Since it had come, the Council was "grateful that the ends to which we are committed are such as we can approve." In words recalling those of Wilson and heavily tinged with the prevailing idealism, the message described the war goals as "freedom" and "the principles of righteousness," and the war as one in which America participated "without haste or passion, not for private or national gain, with no hatred or bitterness against those with whom we contend." Distinguishing between those disciples of Christ who believed in war and those who did not, the message asserted that all were united "in loyalty to our country, and in steadfast and whole-hearted devotion to her service."[24]

But how should the churches express their dual loyalty? In general the message directed them to serve the nation by bringing "all that is done or planned in the nation's name to the test of the mind of Christ."[25] Specifically, they were to pledge themselves to sustain certain ideals and to undertake definite wartime ministries. The dominant themes were penitence, service in the spirit of love, and hope for a final reconciliation. Macfarland called these pledges a "new common creed" for the churches.[26]

> To purge our own hearts clean of arrogance and selfishness;
>
> To steady and inspire the nation;
>
> To keep ever before the eyes of ourselves and of our allies the ends for which we fight;
>
> To hold our own nation true to its professed aims of justice, liberty, and brotherhood;
>
> To testify to our fellow Christians in every land, most of all to those from whom for the time we are estranged, our consciousness of unbroken unity in Christ;
>
> To unite in the fellowship of service multitudes who love their enemies and are ready to join with them in rebuilding the waste places as soon as peace shall come;
>
> To be diligent in works of relief and mercy, not forgetting those ministries to the spirit to which as Christians, we are especially committed;
>
> To keep alive the spirit of prayer, that in these times of strain and sorrow men may be sustained by the consciousness of the presence and power of God:
>
> To hearten those who go to the front, and to comfort their loved ones at home;
>
> To care for the welfare of our young men in the army and navy, that they may be fortified in character and made strong to resist temptation;
>
> To be vigilant against every attempt to arouse the spirit of vengeance and unjust suspicion toward those of foreign birth or sympathies;
>
> To protect the rights of conscience against every attempt to invade them;
>
> To maintain our Christian institutions and activities unimpaired, the

observance of the Lord's Day and the study of the holy Scriptures, that the soul of our nation may be nourished and renewed through the worship and service of Almighty God;

To guard the gains of education, and of social progress and economic freedom, won at so great a cost, and to make full use of the occasion to set them still further forward, even by and through the war;

To keep the open mind and the forward look, that the lessons learned in war may not be forgotten when comes that just and sacred peace for which we pray;

Above all, to call men everywhere to new obedience to the will of our Father God, who in Christ has given himself in supreme self-sacrifice for the redemption of the world, and who invites us to share with him his ministry of reconciliation.[27]

The section of the message titled; "Our Practical Duties," realistically assessed the social disruptions of war and suggested ways to ameliorate them. Men in the armed forces faced novel moral and spiritual problems and the churches should urge ministers of quality and ability to enter the chaplaincy. Liquor and vice sapped the moral and physical strength of men at home. The denominations were called to work for wartime prohibition, and local churches were asked to monitor the sex standards of their communities.[28] War work should not be allowed to detract from effective measures to destroy social blights in the culture. All efforts to promote child welfare and to remove "community conditions that make for defective lives" must be continued. The churches must also sustain the industrial standards established by the Federal Council. They had a clear duty to advocate that the cost of the war be evenly distributed among the different classes in society, for it was nonsense to proclaim democracy to the world if democracy were not an aspect of every sector of the social order at home. Moreover, they should inspire in the people "the determination that the war shall end in nothing less than such a constructive peace as shall be the beginning of a world democracy."[29]

This message spelled out the broad middle ground attitude toward the war better than any other single document published during the conflict. It spoke for those Christians who accepted the war frankly, but who remained primarily concerned to sustain and propagate the basic imperatives of their faith. It reminded them that winning the war at the expense of these imperatives was in reality losing it. It repudiated the crusading spirit and rejected hatred and bitterness as sources of inspiration. It praised the spirit of the pacifists, but argued "that the love of all men which Christ enjoins, demands that we defend

with all the power given us the sacred rights of humanity."[30] It counselled Christians and churches to focus on ministry, not war, and to
search for ways to sustain and extend it. The editor of a Congregational journal declared the meeting "forward-looking" because it was
primarily concerned "that the great things relating to the progress of
the Kingdom of God should suffer no detriment under the shock and
strain of war."[31] The Special Meeting was the second step united Protestants took toward mobilization.

Immediately after it adjourned, the Council communicated the
message to its constituents.[32] A number of the major denominations
held national meetings in the months that followed. These were annual or biennial sessions which happened to fall in this period and
were not special wartime gatherings. The Northern Baptist Convention, meeting in Cleveland, Ohio, May 16 to 22, approved the "initiative action" of the Council in holding the Washington session and
voted to publish a bulletin titled "Emergency War Measures," which
was primarily that portion of the message on "Our Practical Duties."
The General Synod of the Reformed Church in America met in June,
adopted the message in full, and recommended it "to the pastors and
churches for careful consideration." The National Council of the Congregational Churches assembled in October in Columbus, Ohio, and
voted to "approve the work already carried forward by the Federal
Council of Churches for cooperation in Christian work, the success of
which opens the way for further and more intimate unity."[33]

The General Assembly of the Presbyterian Church in the U.S. convened the week of May 17 in Birmingham, Alabama, and decided
"That the message from the special session of the Council being directed to citizens, no action be taken thereon." The Presbyterian
Church in the U.S.A. held its General Assembly the same week in May
as its sister church to the south. The Assembly supported Council
activities in general but made no specific mention of the Washington
meeting or message. It endorsed Council war work at its next annual
meeting.[34]

The reaction of the predominately German denominations varied.
During one of the sessions in Washington the Rev. J.M.G. Darms, a
Vice-President of the Council representing the Reformed Church in
the United States, said that the message would be welcomed by Christian ministers and people of German heritage and that it "will help
them in their own minds, in their own religious thinking, in their own
prayer life, and in their absolute sincere support of the whole proposition, to find what will be a foundation for them!"[35] The representatives

of the General Conference of the Mennonite Church of North America disagreed. This church was a charter member of the Council, but had entertained second thoughts about its membership since 1914. The basic problem was the Council's position on the war. The Mennonite Church was pacifist and found the Council, especially at its Washington meeting, full of the "war spirit."[36] The Mennonite General Conference voted to withdraw from the Council in the fall of 1917, and North could see no way to detain them "if they are moved by the spirit which seems to show itself in their official communication."[37]

Denominational agreement, however important, did not constitute implementation of wartime ministry. That task fell to the Council itself. Since established programs already consumed the time and energy of its staff, a way had to be found to carry out the new programs. The Special Meeting had proposed one when it had recommended: "That the Administrative Committee be empowered to call into counsel an Advisory Committee, if needed, for consideration of emergency matters during the war."[38] Council leaders quickly accepted this general idea but debated for more than a month the kind of committee which would best serve in the situation. One point of view supported the creation of a totally new organization, independent of any existing ones. This proposal failed to gain much support, for it seemed to lead to the duplication of established cooperative procedures. A second plan called for the designation of the Young Men's Christian Association as the official religious war work agency. However, the Association represented individual Christians, primarily laymen, rather than denominations, and did not directly reflect denominational interests. Moreover, President Wilson had already issued General Order No. 57 to the army in late April, informing military leaders that "official recognition is hereby given to the Young Men's Christian Association as a valuable adjunct and asset to the service."[39] Some church officials, concerned about possible church-state conflicts, believed its government assignment restricted the kind of ministry it could perform.

The Administrative Committee resolved the debate by projecting a specifically Council-based organization and authorizing President North "to appoint a War Work Commission of One Hundred upon his assurance, upon consultation, that the cooperation of the constituent bodies and their several agencies would be secured." It also appointed a temporary committee of denominational leaders, under the chairmanship of William Adams Brown, to initiate religious work for the men in the training camps.[40]

These organizational decisions freed Council leaders to channel their energies into establishing the proposed agency. Not everything they did during the summer of 1917 related to it: Charles Stelzle ran the Strengthen America Campaign, a newspaper appeal on behalf of wartime prohibition, and the Council issued a message about food conservation and sent it to all local Protestant churches. Most of their efforts, however, fed directly into the agency. Brown's committee began meetings with denominational officials. It convened for the first time on June 22 in Washington, D.C., with about a dozen persons present. Designated the Inter-Church Committee on War Work, it met frequently during the summer, bringing together executive officers of denominational committees and of the Council who were "appointed for national service in connection with the Army and Navy or other war work."[41]

The Committee readily identified its task. The churches sought to provide for the men in the armed forces a religious environment as normal as possible. One obvious way to do this was to provide adequately trained chaplains, and in the case of training camps in America, to enlist the aid of local churches and ministers near the camps, the latter to serve as voluntary chaplains or camp pastors. The General Committee on Army and Navy Chaplains searched for regular chaplains; the Inter-Church Committee developed a corps of voluntary ones at all the camps which had no regular ones or an inadequate number of them. The draft took place June 5, but the men were not mobilized until September 5. The government needed the summer to train officers and prepare the training camps. The Committee used the time to survey the camp areas, enlist volunteer chaplains, and arrange their assignments. It met the September deadline with considerable success and immediately merged with the larger advisory group which met for the first time that month.

North worked hard to organize the War Work Commission. He did not believe that any of the already organized committees, or even the majority of the thinking Christian men, had an inkling of "the whole task," whereas he was convinced that the new commission, following Council policy, could comprehend it.[42] He and other Council leaders solicited the advice and approval of denominational leaders, especially those directly involved in wartime ministries. When they strongly supported the plan, he turned to the question of leadership. Robert E. Speer, deeply committed to cooperative ministry, agreed to serve as chairman. This new group, renamed the General War-Time Commission of the Churches, met for the first time in September. When it convened, it marked the final step in the mobilization of Protestants united for wartime ministry.

The Roman Catholic Church heeded President Wilson's call for mobilization as rapidly as the Protestant churches and with a similar multitude of responses. Many Catholic leaders, clerical and lay, issued statements reflecting their views and those of their local churches, dioceses or organizations; but the Hierarchy alone possessed the power to speak and act for the whole Church. On April 18 many of the archbishops gathered for their annual meeting at Catholic University of America in Washington. Under the leadership of Cardinal Gibbons they turned their attention to the war and sent President Wilson a public letter of their support. Although not all of them were present to sign the document, a majority affixed their signatures and the Catholic community quickly accepted it as the Church's pledge to the nation.

The archbishops reaffirmed the promises to the nation their predecessors had made at the Third Plenary Council in 1884. They pledged their "most sacred and sincere loyalty and patriotism toward our country, our government, and our flag." They had "prayed that we might be spared the necessity of entering the conflict," but now that the President and Congress had decided, they would work for "the welfare of the whole nation." Echoing Wilson's sentiments they found themselves inspired "neither by hate nor fear," and offered themselves and "all the flock committed to our keeping," to the end that the nation and its cause of liberty might triumph. They concluded by invoking God "to direct and guide our President and our government that out of this trying crisis in our national life may at length come a closer union among all the citizens of America and that an enduring and blessed peace may crown the sacrifices which war inevitably entails."[43] The statement was strongly nationalistic, but lacked any jingoism or appeals to denounce or hate the enemy. The key was loyalty. The archbishops not only promised it, but repeated themselves numerous times by offering to serve, to cooperate, to devote and to demonstrate that "we are all true Americans. . . ." Their underlining doubtless resulted from their awareness of charges by nativists that they had not yet earned a full place in American society.

National attention centered not only on the archbishops' letter, but also on the individual views of the chief prelates among them. Cardinal Gibbons issued his first statement on April 5 before Congress voted for war, and a modified version of it immediately after the declaration. He appealed for support for the President and Congress and said that the primary duty of a citizen was loyalty, "exhibited by an absolute and unreserved obedience to his country's call." Catholic men should step forward and take their places in the ranks. He did not look forward to the agonies of war, he deplored the slaying of men, and he hoped for peace "not later than next Christmas." He added: "I shall pray for peace as fervently as for the success of the arms of the United States." In late May he directed a "Pastoral Letter" to the priests and people of his Baltimore Archdiocese and joined these sentiments to an appeal: "Let it not be said that we were weighed in the balance of patriotism and found wanting."[44]

William Cardinal O'Connell, Archbishop of Boston, and John Cardinal Farley, Archbishop of New York, issued similar statements, each with a personal emphasis. Cardinal O'Connell called for absolute unity behind the President and nation and said that although Americans were of all races, they were also one people. He found remarkable the coincidence of the call for war with Easter and said he saw on Calvary "the strength of sacrifice" that would be needed for the coming struggle. Carefully avoiding any celebration of the war, he decried either "base hate" or "sullen anger" that might dim the glory of the flag. The enemy had to be defeated, but only in ways consonant with justice and honor. Cardinal Farley expressed his opinion in a "Pastoral Letter," sent to his people on April 12. He stressed loyalty less and duty more and the duty was obvious: "We will not shrink from any sacrifice in her behalf. We will render to her what our Catholic Faith and our Catholic teaching sanctions, nay sanctifies. No demand on our American manhood or American citizenship will go unanswered, or will not find us true Americans, true children of our Church, that never was found wanting in any crisis of American history."[45] He celebrated the possibilities of war more than his fellow prelates, largely using Wilsonian language to describe it as the way to vindicate America's cause and to achieve the goals of brotherhood and world peace.

These pronouncements were unequivocal: the Catholic Church had not sought war nor did it celebrate its arrival; it harboured no grudge nor was it motivated by hate; but once the nation officially went to war, it portrayed war as the duty and holy cause of its people and as a possible instrument for the renewal of civilization. Implicit in these pronouncements and explicit in some of their phrases was the traditional Catholic social teaching of the just war. Others were the aggressors, using unjust means for selfish ends. They provoked and finally compelled a non-aggressive state to join the conflict on behalf of high ideals and selfless purposes. In such situations the social teaching led

clearly found the Association's appointment inadequate. They argued that it was a Protestant organization and they lobbied "in the proper quarter" their strong support for recognition of their own group.[50] Fosdick has pled naiveté. He maintained that he discovered only after the vote that the Association's National War Work Council had no Catholic members and that he quickly called a conference with Association representatives, appealing to them to broaden their membership, only to be informed that it would be impossible for them to do so and still retain their widespread support. At a meeting in late June the Commission voted to accept the Knights' offer and admit them to the camps too. Although Fosdick welcomed them and "the strong position which your organization has always taken in regard to the moral hazards surrounding a young man's life," and expressed confidence in their ability to add to the moral tone of the camps, he wrote in his autobiography that the decision was most unfortunate, for it created a stratification which "struck a discordant note in an army whose soldiers were fighting as Americans, not as Catholics, Jews or Protestants."[51] The Commission immediately began receiving angry letters from leaders of numerous fraternal societies, including the Guardians of Liberty and the Masons, demanding access to the camps, and subsequently voted to admit all well established fraternal groups.[52] The organizations that eventually joined the Commission, as distinct from the much larger number that sent representatives into the camps, were the Y.M.C.A., the Y.W.C.A., the K. of C., the Jewish Welfare Board, the War Camp Community Service, the American Library Association, and the Salvation Army.

The Knights were delighted to be invited to serve. Its Board of Directors promptly authorized a War Camp Fund in the amount of a million dollars, a sum multiplied many times through several successful financial campaigns. They eventually operated some 360 recreation centers on the home front manned by over 750 secretaries, and 250 more abroad manned by nearly 1,000 secretaries, and recruited some 27,000 volunteers to assist in their work.[53] However, no sooner had they won from the government their right to serve than they began to see it challenged and qualified from within their Church. The work was commendable, but they neither officially represented the Hierarchy nor fully encompassed Catholic ministry. Specifically, a small handful of Catholic leaders realized that the Knights could not provide the sacramental aspects of the Church's ministry. Recreation and social programs were ministry, but not its heart. The sacraments were central, and they could be provided only by chaplains. Those who saw this need were not so much interested in detracting from the Knights' work as they were committed to the complete ministry through recruiting and equipping an adequate number of chaplains. At the same time they saw a need for some national group other than the Knights to carry it out.

Father Lewis O'Hern, C.S.P., became very much agitated about the chaplain situation in the spring of 1917, and he had every right to be. He directed the Catholic Army and Navy Chaplains' Bureau, and had already experienced difficulties recruiting new chaplains and supplying them. He shared his concerns with Father John Burke, a fellow Paulist, and found him more than a ready listener. If the Hierarchy spoke the mind of the Church, Father Burke represented its vision. When the war began, he was living in New York City and was the editor of *The Catholic World*, a position he had held for almost fifteen years. The work helped him grasp the national character of his Church and its ministry and had led him on several occasions to formulate plans for a national Catholic agency.[54] His specific proposals have been lost, but at least two organizations which reflected his vision emerged during the war. He launched the first of these in late April and early May in response to O'Hern's entreaties. Under the auspices of Cardinal Farley he established the Chaplains' Aid Association. It spread across the nation through many local chapters devoted to making and purchasing the religious supplies and articles the chaplains needed. This was the first step taken under the authority of a member of the Hierarchy along the path leading to the kind of national organization needed to provide adequate wartime ministry.

Father O'Hern was not the only person to seek out Burke. One of his former teachers and a professor of sociology at Catholic University of America, the Rev. Dr. William Kerby journeyed to New York to share his concerns. Kerby was a close friend of Charles P. Neill, a prominent Catholic layman, who had been appointed to the Commission on Training Camp Activities. Neill told Kerby about the deplorable situations the Commission had discovered in camp communities. He feared for the moral and religious life of the soldiers once the camps filled to capacity. Kerby also knew O'Hern and had listened to his problems. These four men met a number of times early in the summer, in both New York and Washington, as an informal discussion group. They became increasingly distressed. Catholic individuals and groups, including the Knights, were stepping forward to help in great numbers, but the result was often chaos, an overlapping of interest, and the neglect of some crucial needs. Moreover, the absence of any official Catholic agency left some government departments at a loss in determining which offers to accept. By June the four concluded that "an attempt must be made for a national meeting of some kind in order to find a national body in the Church that could master the situation, or to create one, if there were none such."[55]

Father Burke took the initiative and presented Cardinal Gibbons with this consensus and perhaps his own long-cultivated plan. The Cardinal gave his cautious approval, subject to the support of the other cardinals, for the convening of a national meeting to discuss the crisis and find ways to resolve it. Burke quickly sought and won the support of the other prelates and on July 17 issued over his signature the call for the meeting.

Invited to this meeting, later described as "the first time in more than 140 years' existence of the Catholic Church in the United States that such a body of clergy and laity had come together for the consideration of problems affecting the Church," were two similar but quite distinct groups of people.[56] Each received its own appeal, although they got the same program outlining the specific concerns for discussion. One appeal went to the archbishops and bishops, soliciting their interest and requesting them to appoint one clergy and one layman as their representatives. The letter described the problems and presented their potential solution in terms of Catholic unity. It emphasized the need to have a truly representative assembly, and its tone throughout was respectful. The other appeal, directed to national Catholic lay societies and the Catholic press, asked them for two representatives each and had a more commanding style. "By the authority and under the direction of their Eminences," Burke began, a meeting has been called to see how best to follow up measures begun to serve Catholic soldiers during the war. In this work "all the Catholics of the country and all Catholic societies must stand as one body doing their best for the common cause."[57] The accompanying program amplified the national character of the crisis, specified some of the potential needs of the soldiers, and raised the following questions: "How shall we best direct our resources? How can each one of us, individually, and as a society unit best help the common cause? What is to be our common Catholic policy in cooperating, in working with non-Catholic bodies for the national welfare, the promotion of which is the common cause of all?"[58]

When Burke called the gathering to order at the Catholic University of America on August 11, he must have been encouraged to see more than 100 delegates representing over 40 dioceses, 28 national Catholic societies, and a substantial portion of the Catholic press. Sixteen other bishops sent words of support.[59] Pleasure soon turned to concern. As delegates presented their views of the needs and their programs, heated exchanges took place. Unity and coordination seemed to be melting away in the face of individual group prerogatives. Whether Burke expected some dissension is unknown, but the speech he made in response to it suggests he did. Michael Williams appropriately called his words "the mind of the Council," and together with the resolutions adopted by this meeting they made specific the need for national action.[60]

The national character of the problems and the obvious and urgent need for unified effort to deal with them formed the central thrust of his argument. He reminded them that Catholic meant unity. Delegates had gathered from distinct dioceses and societies, but they had to see beyond their own boundaries, and "rise above, in thought and action, the parish, the diocese, the particular society to which we belong." Great as the distinct societies may be, "they are all much smaller than Catholic unity." The time had come for parochialism and status seeking to give way to sacrifice and service. Catholics would agree that "it is the Mass that matters—that no Catholic is morally good for any length of time unless he is faithful at Mass, unless he is faithful in the reception of the sacraments," and yet some camps have had no priests available at all. Surely such a need "should move every one of us to work and so to cooperate that they may be able to weather the storm unharmed." The theory and the need of unity were beyond challenge; the practice of unity needed to begin, and the methods should be "sensible, visible, practical, and efficacious." Burke presented an outline for an organization and a list of urgent needs. The organization should be new and special and "harmonize and nationalize the entire work of the Catholic body." It should be founded on diocesan committees, under the authority of the bishops, which would then designate representatives to a national group, a council of the councils, which in turn would have a national executive board. Somehow, it should also "include and give full play to every particular organization." Adopted by the meeting in very much this form it turned out to be cumbersome to create and slow to act.

The comprehensive list of specific needs, later modified by a few additions, served throughout the war as the basis for action. The spiritual care of Catholic soldiers and sailors came first. This meant chaplains, but it also meant, given the vast number of men, extern chaplains. Bishops and religious orders ought to be calculating the number and the cost of such auxiliary chaplains and be ready to supply them. Recreation halls, equipped with the usual games and also with libraries and books on Catholic faith and history were required in the camps and cantonments. Financial campaigns must be mounted on a national rather than a parochial basis. Some were estimating the need at $1 million, but Burke put it at $5 million. No one imagined that the cost would reach the $50 million finally spent. Overseas work should be anticipated and Catholic recreation and rest houses should be built there. A travel bureau for soldiers on the move from one base or town to another might well prevent the young men from falling prey to evil influences. Young women in towns near camps were in special danger and women's groups should look to their interests. A record of Catholic service should be begun at once. The power of the press must be used, as it was being used by other religious groups, to project the Church's point of view. Literature must be published and provided for the men in the armed forces. Vast numbers of prayer books and tracts would be required. Attention would soon fall on dependent families, temporarily bereft of loved ones at war, permanently alone when some of those died. Societies like St. Vincent de Paul already existed, but the need would unfortunately likely be very great. As he drew this catalogue to a close, he challenged the delegates to realize that "the hour for absolute unselfishness, for the perfect manifestation of the Catholic spirit, has come."[61]

The speech cleared the air and placed personal prejudices into proper perspective. Debate continued, but turned to purposeful action. The delegates called upon the Chairman to appoint a committee on resolutions and charged it to make a unanimous report. Burke chose Monsignor M. J. Splaine, Boston; Dr. Kerby; the Rev. P. P. Crane, St. Louis; Mr. John Whalen, New York; Mr. P. H. Callahan, Louisville; Mr. J. Spalding, Atlanta; Dr. J. H. Lyons, Seattle; Mr. Robert Biggs, Baltimore; and Mr. M. J. Slattery, Philadelphia. Six of these represented dioceses: Splaine, Kerby, Crane, Spalding, Lyons and Biggs; and the other three, societies: Whalen for the Federation of Catholic Societies; Callahan for the K. of C. and Slattery for the Catholic Young Men's Association. The delegates adopted their report, in the form of four resolutions, and appointed a committee to organize the National Catholic War Council. The Council represented Burke's second effort to achieve his vision of a national organization. When it met at Catholic University in September, it marked the full mobilization of the Catholic Church. The resolutions constituted the charter of the new agency.

Resolved, That it is the unanimous opinion of this convention that the Catholics of the United States should devote their united energies to promote the spiritual and material welfare of the United States troops during the war, wherever they may be, at home or abroad, and should create a national organization to study, coordinate, unify and put in operation all Catholic activities incidental to the war.

Resolved, That in order to effect this national coordination, a committee of seven be appointed by the chairman of this convention to devise a plan of organizing, throughout the United States, a national body to be called the National Catholic War Council. We suggest that this council be made up of local councils in each diocese, to consist of the ordinary of the diocese and the two delegates to this convention and such others as the ordinary may designate; a National Council, composed of members from all the dioceses in the United States appointed by the ordinaries; and an executive committee of one delegate from each Archdiocese to be appointed by the Archbishop; that this organization be completed and put in operation without further report to this convention and that the executive committee be authorized to collect such funds as may be necessary for the above-mentioned purposes.

Resolved, That this convention most heartily commends the excellent work which the Knights of Columbus have undertaken in cooperating with the Government of the United States in meeting the moral problems which have arisen and will arise out of the war, and it is the opinion of this convention that the Knights of Columbus should be recognized as the representative Catholic body for the special work they have undertaken.

Resolved, That we pledge our best efforts to safeguard the moral and spiritual welfare of our Catholic young men called to the service of our country; that we hold ourselves in readiness to cooperate in this work under the direction of our spiritual leaders the Bishops; that we hereby record our approbation of the admirable regulations made by our War and Navy Departments looking to the safe-guarding of our camps and cantonments and military and naval establishments from the moral dangers incident to camp life; that our most earnest efforts and sincere prayers are with our President and the authorities of our country for the triumph of our cause and complete success in the struggle in which we are engaged.[62]

By September, 1917, Protestants and Catholics had created national and ecumenical organizations to coordinate and carry out their wartime ministries. Each had faced the option of designating a social welfare and recreational group to fulfil its ministry and each had refused. Separately they had concluded that the heart of ministry in war was like the heart of ministry in peace, preaching the Word and celebrating the sacraments. Each had begun with the need to recruit, organize, and equip chaplains and had then moved into other areas. Each had developed about its wartime ministry a point of view that stood between the crusading and pacifist positions and very close to the just war theory. The similarities between the two groups during the period of mobilization are striking, and leaders involved in these developments were aware of them. They worked separately, but with some knowledge of each other's activities, in anticipation of true ecumenical action. Their primary commitments, however, were to their respective groups. Now that they were ready, they turned their full attention to carrying out their wartime ministries.

1. Edward Cuddy, "Pro-Germanism and American Catholicism, 1914–1917," *Catholicism in America*, Philip Gleason, ed., (New York, Evanston, and London: Harper and Row, 1970), p. 93.

2. Daniel M. Smith, *The Great Departure* (New York: John Wiley and Sons, Inc., 1965), pp. 89–90.

3. Quoted in John L. Heaton, comp., *Cobb of "The World"* (New York: E. P. Dutton and Company, 1924), pp. 269–70. See also Jerold S. Auerbach, "Woodrow Wilson's 'Predictions' to Frank Cobb: Words Historians Should Doubt Ever Got Spoken," *The Journal of American History* 54 (December, 1967): 608–17.

4. Quoted in Arthur S. Link, *Wilson: Campaigns for Progressivism and Peace, 1916–1917* (Princeton: Princeton University Press, 1965), pp. 399–400.

5. Woodrow Wilson, *The Public Papers of Woodrow Wilson*, Ray Stannard Baker and William E. Dodd, eds.; 6 vols. (New York: Harper and Row, 1925–27) 5:16.

6. Charles S. Macfarland, ed., *The Churches of Christ in Time of War* (New York: Missionary Education Movement of the United States and Canada, 1917), pp. 8–9.

7. *Ibid.*, p. 105.

8. Wilson, *The Public Papers* 5:22.

9. Margaret Renton, ed., *War-Time Agencies of the Churches: Directory and Handbook* (New York: General War-Time Commission of the Churches, 1919).

10. See Norman Thomas, *The Conscientious Objector in America* (New York: B. W. Huebsch, Inc., 1923).

11. Billy Sunday's wartime sermons were published in many of the religious periodicals of the time. See William G. McLoughlin, Jr., *Billy Sunday Was His Real Name* (Chicago: The University of Chicago Press, 1955), pp. 255–60. See also Newell Dwight Hillis, *German Atrocities* (New York: Fleming H. Revell Company, 1918); Lyman Abbott, *The Twentieth Century Crusade* (New York: The Macmillan Company, 1918); and Granville Hicks, "The Parsons and the War," *The American Mercury* 10 (February, 1927): 129–32.

12. Quoted in Abrams, *Preachers Present Arms*, p. 106.

13. *Ibid.*, p. 109.

14. Quoted in Renton, *War-Time Agencies*, p. 30.

15. Frederick Harris, ed., *Service with Fighting Men* (New York: Association Press, 1922) 2:487–88. For a history of the War Work Council see John R. Mott, *The Young Men's Christian Association* (New York: Association Press, 1947; vol. 4, "The Addresses and Papers of John R. Mott"), pp. 743–906.

16. C. Howard Hopkins, *John R. Mott: 1865-1955* (Grand Rapids: William B. Eerdmans Publishing Company, 1979), p. 525.

17. *Ibid.*, p. 526.

18. Macfarland, *The Churches of Christ in Time of War*, p. iii.

19. *Ibid.*, pp. 20–22.

20. *Ibid.*, pp. 8–9.

21. *Ibid.*, pp. 35–36.

22. William Adams Brown, *A Teacher and His Times* (New York: Charles Scribner's Sons, 1940), p. 228. See also "Our Duty as a Seminary in Time of War," April 18, 1917. Manuscript in the Papers of William Adams Brown, in the library of Union Theological Seminary, New York. Hereafter cited: Brown Papers.

23. Macfarland, *The Churches of Christ in Time of War*, p. 129.

24. *Ibid.*, pp. 130–31.

25. *Ibid.*, p. 130.

26. Charles S. Macfarland, "Spiritual Unity Through Sacrificial Suffering," *The Survey* 39 (December 29, 1917): 358.

27. Macfarland, *The Churches of Christ in Time of War*, p. 133.

28. *Ibid.*, pp. 133–34.

29. *Ibid.*, pp. 135–37.

30. *Ibid.*, p. 130.

31. Howard A. Bridgman, "Putting the Church Behind the Nation," *The Congregationalist and Christian World* 102 (May 17, 1917): 631.

32. *The Duty of the Church in This Hour of National Need* (New York: Federal Council, 1917). A Federal Council Pamphlet.

33. *Annual of the Northern Baptist Convention, 1917* (American Baptist Publication Society, 1917), pp. 300-7 to 300-9; *The Acts and Proceedings of the General Synod of the Reformed Church in America, 1917* (New York: The Board of Publication and Bible-School Work, 1917), p. 147; and *The National Council of the Congregational Churches of the United States, Minutes, 1917* (Boston: Office of the National Council, 1917), p. 59.

34. *Minutes of the General Assembly of the Presbyterian Church in the United States, 1917* (Richmond: Presbyterian Committee of Publication, 1917), pp. 48–49; *Minutes of the General Assembly of the Presbyterian Church in the United States of America, 1918* (Philadelphia: Office of the General Assembly, 1918), p. 118. Several of the largest constituents of the Council did not hold national meetings in 1917. The Methodist Episcopal Church, South, did not meet until May, 1918; and it was not until May, 1920, that the largest denomination, The Methodist Episcopal Church, met in General Conference. The cooperation of

each of these groups in the war work of the Council signified general agreement with its wartime social policy.

35. Quoted in Claudius B. Spencer, "American Protestantism Takes Action As to the War," *Central Christian Advocate*, 30 (May 23, 1917): 5-6.

36. H. A. Bachmann to Charles Macfarland, October 15, 1917, in *Annual Reports of the Federal Council of the Churches of Christ in America, 1917* (New York: Missionary Education Movement, 1917), pp. 16-17.

37. Frank Mason North to Charles Macfarland, December 6, 1917, in the Records of the Federal Council of the Churches of Christ in America, 1894-1952, in the Records of the National Council of the Churches of Christ, Record Group 18, in the Presbyterian Historical Society Philadelphia, Pennsylvania. Hereafter cited: FC Records.

38. *The Federal Council of the Churches of Christ in America: Report of Special Meeting.* Washington, D.C., May 7-9, 1917 (New York: Federal Council of Churches, 1917), p. 20.

39. See Harris, *Service with Fighting Men* 2:488-89.

40. *Annual Reports of the Federal Council, 1917*, p. 109.

41. "Inter-Church Committee on Voluntary Chaplains," *Minutes of the Meetings of the General War-Time Commission of the Churches and Its Executive Committee*, July 3, 1917. FC Records. Hereafter cited: *Commission Minutes.*

42. Frank Mason North to Robert E. Speer, August 6, 1917, in the Papers of Robert E. Speer, in the Speer Library of Princeton Theological Seminary Princeton, New Jersey. Hereafter cited: Speer Papers.

43. J. Cardinal Gibbons to Mr. President, April 18, 1917. Copy in the Archives of the National Catholic War Council, in the library of Catholic University of America, Washington, D.C. Hereafter cited: NCWC Archives. See also "The Hierarchy's Call to Patriotism," *Catholic Mind* 15 (May, 1917): 233-34.

44. John Tracy Ellis, *The Life of James Cardinal Gibbons* (Milwaukee: Bruce Publishing Company, 1952) 2:239-41.

45. John Cardinal Farley to My dear People, April 12, 1917. Copy in NCWC Archives.

46. Williams, *American Catholics and the War*, pp. 88-89. John B. Sheerin, C.S.P., *Never Look Back: The Career and Concerns of John J. Burke* (New York: Paulist Press, 1975), pp. 36-37.

47. Williams, *American Catholics and the War*, p. 91.

48. Maurice Francis Egan and John B. Kennedy, *The Knights of Columbus in Peace and War* (New Haven, Connecticut: The Knights of Columbus, 1920).

49. See Chapters IV, VI, and VII for additional material on the Commission on Training Camp Activities.

50. *The Catholic Soldier In Camp and Out of Camp.* Handbook of the National Catholic War Council of America (Executive Committee, National Catholic War Council, n.d.), pp. 7-8.

51. Raymond B. Fosdick, *Chronicle of a Generation: An Autobiography* (New York: Harper and Brothers, 1958), pp. 149-50.

52. *Minutes of Meetings*, November 24, 1917. World War I Organization Records, Commission on Training Camp Activities, in Record Group 120, in the National Archives, Washington, D.C. Hereafter cited: CTCA Records.

53. Sheerin, *Never Look Back*, p. 37.

54. *Ibid.*, pp. 39–40.

55. The words belong to Dr. Kerby and are quoted in Loretta Lawler, *Full Circle* (Washington: Catholic University of America Press, 1951), p. 8.

56. *Ibid.*, p. 10.

57. Williams, *American Catholics and the War*, p. 108.

58. "Memo Enclosed with the Invitation to the Bishops," July, 1917. Copy in NCWC Archives.

59. These figures were derived from a list of "Delegates," in NCWC Archives. Williams says sixty-eight dioceses were represented, but only forty are named in the list. *American Catholics and the War*, p. 113.

60. *Ibid.*, p. 117.

61. *Ibid.*, p. 117–33.

62. *Ibid.*, pp. 135–36. *Ordinary* as used here means *bishop*.

II

The General War-Time Commission

The General War-Time Commission of the Churches served the Federal Council as its special Commission to fulfil its wartime ministry from September, 1917, until April, 1919. It brought together one hundred Protestant leaders. Chosen by Chairman-designate Robert E. Speer in consultation with Council President North, they represented a variety of constituencies. The largest group came from the denominations associated with the Council and were leaders of their respective denominational wartime committees. Their choice was largely predetermined by their denominational responsibilities. Another large group represented other Council commissions and committees which were already involved in wartime ministry, like the General Committee on Army and Navy Chaplains, or with which regular contact seemed important.

Speer had relatively little control over the choice of individuals who represented these two groups; he had much greater power to select other members. He chose a number of prominent laypersons and pastors, educators, publishers of religious periodicals, and leaders of groups like the Y.M.C.A. and the Y.W.C.A. Those who agreed to serve included the Rev. Harry Emerson Fosdick and the Rev. Henry Sloane Coffin, famous preachers; John M. Glenn and Fred B. Smith, noted laymen; J. Ross Stevenson, President of Princeton Theological Seminary; William Douglas Mackenzie, President of The Hartford Seminary Foundation; Shailer Mathews, former President of the Federal Council and Dean of the University of Chicago Divinity School; William H. P. Faunce, President of Brown University; the Honorable Gifford Pinchot, former Cabinet member; and Governor Carl E. Milliken of Maine. John R. Mott represented the Y.M.C.A. and Mabel Cratty represented the Y.W.C.A.[1] North had suggested that it might be well in addition, "to have the Commission organized with a view to bringing into line even those who are less clear that the Federal Council can effectively work out so large a program."[2] Speer followed this lead and secured the participation of representatives of several such groups, including the largest of the non-Council churches, the Southern Baptist Convention.

Despite the fact that Commission members were chosen these several different ways and that they represented a wide range of special interests, they possessed a uniformly high quality of religious insight and a strong commitment to cooperative Christian action. They also quickly demonstrated a willingness to follow Council wartime policy as developed at the Special Meeting in May. Few if any militant churchmen were on the Commission and none of those who espoused an excessive nationalism. Membership fluctuated somewhat during its life, but not in any way unaccounted for by the dynamic circumstances of war. Disagreements over programs occurred occasionally, but they were resolved without any major disaffections or disruptions.

The Commission held its first meeting on September 20, 1917, in the Federal Council offices in New York City. It decided the issues of leadership and purpose and provided a forum for consultation between denominational wartime leaders. Chairman-designate Speer ran it, with assistance from several Council officers. The Commission elected Speer Chairman and Bishop William Lawrence, the Protestant Episcopal Bishop of Massachusetts, Vice-Chairman. William Adams Brown of Union Seminary agreed to be Secretary. Brown quickly became Speer's right-hand man. One Associate Secretary, Professor Gaylord S. White, and five Assistant Secretaries, including Professor Harold Tryon, Professor Eric North, the Rev. Samuel McCrea Cavert, the Rev. Jasper T. Moses, and the Rev. W. Stuart Cramer, served during its lifespan. Four of these men, White, Tryon, North, and Cavert, were graduates of Union Seminary; and two of them, White and Tryon, were on the faculty. North and Cavert had each served Brown at Union as an Assistant in Systematic Theology. It would be fair to say that the liberal social and theological element of the Seminary greatly influenced Commission work. Brown later described the Seminary's wartime contribution as greatest "for the cause of interdenominational cooperation in connection with the General War-Time Commission of the Churches."[3]

The Commission decided to turn most of its work over to these officers and an Executive Committee. It appointed to that Committee key denominational leaders, several Council officials, and a few prominent churchmen. The full Commission met only four times, whereas the Executive Committee met twice a month, usually in the offices of the Council, with an average of fourteen members and seven secretaries or Council officers present. Speer, Brown, North, and Macfarland were very active; Lawrence was less so. The secretaries were extremely diligent. The other active participants were the Rev. Alfred Williams Anthony of the Home Missions Council; Bishop William F. McDowell of the Methodist Episcopal Church and Chairman of the General Committee on Army and Navy Chaplains; the Rev. William I. Haven of the American Bible Society; the Rev. Albert G. Lawson, Chairman of the Administrative Committee of the Federal Council; the Rev. Worth M. Tippy, Executive Secretary of the Commission on the Church and Social Service; John M. Glenn, Episcopal layman; the Rev. Samuel Z. Batten of the Northern Baptist Convention; and the Rev. Reinhold Niebuhr of the Evangelical Synod of North America. Niebuhr joined the Executive Committee in the summer of 1918.[4]

Speer directed the initial meeting along two lines. First, he called on representatives of various groups to share the wartime ministries they had already developed. Eric North reported that presentations were made "for the Presbyterians, the Protestant Episcopalians, the Baptists, the Methodist Episcopal Churches, the Methodist Church, South, the Congregationalists, the Lutherans, and the African Methodists."[5] In addition, Mott, Cratty, and Haven spoke for their particular groups. The reports highlighted the need to provide ways to coordinate the work so as to avoid duplication and to promote the fullest possible ministry.

The second task Speer set before the Commission was the formulation of a statement of purpose. His personal view was that the primary function of the Commission would be to encourage the various denominational and inter-denominational programs to go in the direction of cooperative ministry. He saw no need to abrogate programs already begun, just in order to build cooperative ones, but chose rather to use the mechanisms already in place as the basis for cooperation and to create new ones as new needs arose. He had a draft statement of purpose ready for the meeting and turned it over to a Committee on Plan, Purpose, and Organization. They reworked his proposal and recommended the following statement of purpose:

1. To coordinate existing and proposed activities and to bring them into intelligent and sympathetic relationship so as to avoid all waste and friction and to promote efficiency.

2. To suggest to the proper agency or agencies any further work called for and not being done.
3. To provide for or perform such work as can best be done in a cooperative way.
4. To furnish a means of common and united experience when such is desired.
5. To provide a body which would be prepared to deal in a spirit of cooperation with any new problems of reconstruction which may grow out of the war.[6]

The Commission adopted this but paused to underline the first two points, defining itself as "a clearing house of information," and "an agency of sympathetic co-ordination."[7]

It used these decisions to interpret itself to its various publics, including member churches. It modified the statement once by adding a clause affirming its temporary, wartime nature, but it never substantially changed it. However, it gradually shifted the emphasis from the purely advisory and coordinative activities to the more executive ones, especially those suggested in points three and four. Experience showed that the original orientation toward advice and counsel often fell short of meeting the immense needs created by the war. Brown pointed out in his report to the Annual Meeting of the Council in December, 1917, that counsel was not enough: "There were things which needed to be done which no one was doing, and for these it was necessary for the Commission to make provision."[8] Discussions increasingly centered on the appropriate degree of executive power useful in specific instances, not whether the exercise of such power was part of the task.

On October 5, the Commission began to function through its Executive Committee. It quickly developed a number of basic working principles that it used throughout its period of service. It maintained a small operating staff. Speer called its members "liaison officers" because of the way they brought together the churches and agencies for exchange of ideas and programs.[9] Moreover, whenever it decided to operate a program, it had at hand not only the denominational war commission offices and personnel, but the offices and staff of the Council. It did not hesitate to call on the latter. For example, it asked Roy B. Guild, Secretary of the Commission on Interchurch Federations, to serve as secretary of one of its important committees, and it chose the Commission on the Church and Social Service to function as its committee for investigating industrial conditions. The formal staff of the Commission was not only small, but also largely voluntary.

It had a cooperative budget. The Council stressed denominational responsibility for cooperative programs and used an apportionment process to set a yearly cash contribution from each participating denomination. The Commission followed the same procedure. This system of financing had never worked well for the Council, and it failed to turn up many contributions for the Commission. Like the Council it had to mix small denominational gifts with large ones from interested individuals in order to balance its budget, but even this combination failed to provide enough money. In its first year it received $20,130 and spent $22,949. Monthly reports showed small but continuous deficits. These total expenditures represented only administrative expenses, since the churches or the Council carried most of the program ones. The churches, for example, underwrote the major costs of the Liberty Church project. The Y.M.C.A. and the Y.W.C.A. had their own completely separate budgets and although they occasionally contributed small amounts to the Commission, they never asked for or received any monies from it.

In the spring and summer of 1918 the Commission launched some new projects and faced the need for substantially larger sums of new money, money that did not appear to be readily available from the traditional sources. At the same time it began to receive suggestions that it sponsor some kind of joint financial campaign, in cooperation with its associated churches. In response it called an elaborate and very well attended conference of denominational war work agencies for June 5. Speer presided. Estimated costs for war work including reconstruction needs approached $10,000,000. The Council and the Commission had some basic organizational machinery and could help raise the money, but the kind of major campaign needed would require a larger organization. Speer stressed, however, that the question of organizing a campaign was secondary to the strength and extent of the cooperative spirit necessary to sustain such an effort.[10]

Worth Tippy and other Council officials spoke in favor of a cooperative drive. Tippy told the delegates that the great financial campaigns, like those of the American Red Cross and the Y.M.C.A., had impressed him. Surely the churches could mount a similar program. Several denominational representatives joined the discussion, and a lively debate ensued on the degree of cooperation required. A preliminary vote favored a joint appeal for funds only. As the discussion zeroed in on the various implications of this appeal, several delegates, in particular those of the Presbyterian Church in the U.S.A. and of the Southern Baptist Convention, argued for denominational prerogatives and stressed that the churches would have to take the lead. These delegates proposed to postpone any further action until they could consult with their official bodies.

North, troubled by the apparent failure of the conference to approve the idea of a cooperative campaign, interjected a plea that the delegates at least put themselves on record as individuals that they favored the proposal. Speer immediately came to North's support. He outlined four possible levels of cooperation which had emerged in the discussion. At the first and lowest level each denomination would make its own appeal; at the second level there would be some attempt to standardize the denominational budgets by submitting them to a central committee; at the third level there would be an appeal to the Christian constituency at large, irrespective of denominational lines; and finally, there would be full cooperation and a common administration of funds. Further discussion revealed resistance to the last level, largely because of fear of over-centralization. The conference finally agreed: "That we seriously undertake to make a united appeal for funds to the common Christian constituency, disregarding denominational lines and stating the appeal in maximum terms; that a committee be appointed to prepare a plan for making such an appeal and providing also for the common direction of the work in such measure as may be feasible, this plan to be submitted to this body reassembled at a convenient time, and after approval to be submitted also to the denominational agencies interested."[11]

The proposal for a joint financial campaign received the consideration of a large and representative body of churchmen again in early September. The group confirmed the decision to hold the campaign and then turned its attention to the crucial issue of the degree of cooperation. The choice had narrowed to a united campaign for a common fund, with joint publicity, or a joint publicity campaign and simultaneous campaigns for funds by the various denominations. Both plans included a designated sum for the cooperative agencies, especially for the Commission and its various committees. After a lengthy and involved discussion the representatives voted to support "a united campaign for a common fund."[12] The Commission approved this plan on the condition that at least six denominations, including at least four of the numerically largest, would agree to participate. Commission members believed that the united campaign for a common fund would promote the spirit of unity among the Christian people of the nation as well as raise more money than separate appeals.[13]

Fourteen denominations agreed to participate in the drive. They established a Central Committee, hired the Rev. George O. Tamblyn as their Campaign Director, and designated the effort the Interchurch Emergency Campaign. The end of the war as they were formulating their final plans did not deter them, for they believed that special post-war ministries would be as vast as wartime ones had been. The Central Committee received and approved denominational budgets and set aside $250,000 for cooperative work. It sought to tie existing denominational campaigns together and stressed in a barrage of publicity that they were all part of one large, new Campaign, and that a portion of each denomination's giving went for cooperative work. In addition, the Committee developed a genuinely joint appeal and scheduled eleven large inspirational conferences in eleven of the largest cities. It set the week of February 9-16, 1919, for the Campaign and asked churches to designate the final day Interchurch Sunday. Services on behalf of the drive were scheduled in many cities on this Sunday.[14] The largest one in New York City took place at the Cathedral of St. John the Divine where an overflow audience listened to Secretary of the Navy Josephus Daniels, Episcopal Bishop David H. Greer, Bishop William F. McDowell, and William Adams Brown. Speaking for the Commission Brown said: "The financial aspect of our campaign is the least important feature of it. It is the symbol and pledge of a new spirit, the spirit of practical Christianity, that has learned how to agree even while it differs, and found in a common faith and a common task a bond of union strong enough to unite men of different beliefs and different traditions."[15]

The Interchurch Emergency Campaign succeeded. In the spring of 1919 the Commission received the first quarterly payment of the amount set aside for cooperative work. Money aside, it marked a more important victory of the cooperative spirit. Some churches declined to share in the drive, notably the major southern ones, and some of those which joined it did so only in casual ways. In addition, some of those which were most involved were partly motivated by the efficiency of a large and united effort. These qualifications did not, however, detract from the fact that the united Campaign for a common fund achieved cooperation of a more comprehensive nature than had been accomplished before.

The Commission carried on much of its work in small groups. The leadership realized that bringing responsible denominational executives together for general round table sharing provided only a partial answer to the religious needs of the times. Such sharing often resulted in better informed executives and occasionally even in cooperative programs, but there were too many executives and too many needs to make this approach efficient. The Commission turned to small comittees. Executives with special responsibilities and interests met with others similarly commissioned to study and propose action. The procedure is so commonplace that it seems unworthy of mention. However, denominational individuality was so strong that such interchanges were rare before 1917, and unheard of on the wartime scale. This exchange of opinions of specific problems was particularly novel for those denominations which traditionally had no inter-denominational contacts and those non-denominational groups which had only limited denominational ties. Macfarland, reflecting on the committee procedure, said: "It would be hard to think of any agency or area of service which was overlooked. Thus, by the time the war was well under way an administrative agency was developed which reduced duplication of effort and unified the Protestant bodies, both denominational and interdenominational, to a degree hitherto deemed impossible."[16]

The Commission devoted large amounts of time to formation of committees. It multiplied them at great speed in the early months so that by the end of 1917 it had no fewer than eighteen distinct ones, each with a chairman or convener. Before it closed out its work it created eleven more. These figures exclude many small groups which never achieved formal status. The Executive Committee formed the committees in response to definite needs or proposed programs. Most of them began quite small and grew until they reached a membership of about ten, large enough to make possible genuine representation and intimate enough to give opportunity for discussion and interchange of ideas. Some, like the Joint Committee on Welcoming the Returning Soldiers and Sailors, rivaled the Executive Committee in size. Not all of them operated throughout its life, but a substantial number met regularly until it dissolved.[17]

Speer and his fellow workers utilized several distinct kinds of committees. Standing committees functioned throughout the life of the Commission and maintained a stable membership. Most of them organized at the first meeting or soon thereafter in order to give constant attention to major areas of concern. They included those on Finance, Literature and Publicity, Survey of the Field and Work, Camp Neighborhoods, and the Welfare of Negro Troops. The Commission recognized the General Committee on Army and Navy Chaplains as a standing committee although it continued to serve as a special committee of the Council. Standing committees formed after the initial group concerned Interchurch Buildings; Days of Prayer and Devotional Life; Interchange of Preachers and Speakers between the Churches of America, Great Britain, and France; and Recruiting and Training for the Work of the Churches at Home and Abroad.

Special committees made up a second large category. They focused on specific short-term problems or programs and most of them survived only a few months. The Committee on Interned Aliens operated in the fall of 1917. It ceased to function when the Commission determined that the program for providing religious instruction for interned aliens had achieved approval of the churches and the government and that it was under way. The Committee on a Church Flag worked from the fall of 1917 until the spring of 1918. After considerable negotiation this Committee reached an agreement with the National Catholic War Council to recognize one official Church flag. The Committee on National Prohibition as a War Measure convened in November, 1917, and spent some months drawing up a petition. Sent in May, 1918, to the President and the Congress, the petition called on the government to prevent by law the manufacture, importation, and sale of all kinds of intoxicating beverages. In this instance no agreement of support could be secured from the War Council because of its concern for the availability of sacramental wine. The Committee on the Observance of Memorial Day served for several months in the spring of 1918 and disbanded when it succeeded in having the day set aside for prayer. The Committee on Investigation of Conditions in France organized late in 1917 and met intermittently until the end of the war.

A few special committees opened up wide areas of ministry, requiring more resources than the Commission possessed, and led to the formation of joint committees. The studies the Committee on Industrial Conditions made of life in industrial communities turned up needs already on the agenda of the Home Missions Council. The two groups organized a Joint Committee on War Production Communities in June, 1918, to consider and carry out a united ministry. The special Committee on Health and Moral Conditions led, in July, 1918, to the Joint Committee on Social Hygiene, in this instance with the Commission on the Church and Social Service. Other joint committees included ones on Chaplains, Welcoming Returning Soldiers and Sailors, and War-Time Work in the Local Church and Cooperation with the American Red Cross.

Committees on conference constituted a final type popular with the Commission. They were appointed for many reasons, the two most common of which were to establish new relationships, often with non-Council groups, or to resolve misunderstandings. Conferences of the first kind were held with the War Camp Community Service and with the Faculty of the Training School for Chaplain Candidates. Those of the second type were held on numerous occasions with the Y.M.C.A. Brown reported that these latter conferences "have led to the clearing up of not a few misunderstandings, and to the taking of steps which will in time clear up others."[18] Assistant Secretary Cavert did not dispute this, but later recollected that the churches and the Y.M.C.A. never fully resolved their wartime differences. The Association, "although it leaned heavily on the churches for personnel and support, was launched without any clear agreement with them. Its War Work Council was set up without consultation with either denominational or interdenominational leaders."[19] The key to the constant negotiations and efforts at reconciliation between the Association and the churches and the main reason disagreement never fell into disruption was "relations of personal friendship and trust between the leaders on both sides," especially to the long and deep relationship between Mott and Speer.[20]

The work of the Commission fell into three periods, each approximately six months long and each concluded by a meeting of its entire membership. The three meetings, one in February, 1918, one in September, 1918, and one in April, 1919, were occasions for reflection, inspiration, and exploration of new ideas, and mark definite stages in its existence as an institution. The first period was a time of initial cooperative action, the second of the extension of the cooperative ministry, and the third of intensive cooperation. These periods coincided with similar ones in the participation of America in the war, not in terms of official government actions, but in relation to the preparation and deployment of troops. American soldiers were almost ready for battle by February, 1918, but did not achieve full effectiveness until mid-summer when they helped initiate an Allied counteroffensive at the Marne Salient. Although the Armistice was signed in November, the bulk of Americans in khaki "somewhere in France" did not return home until the spring of 1919. The meetings were remarkably similar in their emphasis on ministry and ecumenicity.

The full Commission gathered on Washington's Birthday in 1918, at the National Headquarters of the Y.W.C.A. in New York City. It marked the end of the period of initial cooperative action, largely defined by committee formation. Speeches and reports dominated the sessions. Speer called attention to the widespread concern for ministry: "We have zeal here, but most of it has risen from a feeling of pastoral responsibility and has been animated by no sectarian spirit and no desire on the part of the different churches "to run their own show" for their own glory, but to make sure that the Church of Christ is doing its work and making its impact on the lives of the young men and the nation."[21] North asked if the time had come for the churches to face the difficult question of whether their ideal of a Kingdom of God was something off in the sky, or whether it was a new human society on earth. If it were the latter, then they had to re-evaluate their understanding of brotherhood in the light of Christ's vision of brotherhood. The denominations had to determine ". . . whether the inheritance of the splendid but narrow conscience of our fathers necessarily creates for us a proper barrier between ourselves and Christians of another name; whether, after all, the essentials in which we are all one, if they are really set on fire, may not burn the barriers away and give us a common life in the fellowship of our Lord Jesus Christ."[22]

Council General Secretary Macfarland's report revealed some of the organizational strains associated with the development of the Commission. He shared the feelings of some of his co-workers that the Commission frequently usurped their work in the name of wartime ministries. Was the Commission "securing genuine and adequate cooperation," he asked, or was the allegation true that "we are in danger of sealing sectarianism with the approval of the Federal Council and of giving it encouragement and impetus"?[23] His words veiled, but only slightly, the feelings of some Council officials that war work was getting out of hand. New committees were numerous, plans abounded, and new faces in the Council offices exercised new authority; but actual programs were still few and financial support remained uncertain. The Commission made no specific response to these inquiries and they stand simply as testimony that wartime mobilization had a clear impact on Council bureaucracy.

The Commission met six months later, on September 24, at the New York Avenue Presbyterian Church in Washington, D.C. The meeting marked its first anniversary and brought to a close the period of the extension of cooperative ministry. The gathering was the largest ever for a Commission meeting and included half the membership, 8 secretaries of the Council, and about 175 guests. Among the latter were Secretary of the Navy Josephus Daniels; Frederick P. Keppel, Third Assistant Secretary of War; The Rev. Arthur T. Guttery, President of the Free Church Council of England and Wales; Bishop Charles Gore, Bishop of Oxford; other government and church officials; numerous chaplains; and a large delegation from the welfare agencies, especially from the Y.M.C.A. and the Y.W.C.A. President Wilson had been invited, but was unable to attend. General John Pershing sent a special message, as did Chaplain Charles Brent, Chief of Chaplains of the American Expeditionary Force (A.E.F.).

Many of the guests brought greetings and the chairmen of the major committees made reports, but the highlight of the gathering was Brown's summary of the work of the Commission for the year and of its efforts to achieve cooperative ministry. The Commission had an encouraging story to tell, he said, and "The progress appears in our more vivid consciousness of unity, in our closer practical cooperation, in the clearer definition of the function of the different agencies that are working together in the common task, and, above all, in our enlarged program for the future."[24] He listed as outstanding instances of cooperation the efforts on behalf of the soldiers and chaplains, the attempts to sustain the moral tone of the nation at a high level, and the proposals for cooperation in the war production centers. Although he recited a catalogue of deeds, he also shared his personal sense of gratitude and that of the Commission for the new cooperative Christian spirit which had come with the war. "Above all," he concluded, "I want to voice our thanksgiving to Almighty God for the best gift of the year, that ever deepening and more vivid consciousness of a unity of the Spirit that has become to some of us just as certain a fact as the things our eyes can see."[25]

In the spring of 1919 the Commission began to think of disbanding. It had been established as a special wartime agency and the war was over. Moreover, many of the wartime groups which it had been founded to bring into cooperative work were beginning to dissolve. In mid-March, Assistant Secretary Cramer reported that some of the denominational service commissions had concluded their work and that all of them were considering doing so in the near future. The Commission set April 29 as the date for its final meeting.

It did not attract many people. Approximately one-third of the members and a very few guests came. It agreed to disband when the meeting adjourned. It also approved a brief statement containing the record of its service. Considerable discussion revolved around provisions for those portions of its work which were to continue. These were mainly housekeeping matters, but they show how much of its work carried over into the regular work of the Council. The General Committee on Army and Navy Chaplains continued to function as a special committee of the Council. The Committee on the Welfare of Negro Troops also survived with the provision that it return to its pre-war status as the Committee on Negro Churches. The Joint Committee on Social Hygiene merged into the Commission on the Church and Social Service. The Committee on Recruiting and Training for the Work of the Church at Home and Abroad accepted a commission to continue under the Council until it finished its work. All the other committees broke up with the adjournment of the Commission. Most of the final reports stressed the unusual experience in cooperation it had provided. Both Brown and Speer claimed that it had discovered new methods of cooperative action and enlarged Christian unity.

The General War-Time Commission had a useful and fruitful life. Its unique structure, based on Federal Council membership but extending far beyond it to include non-Council churches and many special ministry agencies, enabled it to be a genuine vehicle for cooperative Protestant wartime ministry. Its committee structure and emphasis on consultation reflected a concern for a broad and complete ministry. Time after time, the programs these committees generated successfully used Council strategy of cooperation and unified effort. The Commission worked tirelessly to prevent any narrowing of the ministry in the name of war and tried to avoid the pitfalls of belligerency and hatred which clearly existed. Its success in these efforts derived partly from the guidance of Council wartime policy as defined at the May meeting, and partly from the character and orientation of its leadership.

1. The members of the Commission are listed in Renton, *War-Time Agencies*, pp. 149–51.

2. North to Speer, August 6, 1917, Speer Papers.

3. William Adams Brown, "A Retrospect of Thirty Years, A paper read at the Social Meeting of the Faculty," April 25, 1922, Brown Papers.

4. For data on attendance see *Commission Minutes, passim.*

5. "Working Together in War Time," in the Papers of Eric M. North, in the possession of Eric M. North.

6. *Commission Minutes*, September 20, 1917.

7. *Ibid.*, December 5, 1917.

8. *Annual Reports of the Federal Council, 1917,* p. 227.

9. Committee on the War and the Religious Outlook, *Christian Unity: Its Principles and Possibilities* (New York: Association Press, 1921), p. 31.

10. "Minutes of A Conference of Representatives of Denominational Agencies Engaged in War Work," June 5, 1918, in *Minutes of the Meetings of the Various Committees of the General War-Time Commission of the Churches.* FC Records. Hereafter cited: *Minutes of Committees.*

11. *Ibid.*

12. "Minutes of a Conference of Representatives of Denominational Agencies to Consider a United War-Time Program of the Churches," September 11, 1918, *Minutes of Committees.*

13. *Commission Minutes*, September 24, 1918.

14. See "Minutes of the Joint Meeting of the Central Committee and the Advisory Committee on Publicity of the Interchurch Emergency Campaign," December 18, 1918, *Minutes of Committees*; "The Interchurch Emergency Campaign," *Federal Council Bulletin* 2 (February, 1919): 35–36. Hereafter cited: *FC Bulletin.*

15. Quoted in "Climax of the Interchurch Emergency Campaign Day Observed in New York City Churches," *FC Bulletin* 2 (March, 1919): 47.

16. Charles S. Macfarland, *Christian Unity in the Making* (New York: The Federal Council of the Churches of Christ in America, 1948), p. 137.

17. The collected minutes of these committees number almost two hundred. See *Minutes of Committees.* Much of the work of the committees is described in Chapters VI–IX.

18. *Annual Reports of the Federal Council, 1917*, pp. 239–40.

19. Samuel McCrea Cavert, *The American Churches in the Ecumenical Movement: 1900–1968* (New York: Association Press, 1968), p. 96.

20. *Ibid.*

21. "Opening Address: Meeting of the General War-Time Commission," Speer Papers.

22. "Address of President Frank Mason North," February 22, 1918. Manuscript in the Papers of Frank Mason North, in the possession of Eric M. North.

23. Charles Macfarland to Frank Mason North, February 8, 1918, FC Records. See also "Questions Raised by Dr. Macfarland in His Address at the Meeting of the General War-Time Commission," February 22, 1918. Appended to *Commission Minutes*, February 22, 1918.

24. William Adams Brown, *The Record of a Year*, September, 1918. A General War-Time Commission Pamphlet.

25. *Ibid.*

III

Protestant Leadership

The leaders the Federal Council chose to run its General War-Time Commission were a nationally recognized and ecumenically experienced group. Their tasks were to organize the work, develop programs for cooperative ministry, and interpret wartime policy on ministry. Their ecumenical experience varied, but a number of them had served the Council through its several commissions, and many of them attended the Special Meeting in May and had participated in formulating the outline of the wartime ministry. They organized their work quite rapidly and with little controversy, with the exception of some clashes with Council bureaucrats. They developed programs a little more slowly, but they created quite a number in the relatively short time they had.[1] They also interpreted the Council's view of wartime ministry. Commission records suggest different degrees of self-consciousness among them in this latter task. As might be expected, the officers were the ones who were primarily aware that their words would be regarded by the public as representative of Council views. Yet the ideas of a remarkable number of the wider membership coincided with those views. Such similarity of perspective reflected the unity of mind among ecumenically committed Protestant leadership, more than it represented any school of thought. A serious risk complicated the interpretative task. The Council view of ministry did not agree with what the militants, those taking the one hundred percent American line, or from a different angle the non-cooperating Protestants, those who guarded their individuality, regarded as normative. Risk of public censure accompanied espousal of cooperative ministry. Commission Chairman Robert E. Speer, above all others, accepted the task and faced its risks.

Speer was one of the truly outstanding Christian leaders of his day. He was born in the small Pennsylvania town of Huntingdon two years after the Civil War. His family was profoundly committed to the Christian faith, so much so that he once said: "Our real religious education was at home."[2] "Rob" attended Phillips Academy at Andover, Massachusetts, and Princeton University. He went to college to study law, intending to enter the profession of his father. In his second year visitors to the campus from the Student Volunteer Movement persuaded him to change his plans. After graduation he entered the theological seminary at Princeton in order to prepare fully for a missionary vocation, but he never finished the seminary. In his middle year he left to accept a call to become secretary of the Board of Foreign Missions of the Presbyterian Church in the U.S.A. He remained with the Board for forty-seven years. It is difficult to characterize him and his work fully, for he was so many things to so many people. He served not only his denomination but also student work and the ecumenical movement. He was identified with the Student Volunteer Movement and served as chairman of its Executive Committee for many years. Working on several commissions of the Federal Council, he was chairman of its Commission on Foreign Missions from 1913 to 1915, and president of the Council in the quadrennium from 1920 to 1924. His biographer said of him that he was "a man sent from God," and the brilliance of the light cast by his life gives impressive warrant for the claim.

One of the more challenging assignments of his career was his work with the Commission. He was strongly sympathetic to the nation's efforts in the fall of 1916 and the early months of 1917 to find a way to bring about peace and to keep out of the war. When these failed and President Wilson and Congress made the decision to enter the war, he supported the new policy. However, he was not enthusiastic about taking a leadership role in the churches' war effort. North talked with him several times in July in an attempt to persuade him to chair the proposed wartime commission. He demurred each time, arguing that others like Harry Emerson Fosdick or William Adams Brown were more suited and that his personal wish was to be a "private in the ranks."[3] North was not to be denied. He wrote him and argued that the proffered job was a question of duty. He shared his growing feeling that the times ahead were critical ones for the church as well as for the nation and stressed his apprehension "that unless men like yourself come out into the larger leadership which existing conditions seem to require, and which seem to be planned in the mind of the Master, days of regret, if not disaster, are before the Church."[4]

The argument apparently convinced Speer, for within two weeks he was busily at work selecting members for the Commission and writing letters announcing the organizational meeting. The key to his acceptance probably lay in North's concern for "larger leadership." Many denominations had already established separate war service groups. In addition, warmongering began to appear in a number of pulpits and religious periodicals. "Larger leadership" was needed to bring unity and coherence to a fractured ministry and to raise a voice of moderation and restraint in the message the church spoke to a nation at war. It was also needed if postwar reconstruction plans were to measure up to the Kingdom of God.

Speer already had articulated his position on these points in the context of the Special Meeting. In his speech on "The War and the Nation's Larger Call to World Evangelism," he had urged the denominations to greater cooperation and an enlarged ministry. He had told the delegates that the missionary movement was "an expression in flesh of our conviction that humanity is one."[5] It was through the missionary enterprise that men had seen the great possibilities of interdenominational, international, and interracial service. Now was the time to further extend cooperation on all fronts. However, unity of action was not enough. The churches must also speak out clearly on the issue of internationalism. Too often they had simply sanctioned the existing order without exercising their prophetic imperative to look beyond that order to other possibilities. He believed that nothing should be permitted to limit their policy: "We betray our mission and fail God if we shrink into a nationalistic sect that can conceive only of our own national functions, unless those national functions include for us the whole human brotherhood and the duty of speaking and thinking and living by the law of a world love."[6] He held these views throughout his leadership of the Commission. They were the substance of his intellectual convictions about the relation of the Christian and the church to war and peace, convictions that were tested in a public confrontation and later refined and clarified in a number of articles and books.

The public confrontation came rather unexpectedly. Speer was a popular writer and speaker, much in demand to reflect on the mission of the church in light of the war. He had given many speeches and written several articles in the closing months of 1917 and received little if any critical response.[7] Therefore, when he spoke at a mass meeting held under the auspices of the Intercollegiate Y.M.C.A. of New York City in the gymnasium of Columbia University on February 18, 1918, he had no reason to expect the furor his words would arouse. He had come on behalf of an innocent cause. His task was to interest students in enrolling in a study course sponsored by the Y.M.C.A. on the Christian program of reconstruction, and he was charged to emphasize the religious and democratic elements of that program. He had been warned by the General Secretary of the Intercollegiate Association that the audience would include members of a radical group, evidently so named because of their non-Christian orientation, and he had been advised that he should speak in such a way as to interest and challenge them too.[8]

He organized his address around the title "World Democracy and America's Obligation to Her Neighbors." In the initial part of his presentation he analyzed five main elements in the world problem which had helped precipitate the war and had to be resolved if the future were to be different from the past. These elements were as follows: (1) "the imperfect development of democracy," (2) "the contested claim of nationalism to be above the moral law," (3) "the retarding or the breaking down of the process of social evolution and human progress for the want of adequate agents to carry them forward," (4) "the persistence of race prejudice and suspicion," and (5) "the resistance of national individualism to the spirit of world brotherhood and to common human interests."[9] He illustrated each of these elements with examples from all belligerent nations, including the United States. To make his point on race prejudice, for example, he cited not only German racial attitudes but also American attitudes towards the Japanese and the American Indians. In reference to the fifth element he pointed to American movements in the interest of "pure national individualism," and argued that they could easily destroy the nation's ability to hold onto "universal ideals and the universal spirit."[10] In the second half of his speech he showed how the phases of this problem had their solution in the Christian ideas and spirit as they were expressed in the missionary movement.[11] The main thrust of the entire speech was against those things, including a narrow patriotism, which limited the growth of world-wide democracy and the international spirit, however dear such things were to the hearts of many Americans.

At first it seemed that the speech would go all but unnoticed. It was briefly reported in the New York *Times*, but received no editorial comment.[12] The anticipated reaction from the radicals did not materialize. Then on February 22, the same newspaper published a letter from Henry B. Mitchell, Professor of Mathematics at Columbia University, under the title "Weakening Patriotism." Mitchell had attended the Y.M.C.A. meeting, and he turned out to be a much more dangerous kind of radical than those about whom Speer had been warned. Speer was a man of reputation, reported Mitchell, a man who held important posts in the Presbyterian Board of Foreign Missions and in the General War-Time Commission of the Churches; but his speech at the University was "insidiously corrupting, both to the will and the intelligence, because it breathed throughout the spirit of pacifism and minimized the infamies that Germany had perpetrated." Mitchell continued: "His argument was the stock one of pro-German agitators in this country—that Germany had only done what all other nations had done, or would do if they had the power." He was disturbed because Speer had made no "appeal for aid in the prosecution of the war." Were men such as this, he asked, making similar speeches on behalf of the Y.M.C.A. all over the nation?

This single letter brought a storm of criticism raining down on Speer and the Association. Within two weeks the *Times* printed no fewer than ten letters and three editorials commenting on Mitchell's version of the speech. The authors of most of the letters followed Mitchell in soundly chastising Speer for his pacifism, and denying the right of any man to speak words which might detract from the nation's glory in time of war. The temper of the times was captured by two of the correspondents. The chaplain at Dartmouth College wrote: "The war with Germany is the whole thing now, and none of our other problems will suffer, while we bend every energy to secure the right conclusion. Surely on this point there should be no wavering."[13] More damning publicly was the opinion of Professor Charles Fagnani of Union Theological Seminary. He substantiated the pro-German label Mitchell had pinned on the speech and said he recognized many Germans and those with "Teutonic susceptibilities" at the meeting. He concluded: "The German-American Alliance would have found absolutely nothing to object to in Mr. Speer's address, on the contrary."[14]

The editorial remarks in the *Times* were all pro-Mitchell. The editor accepted without question the accuracy of his reporting and declared that he had performed a patriotic duty which should receive the praise of all sane Americans.[15] The editor added that those accused would likely scold him, but that was a small thing compared to the service he rendered, for pacifism was "no less harmful, no less despicable, when done under Y.M.C.A. auspices than when it is the work of the Kaiser's secret agents."[16] Fletcher S. Brockman, Associate General Secretary of the National War Work Council, quickly responded to the jibes and incriminating remarks of Mitchell and the newspaper with a staunch defense of the Association's purposes. He declared that it was for win-

ning the war and pointed to the many services it was rendering the
nation as proof of its devotion to this goal. He denied that Speer had
made any pacifist utterance, but did not unequivocally approve of his
speech. In fact, Brockman's statement was somewhat less than generous to Speer.[17]

Several days after Mitchell's attack Speer spoke for himself. He said
he was amazed and indignant at the response made to his address.
There never was any uncertainty in his own mind about the rightness
and necessity of the war, and that it should be continued until "everything has been done that can be done by the war to establish an order of
justice in the earth." "I hate war," he continued, "but I believe that
this is a war against war and that it must be waged in order that war
may be destroyed."[18] He explained to the readers of the *Times* that the
speech was not on the war, but on world problems related to it. However, he was not prepared to retract his attitudes toward loyalty and
patriotism despite the attacks made on them. He did not feel it was
necessary for the patriot to affirm the "impeccability" of the nation's
past or the "perfection" of its present. He added that "whoever takes
any other view and requires of the man who would be loyal that he
must deny facts or tolerate in America what he is warring against
elsewhere comes perilously near to the 'insidious disloyalty' of whom
(sic) one of your correspondents speaks." The task before the nation
was "to replace an order of selfishness and wrong and division with an
order of brotherhood and righteousness and unity." He believed that
the war with Germany was only a part of this task.

The editor of the *Times* was far from satisfied with either of these
defenses. He approved of the speed with which the Association denied
pacifism, but wrote that its statement should have contained some
public repudiation of Speer.[19] As for Speer's defense, it simply revealed
the reason for the controversy, for he really was a kind of pacifist.[20]
The editor, recalling his statement that the war was only part of the
problem, argued that this was not the point. There were other problems in the world but the war was the only important one at the moment. To divert attention from it was to risk the label "pacifist." Speer
took the risk and deserved the label.

During the entire controversy the *Times* published only one pro-
Speer letter. It affirmed that the Columbia meeting had been held to
probe the deeper issues of the war, not to arouse patriotism. The militant spirit of the times dictated its anonymity.[21] The mood of the people was so much against utterances which sounded pacifist that the
New York *Evening Post* could seriously propose that every speaker,

whatever his topic, was obligated to state his position on the war as a preface to his remarks. Such a "patriotic grace" would enable speakers to show their patriotism without dwelling on it at length.[22] Speer clipped out a response to this suggestion which the same newspaper published in early March. It was a letter from "True-Blue," who had been accused of being soft on Germany when he failed to make a patriotic appeal at the opening of a speech on "Plumbing." He suggested, perhaps seriously but evidently Speer took it in a different humor, that it should be the rule "that every public speaker and preacher during the war should begin his remarks with the words, 'God Damn the Kaiser,' and that the audience should stand during the repetition of this prayer."[23]

As a result of this extensive publicity Speer received a number of letters from friends and acquaintances, some attacking his point of view and others approving it.[24] Members of the Commission wrote many of the supportive letters. Their attitudes provide an index of the thinking of representative Protestant leaders. The Rev. Henry A. Atkinson, Congregationalist, said: "I have been very much interested in following the attacks that are being made on you through the New York *Times*, and am amazed at this attitude. In my mind it simply indicates one thing, and that is there is a determined effort being made throughout the country to put over a harsh militaristic regime for America . . . You and I and the rest of us are agreed that we must win the war. There is nothing else to be done. But that does not commit us, soul and body, to the military party, junkers and profiteers, who are trying to make the cloak of patriotism long enough to hide their forked tails and cloven hooves."[25] The Rev. Frederick H. Knubel, Lutheran, wrote: "Very, very many thoughtful men stand with you in your patriotism and abiding devotion to the best interests of your country. It would be a strange and weak loyalty and patriotism which could sustain itself only by remaining blind to facts of the past and present. If we cannot stand the truth then there is something false in our present position."[26] The Rev. Henry Sloane Coffin, pastor of the Madison Avenue Presbyterian Church and an Associate Professor of Practical Theology at Union Seminary said: "You have my genuine sympathy, for not a week has passed, I think, without some objection or criticism coming to me, on account of an expression or phrase in prayer or sermon. I would gladly relapse into total silence, if God would make that possible for me. One is misunderstood in the most amazing fashion, and men simply will not look at the situation we face from the Christian point of view."[27]

One letter sent to him reveals very precisely the relation of his position to the point of view of the pacifists. He thought of himself as neither pacifist nor militarist, but believed that the greatest danger to the nation in the long run lay in the militant mentality. His position, therefore, could sound as it did to Mitchell and others, like the position of the pacifists. Pacifist leader Norman Thomas was quick to pick this up.

Christianity suffers by the abject tone apparently adopted by the Y.M.C.A. authorities in expressing their stand and yours. Surely your patriotism is above reproach. Surely it is possible to call upon men and women to repent of their own sins without being accused of apologizing for others. I know you do not at all share the views of some of us with regard to the absolute incompatibility of war and Christianity, but however we may differ on this, it seems to me that we must be united in believing that it is the high function of Christianity to call for a national penitence and a new effort for the kingdom of God. Neither the Y.M.C.A. nor the Church can be true to their mission if they have no other conception of their duty that (sic) that of auxiliaries to the Security League in promoting patriotic ardor. Christianity will lose her distinctive message to the world unless she speaks with a prophetic voice now . . . Your address struck the right note and needs praise and not apology.[28]

Sometime before Speer spoke at Columbia he had written a book setting forth his basic views on the war. Once the crisis passed he was able to devote time to getting this volume ready for publication. He was working on galley proofs of it in April when he wrote to his son that he did not know whether it was substantial enough to win anyone to his perspective. His recent experience exposing his views to the public led him to expect it to be "criticized both by the ultra-militarists and by ultra-pacifists."[29] Another reason for his uncertainty became evident when the book was published in May, for its final chapter, "The World Problem and Christianity," was written on the same outline as his Columbia speech. The volume did not inspire a public uproar and was important primarily as a forthright and extensive statement of his position.

His analysis of the relation of the Christian and the church to the war hinged on the reality of a world already at war. He spurned those who spent their energies decrying the involvement of the United States, as well as those who ignored wartime dilemmas in the name of planning for the postwar peace. He was troubled that his nation had become a partner in the war and he was vitally concerned about projecting plans for peace, but he believed these perspectives were realistic only if they were coupled to a clear commitment to grasp the meaning of the war itself and to carry out a ministry during the war. The Christian should "take Paul's counsel and seek to behave as a citizen in a manner worthy of the Gospel, believing that his present duty is to be a Christian not in some other world but in this one, and that this duty can be done in the highest loyalty both to humanity and to Christ."[30]

Peace was far better than war, but there was no peace. It was all right to think about a future day of peace, but "we shall never bring that other and better day in if we do not do our duty now."[31] He regarded as foolish the argument that the way to stop the war was simply to stop fighting. That kind of behavior would constitute a clear surrender to the militaristic powers of the world. It was ridiculous to think that an aggressor nation would hesitate to attack a pacifist one which possessed valuable land and resources. America's failure to arm for three years did not prevent attacks on her property. The evil which could grow out of abject surrender to a warring nation could be the tyranny of injustice, and in the present case it could have led to a world-wide tyranny. He believed that life in such a world would be intolerable, and if war were the only possible way to prevent the loss of justice and righteousness, then war must be accepted. "There are days in human history," he said in an article written in the fall of 1917, "when war is the lesser evil and when its necessary work must be done."[32] Ten years later in the pacifist era and while he was serving as Moderator of the General Assembly of the Presbyterian Church in the U.S.A., he refused to endorse a statement on behalf of the pacifist position and is reported to have said: "There are occasions in history when criminal nations emerge and these nations must be restrained."[33]

Accepting war did not mean embracing it. He was not a crusader. However, specifying his position is not a simple matter. Historians of World War I have so polarized the participants that fine distinctions continually fall into the crevices they have created. Speer saw all war as evil; but when he judged that a particular engagement was a lesser evil in a given social and political context, he did not hesitate to call it, in relative terms, right. The World War was right when it was understood as a "war in defense of human rights, of weak nations, of innocent and inoffensive peoples, an unselfish war in which the nation seeks absolutely nothing for itself and is willing to spend everything in order that all men, including its enemies, may be free."[34] He turned to this familiar Wilsonian terminology of the defensive war whenever he wrote of the war in a favorable light. Although these words convey the values of the traditional just war theory, he expended very little effort in the task of intellectualizing those values. Convinced that there was a rationale for the war which the Christian could adopt, he devoted himself to delineating acceptable ministries for the individual and the church.

Of the other possible stances the Christian could take, he found those labelled either pacifist or militarist unacceptable. He rejected the pacifist dogma that "in our present state of social and political development all war is in principle wrong," for it was based on an unreal estimate of the world's progress.[35] Christian pacifists repudiated war for other, more specifically religious reasons. One of these was that it was wrong to kill. He quarreled only with the application of this point of view to the present conflict. It was a war against war. The remedy was dreadful, but "if it is the only remedy, the greater wrong is in flinching from its use."[36] A more central reason was that war is "contrary to the teaching and spirit of Jesus."[37] He concurred with this estimate, but added that the real problem arose when another nation started a war and involved the Christian in it. In that case he did not believe that it was required of the Christian that he stand aside and let those who used war for selfish gain win without opposition. The error involved in the total rejection of war on the basis of Jesus' teaching was in seeing Him and His words in terms of love and compassion alone, and not also in terms of justice and truth: "He taught the duty of pity and unselfishness and forgiveness, but He never abrogated or compromised the principles of righteousness. Neither in His example nor in His teaching is there any warrant for the surrender by society of the political order of human life to the power of evil and wrong-doing."[38] The pacifist arguments were relevant to a war of aggression, but they could not be applied to the present primarily defensive conflict. Nevertheless, he did not impugn the integrity or loyalty of those who held such convictions.

The militarist stance did not receive similar approbation. He defined this position as the belief that war in itself was a good thing and even a creative thing.[39] He saw any argument for the war based on national glory or pride, racial superiority, or territorial acquisition as essentially militaristic. Germany was the chief proponent of these views, but they were not absent from the British or American scene, and he did not hesitate to cite examples from all three nations. He may not have perceived the extent to which selfish nationalistic forces dictated his own nation's policies, but he was aware of numerous instances of overt racism and jingoistic nationalism and he quoted many of them. He cited one newspaper that appealed to its readers to help stop the war between the white races and to unite to fight the real enemies, the yellow races, and he noted a pamphlet that enjoined hatred for the German nation and argued that after the war it should be ostracized for a thousand years.[40] Repudiation of such statements at Columbia had turned out to be extremely unpopular. Reaction had not forced a retraction then, nor did it change his mind when he published his views.

The true Christian wartime life style, neither pacifist nor militarist, was a middle way. He was not dogmatic on this point and he had no label for his perspective. He believed Paul's advice was sound. The Christian ministers to others in all circumstances, including war. This ministry should christianize the present situation insofar as possible.

> It bids us be rid of our prejudice and passion, to chant no hymns of hate, to keep our aims and our principles free from selfishness and from any national interest which is not also the interest of all nations, to refrain from doing in retaliation and in war the very things we condemn in others, to avoid Prussianism in our national life in the effort to crush Prussianism, to guard against the moral uncleanness which has characterized past wars as against pestilence, to magnify the great constructive and humane services for which humanity calls in every such time of tragedy, to love and pray for our enemies, to realize that the task set for us is not to be discharged in a year or five years, nor by money and ships and guns, but by life, that it is a war to the death against all that makes war possible.[41]

The terms are from World War I, but the mood is akin to that explored in greater depth by the Christian realists in World War II.[42] Indeed, he signed as a founding sponsor of the realists' journal, *Christianity and Crisis*, in February, 1941.

Among the specific aspects of his version of Christian realism which were like those of his successors were his concern for the humanity of the enemy and his readiness to repent for doing violence to it. He set forth this view many times during the war. One of the clearest and most forthright expressions of it came in the fall of 1917 when he signed *A Call to Prayer* which the Commission issued for use at Thanksgiving. This pamphlet carried a strong note of national penitence and one part of it called for prayer "for all men, for the suffering and the destitute, for our allies and for our enemies, . . . for all mankind and for the coming of its one hope and deliverance in the reign of Jesus Christ our Lord as king of all the earth."[43] The Lutherans felt more deeply than most Protestants in America the errors expounded by irresponsible patriots. The editor of *The Lutheran* praised him and the Commission for "calling attention to the fact that we must not give ourselves so exclusively to confessing other nations' sins; America has a few of her own." National penitence was "a new note in our wartime literature, and we shall watch with interest its effect on those among whom Robert E. Speer is a name to conjure with."[44] In the postwar period he recollected that the theme of repentance encountered resistance during the war. Doubtless referring in part to the Columbia episode, he said: "Any reminder that we had motes or beams in our own eyes, that the hands that held the chalice in the name of God must be clean, . . . was denounced as the seditious talk of a pacifist, forgetting that the battle is in God's hands and that we have Him to deal with as well as the enemy."[45]

Christian ministry was for the church as a whole as well as for individual members. It constituted the one group in American society that could adequately handle the task of bringing social realities into conformity with social ideals. He was careful to preserve an independent role for the church in relation to the state. It was in no sense an appendage of the state and if it should ever assume such a stance it would quickly be reduced to a "nullity."[46] Since the church judged this war to be right, it committed itself to a two-fold task. In the first place, it was called to serve as the moral conscience of the nation and to bear witness to the elemental principles of justice and rightousness. In Pittsburgh in early October, 1917, he defined this responsibility in an address to the Congress on Purpose and Methods of Inter-Church Federations.

> Every influence which Christianity can bring to bear upon America today is necessary to keep us from destroying for ourselves what we are fighting to keep others from destroying for us. As we war against injustice and wrong, are we preserving only justice and right among ourselves? As we fight the spirit of racial self-aggrandizement and ill will, are we cherishing only the spirit of brotherhood and equal judgment toward other nations? Are our own hearts pure of hatred and passion and our hands so clean that we can hold the sword of God? The Christian faith must make us ask these questions. It alone can help us to answer them right.[47]

In the second place, it was called to render unselfish service. This service should be united, as in the Commission, and it should include definite elements, such as providing the young men in the army and

navy with every needed religious ministration. These were no easy
tasks and it was certain that the church would never accomplish them
except "by the power of God living in the Risen Lord."[48] The need of the
world and the capacity of the church to meet it were in the final analysis beyond the power of man. The new life required of men and nations
was available "in one place alone, that is in God in Christ. To believe
this and to try to live in this belief is the highest loyalty."[49]

The practical politician in ecclesiastical or public affairs might pass
over this appeal to the "power of God" as a pious platitude. In doing so
he would miss the essential spirit of Speer, the spirit of a truly evangelical Christian. During the war and in the subsequent peace he never
dealt with small or inconsequential themes, but cast his ideas on a
universal stage. He was a citizen of the United States, but he was
really an internationalist. He was white, but he was really a humanist,
"of one blood" with all humanity. He was a Presbyterian, but he was
really an ecumenist. His vision was a new world order formed by and
infused with Christian ideals: the Kingdom of God.

Speer was not a lonely prophet. Prominent members of the Commission agreed with him, although each had his individual views. The
perspective of William Adams Brown matched Speer's very closely.
Brown was one of the outstanding and most influential theologians of
his day. *Christian Theology in Outline* stood as one of the pathmaking
statements of evangelical liberal theology.[50] As Roosevelt Professor at
Union Seminary he occupied one of the principal theological chairs in
the nation. Born in New York City several months after the end of the
Civil War, "Will" Brown, as he later signed his name, attended Yale
University and Union Seminary. At Union he won a travelling fellowship to study in Europe and chose to do his work in historical studies at
the University of Berlin under Professor Adolf Harnack. Deciding not
to take his Ph.D. there, he returned to America where he joined the
Union faculty. In 1893, he was ordained to the Presbyterian ministry,
and a few years later earned his Ph.D. at Yale. Ordination and a doctor-
ate did not lead him away from Union. At the end of his teaching career
he could look back on forty-four uninterrupted years of service to the
Seminary.

Social problems interested him as much as did theological ones.
Shortly after the turn of the century he participated in the founding of
Union Settlement, a social center on New York's upper East Side. From
1913 to 1915 he served on the Commission of Home Missions of the
Federal Council, and in 1916 he was appointed to the Administrative
Committee. After the war he was chairman of the Department of

Research and Education from 1920 to 1936 and served as co-president of the 1937 Oxford Conference on Church, Community, and State.

Brown thought deeply about the participation in the war of the nation and the church. He helped draft the Council's plan for wartime ministry. His views remained substantially the same throughout the war. He continued to advocate, for example, the need for repentance by all Christians. Those who argued that the needs of the moment precluded time for self-examination and penitence were short-sighted, for repentance alone provided "a foundation on which the new and better world order for which we profess to be fighting can safely be built."[51] The experience of war convinced him that the major problem for the church was not that its message was inadequate, but that its members often failed to live in accord with its demands. "We have heard much of God's love for all mankind, of prayer for the coming of his kingdom, of sin as social as well as an individual fact, of salvation by sacrifice, of complete consecration; but we have seen Christians living narrow and selfish lives and limiting the horizon of their Christian sympathy to those who are personally congenial to them."[52] The church's task was to help individuals witness to their faith.

Individuals constituted only a part of the mission of the church. He saw it as the source of the inner unity of a future world democracy. It was to be hoped that the war would result in a world unity, but such unity would be unstable if mankind at large did not have some principle to bind it together in the way that patriotism bound a nation together. The opportunity of the church in the future lay in its ecumenical character; that is, in its capacity to provide a common tradition, symbol, and leader for all men. Its mission in America was to serve the nation in the light of and in ways compatible with its international ministry, which the war had curtailed but could never destroy.[53]

One of Brown's fellow professors at Union Seminary and a man who had an established reputation as an eminent preacher was Harry Emerson Fosdick. Shortly after America entered the war Fosdick preached a series of sermons on the challenge of the war to Christians and Christianity.[54] He was convinced that the important thing for Christians was the mood in which they approached the war. Some had already capitulated to cynicism. For them bitterness and hatred replaced goodwill and love, and the war was crisis without hope. He understood how such feelings could grow, but he affirmed that there were also reasons for looking upon the war as a challenge. Primary among these was the widespread feeling that Christianity should have prevented it. It was a hopeful sign that men were beginning to understand that Christianity and war were incongruous.[55] Men who once argued that their faith had nothing to do with social questions now grasped the sharp contrast between the spirit of Jesus and the spirit of war.

The extension of this new vision of the faith was a great wartime challenge. Christians were called to share love with all men. Love and force were not always antithetical as some persons, especially some pacifists, believed; however, love could never simply forget itself in the embrace of force so as to sell itself to the cult of hatred. He prayed: "O God, bless Germany! At war with her people, we hate them not at all . . . Our enemies, too are sons of God and brothers for whose sake Christ died. We acknowledge before Thee our part in the world's iniquity that rolls this burden on Thy heart and crucifies the Son of God afresh. We dare not stand in Thy sight and accuse Germany as though she alone were guilty of our international disgrace. We are all guilty."[56]

Christians were called to hold high the goal of peace. He had no fondness for war. It was "the last word in idiocy," and from every standpoint "unchristian—essentially, hideously unchristian." War was simple surgery, the cutting out of evil, and had no positive, creative capacities. Yet Christians were often seduced by the glories of war into thinking that militarism was a positive good. Posing as the "angel of peace," militarism was nothing less than "the most feckless and muddle-headed sham in history."[57]

Christians were called to join their efforts on behalf of peace to an effort on behalf of a federation of the world. Present international relations were based on selfish nationalism, and Fosdick perceived that internationalism on that basis doomed the world to perpetual war. Christians, almost alone among men, possessed a true international mind. Their task was clear: they had to convert the world to genuine internationalism. Finally, Christians were called to examine their faith and renew their devotion to their cause. He affirmed that the biggest problem facing the faithful was division and sectarianism. The challenge of the crisis was for them to unite in order that they might "speak great words about God and the Kingdom."[58]

Fosdick later wrote that the book containing these sentiments on the war was "the only book I ever wrote that I wish had not been written."[59] He said this because he converted to pacifism shortly after the war and thereafter felt any support of war unchristian. It is ironic that there were some churchmen who opposed the basic themes in the book when it was first published for the very reason that they were too pacifistic. Professor Mitchell, the man who led the attack on Speer, also spoke out against Fosdick. Mitchell and several friends, representing the War Commission of the Parish of the Chapel of the Comforter, excoriated him for having advocated love for the Germans. They charged that he was a pacifist who did not see the Christian side of hate. Since the Y.M.C.A. distributed this book, they branded it a pacifist organization. What Mitchell and his friends desired was ". . . that all talk of loving Germany or Germans shall cease, and that Pacifism in any form, and particularly in its more subtle and plausible forms, shall be recognized as support of the German cause and as treason both to this country and to the Cause of Christ."[60]

William H. P. Faunce was one of several college presidents who worked on the Commission. This respected Baptist educator of Brown University did not contribute much to the early life of the Commission but did join fully in its later efforts to study the post-war period. His position on the war had strong affinities with Speer's, and was informed throughout by the international scope and mission of Christianity. Faunce did not hesitate to justify the participation in the war of American Christians. It was a necessary war, fought because it was apparent after two and one-half years of neutrality that to avoid direct involvement was a greater evil than not to avoid it.[61] The main point for the Christian to remember, however, was that war was not a permanent part of his world order. He tolerated it as he tolerated famine, and he spent his main energies awakening his nation and the world to its causes and working to overcome them.

Christianity's answer to the world's problems was Christian goodwill or love. Such love required two specific duties of all Christians during the war. Their first task was to extend the horizon of their patriotism. Narrow, conceited patriotism was not becoming to a man of faith. Some loud orators were appealing to Americans, " 'Don't talk, don't parley, don't think, just win the war,' " as if blind devotion to nationalistic interests was the greatest good.[62] These attitudes inspired hatred of the enemy, whereas the Christian was called to love his enemy, "to love his inner self . . . and by relentless love to make him at last lovable. . . ."[63] He wanted to Christianize patriotism so that the Christian patriot thought of his nation as the servant of all mankind. The charge Christianity gave patriotism was not just to overcome an evil state, but to incorporate it again into the fellowship of humanity. He wrote: "The State wins a war when it has administered a military defeat. Christianity never wins until it has changed the mind and heart of the enemy. It uses physical force as the necessary means to a moral triumph. It looks beyond the capture of guns and men to the defeat of the lust for world-dominion, and to the establishment of the principle that greatness among nations, as among individuals, is measured simply by capacity and willingness to serve in the cause of all humanity."[64]

The second duty followed directly from the first: Christianizing patriotism should lead to the supreme goal of creating a true internationalism. He became mystical in speaking of this. He was aware of the obstacles in the way of establishing it and did not simply equate it with any specific plan; yet he was inspired by a vision of a "Christian civilization," in which the world would be rebuilt on the basis of Christian goodwill. The reconstruction period was the great opportunity of the church, and he believed that it was "divinely and imperatively summoned now to lead, to set men dreaming of the day of God, to unite men in executing the great new structure of international life."[65] His perspective on the war and his vision won the approval of the German churchman Adolf Deissmann. Shortly after the war Deissmann commented that despite certain "false judgments concerning our people," Faunce took a position "which will make possible the bringing together again of the Christians of America and Germany."[66]

Speer, Brown, Fosdick, and Faunce were important members of the Commission. They were not alone in directing its policy, but they were at least as influential as any other group who might be chosen to represent its leadership and wider membership. It is perfectly evident that they had some differences of opinion. It is just as clear that they were in fundamental agreement on many issues and attitudes. They shared a trust in democracy, a sense that the war and the participation in it of the United States were just, a belief that peace was the only ultimately true order in national and international life, a conviction that the Christian could and should minister to the nation in wartime, and a profound hope in the Christian religion. They all sought to balance their commitments as citizens with the transnational imperatives of their faith. They believed that these imperatives spoke to their needs and to the needs of all Christians in a nation and a world at war in some way other than the ways chosen by the pacifists or the militants. The articulation of this other, middle way, was not easy. The misunderstanding which confronted Speer shows this.[67] Nevertheless, they maintained their point of view. These public statements, all made during the war, are convincing testimony that these men preserved in varying degrees a significant critical Christian detachment from the nation and the war.

1. See Chapters VI–IX for the specific programs.
2. Quoted in W. Reginald Wheeler, *A Man Sent From God* (Westwood, New Jersey: Fleming H. Revell Company, 1956), p. 32.
3. Robert E. Speer to Frank Mason North, July 30, 1917, Speer Papers.
4. North to Speer, August 6, 1917, Speer Papers.
5. Macfarland, *The Churches of Christ in Time of War*, p. 102.
6. *Ibid.*, p. 106.
7. The speeches and articles are very numerous. He kept meticulous records of his work and responses to it, and his papers show no critical responses to his activities in 1917. Further search in the periodical literature of the time failed to turn up anything he might have missed.
8. Harry E. Edmonds to Robert E. Speer, February 14, 1918, Speer Papers.
9. The New York *Times*, February 26, 1918.
10. Robert E. Speer to John Greene, March 8, 1918, Speer Papers.
11. Because no copy of the speech was found in the Speer Papers, it had to be reconstructed from various sources. See especially the letter to John Greene and the articles in the *Times* of February 26, cited above.
12. The *Times*, February 19, 1918.
13. *Ibid.*, March 1, 1918.
14. *Ibid.*, February 26, 1918. For the other letters see the following issues: February 23, 25, 27; March 1, 3, 7, 13. An unsigned article in *The Congregationalist and Advance* also agreed with Mitchell, and called Speer's address "an ill-proportioned speech and not the full-orbed presentation of the matter which that particular occasion called for." "An Unfortunate Start in New York," 103 (March 7, 1918): 293.
15. The *Times*, February 22, 26, 1918.
16. *Ibid.*, February 22, 1918.
17. *Ibid.*, February 24, 1918. If Speer received from officials of the Y.M.C.A. any letters which supported his position, he did not save them. John R. Mott sent him a copy of a letter he wrote to George W. Pepper, dated July 2, 1918, in which he said: "I consider that a grave injustice has been done to him and that there will be a few things more pleasing to our enemies than to have any doubt associated with his name and attitude with reference to the war." Speer Papers.
18. The *Times*, February 26, 1918. See also "Robert E. Speer a True Patriot," *The Presbyterian* 88 (March 14, 1918): 4.
19. The *Times*, February 26, 1918.
20. *Ibid.*, February 27, 1918.
21. *Ibid.*, March 7, 1918. For another pro-Speer letter see "Dr. Speer Defended," *The Congregationalist and Advance* 103 (April 4, 1918): 434.
22. The New York *Evening Post*, February 28, 1918.
23. Speer Papers.
24. Raymond C. Knox, Chaplain of Columbia University, wrote "in a spirit of sincere friendship," to say that Mitchell's report was correct. February 26, 1918. Eugene Thwing, President of Western Reserve University, sent Speer a

note which contained simply the following quotation: "When men persecute you and say all manner of evil against you falsely, for my sake, Rejoice and be exceeding glad, for so persecuted they the prophets which were before you." Speer Papers.

25. Henry A. Atkinson to Robert E. Speer, February 28, 1918, Speer Papers.

26. Frederick H. Knubel to Robert E. Speer, February 27, 1918, Speer Papers.

27. Henry Sloane Coffin to Robert E. Speer, February 25, 1918, Speer Papers.

28. Norman Thomas to Robert E. Speer, February 25, 1918, Speer Papers.

29. Robert E. Speer to Elliott Speer, April 9, 1918. Quoted in Wheeler, *A Man Sent From God*, p. 147.

30. Robert E. Speer, *The Christian Man, the Church, and the War* (New York: The Macmillan Company, 1918), p. iii.

31. *Ibid.*, p. 29.

32. Robert E. Speer, "Looking Through the War Clouds," *The Missionary Review of the World* 41 (January, 1918): 14.

33. Quoted in Wheeler, *A Man Sent From God*, p. 150.

34. Speer, *The Christian Man*, p. 15.

35. *Ibid.*, p. 8.

36. *Ibid.*, p. 17.

37. *Ibid.*, p. 19.

38. *Ibid.*, p. 8.

39. *Ibid.*, p. 12.

40. *Ibid.*, pp. 86–87; p. 58.

41. *Ibid.*, pp. 30–31.

42. For some typical comparisons of the two world wars see Roland H. Bainton, *Christian Attitudes toward War and Peace* (New York: Abingdon Press, 1960), p. 221; James Hastings Nichols, *Democracy and the Churches* (Philadelphia: The Westminster Press, 1951), p. 220; Ray H. Abrams, "The Churches and the Clergy in World War II," *The Annals of the American Academy of Political and Social Science* 256 (March, 1948): 112, 116; and Ralph L. Moellering, *Modern War and the American Churches* (New York: The American Press, 1956), p. 83.

43. *A Call to Prayer*, Thanksgiving, 1917. A General War-Time Commission Pamphlet.

44. "Robert E. Speer's Call to Prayer," *The Lutheran* 22 (December 6, 1917): 3.

45. Robert E. Speer, *The New Opportunity of the Church* (New York: The Macmillan Company, 1919), p. 25.

46. Speer, *The Christian Man*, p. 38.

47. "Address by Dr. Robert E. Speer, Thursday Afternoon, October 4, 1917," Speer Papers.

48. Speer, *The Christian Man*, p. 38.

49. *Ibid.*, p. 62.

50. (New York: Charles Scribner's Sons, 1906). See Kenneth Cauthen, *The Impact of American Religious Liberalism* (New York and Evanston: Harper and Row, 1962).

51. William Adams Brown, "The Place of Repentance in a Nation at War," *The North American Student* 6 (May, 1918): 366.

52. William Adams Brown, "The Church's Message for the Coming Time," *The Homiletic Review* 75 (April, 1918): 273.

53. William Adams Brown, "The Contribution of the Church to the Democracy of the Future," *Religious Education* 13 (October, 1918): 346f.

54. These sermons were preached at Stanford University and later published as *The Challenge of the Present Crisis* (Philadelphia: American Baptist Publishing Society, 1917).

55. *Ibid.*, pp. 14ff.

56. *Ibid.*, p. 54.

57. *Ibid.*, p. 70.

58. *Ibid.*, p. 90.

59. Harry Emerson Fosdick, *The Living of These Days* (New York: Harper and Brothers, 1956), p. 121.

60. These words appeared in a pamphlet printed as a form letter, signed by the "War Committee, Parish of the Chapel of the Comforter," and dated April 23, 1918. Speer Papers.

61. William H. P. Faunce, *Religion and War* (New York: The Abingdon Press, 1918), p. 69.

62. *Ibid.*, p. 113.

63. *Ibid.*, p. 183.

64. *Ibid.*, p. 70.

65. *Ibid.*, p. 129.

66. *Evangelical Weekly Letter*, Numbers 107–108 (March 3, 1919), p. 4.

67. Speer and others were misunderstood after the war, too. See Kirby Page, *The Sword or the Cross* (Chicago: The Christian Century Press, 1921), pp. 83–84.

IV

The National Catholic War Council

The National Catholic War Council served as the agent of the Catholic Church to create and carry out its wartime ministry from September, 1917, to September, 1919. It was official in character, sanctioned by the Hierarchy, and national in scope, embracing the entire Church, and at least potentially every aspect of Catholic life. Two different groups of leaders joined their efforts to make the Council work, the Hierarchy and the officers of the Council. They came to their tasks in separate ways, and that largely determined the nature of their involvement.

The Hierarchy, in the persons of the cardinals, archbishops, and bishops, participated in war work by virtue of their administrative roles. They were elevated to their offices prior to the war, with several exceptions and for reasons totally unrelated to it. The war simply added to their already large work loads. The majority of the bishops were not directly involved in the national work although a number of them became active after Council reorganization in January, 1918. At that time four bishops, led by Bishop Peter J. Muldoon of Rockford, and including Bishop Patrick J. Hayes of New York, Bishop Joseph B. Schrembs of Toledo, and Bishop William T. Russell of Charleston, became a new Administrative Committee. The archbishops participated through their discussions at their annual meetings, but they were rarely all able to attend even those.[1] Eight signed the April, 1917, pronouncement pledging the loyalty of the Church to the nation. Two of them, Archbishop Edward J. Hanna of San Francisco and Archbishop George W. Mundelein of Chicago, kept reasonably close contact with Council affairs. The cardinals, especially Gibbons and to some degree Farley, assumed most of the responsibility and took a much more public posture, but not because they were specifically called to war work; rather, because the faithful looked to them to do so. The Hierarchy was the source of authority and of some program ideas, but not of most of the planning and action.

The people who actually fulfilled the wartime ministry were distinct from the Hierarchy not only because they did not belong to it, but more importantly because without exception they were carefully chosen for their particular tasks. Moreover, they came from a strikingly similar background. Almost every one of them had a history of direct involvement in American society on behalf of some specific aspect of Catholic social ministry. Many of them had worked together in one or more of the Catholic social welfare agencies or educational institutions, and often were, as the records of their wartime meetings show, of like mind on what constituted the most urgent social needs. These coincidences indicate the existence of an informal but widely recognized fellowship, clerical and lay, which had established itself in the fields of social thinking, organization and action.[2] Those who selected the wartime leaders saw the war as a time of social upheaval, requiring new ministries, and turned to those who had reputations as interested in and able to organize them. The war did not so much create new leaders as it drew to a common forum those who already worked in separate areas.

Cardinal Gibbons made the initial and most momentous decision when he accepted Father Burke's analysis of the problems the Church would face during the war and his proffered solution in the form of a national Catholic agency. When the Committee of Seven, designated by the August meeting to organize a War Council, met on September 2 at Catholic University of America, it reorganized as the Executive Committee of the War Council and then followed Gibbons' lead and elected Burke as Chairman. It also established six major committees: Legislation, Chaplains, Finance, Historical Records, Recreation and Recreation Halls, and Women's Organizations. Burke shortly opened an office in Washington, D.C., and hired Walter G. Hooke to be the Executive Secretary. At the time of his move Hooke was working as Secretary of the Committee of Fourteen, a New York City based anti-vice organization, led by William Adams Brown.

Most of the initial Council appointments were the responsibility of Father Burke. After Bishop Muldoon joined the work, Burke consulted him fully on all major personnel decisions. The committees generally had two officers, a chairman and a secretary, and a very small membership. Charles I. Denechaud who chaired the Men's Committee was a layman from New Orleans who had been active in the American Federation of Catholic Societies, both as its president and as a member of its first Social Service Commission. Michael J. Slattery, the Secretary, came to the work from the Catholic Young Men's Association. Two faculty members of Catholic University of America led the Women's Committee. Professor Kerby, long an outspoken advocate of social reform and one of the organizers of the National Conference of Catholic Charities, chaired it, and Professor John W. Cooper served as the Secretary. Monsignor M. J. Splaine joined the Council as a representative of the Boston Archdiocese and directed first the Women's Committee and later the Committee on Reconstruction. The Rev. John F. O'Grady began his involvement as Secretary of the reconstruction work and later took Splaine's place as Chairman. A sociologist, O'Grady had worked with the National Conference in the area of immigrant work and was instrumental in launching the post-war Civic Education Program. Monsignor Edward A. Kelly of Chicago chaired the Committee on Legislation, with Executive Secretary Hooke acting as Secretary and chief lobbiest in Washington. Monsignor Drumgoole, Rector of St. Charles Seminary in Overbrook, Pennsylvania, and former President of the American Catholic Historical Association, gave direction to the Committee on Historical Records. The Rev. Peter Guilday, Associate Professor of American Church History at Catholic University, assisted him. John G. Agar chaired the Committee on Finance throughout the war. Burke continued to lead the Chaplains' Aid Association. After reorganization, the Rev. John E. Fenlon, S.S., served as Secretary of the Administrative Committee.

A few people held committee offices for short periods, including Monsignor Michael Lavelle in chaplain's work, but turnover among the leadership was minimal. Dr. John A. Ryan, on the faculty at Catholic University of America, never formally served on the Council but worked closely with it on its reconstruction programs. No women held leadership positions, although the Women's Committee worked directly with women's organizations and chose a woman to lead the National Service School for Women. A number of women were present in advisory capacities and on the office staff, and some of them worked more as administrative assistants than as secretaries. When the United States Government presented Father Burke the Distinguished Service Medal, he in turn gave it to Grace Murray, his assistant at *The Catholic World*, for he felt her skills had freed him for the war work.[3] The Knights of Columbus constituted the one area of appointment that lay beyond the control of Burke or Muldoon. Mr. Patrick H. Callahan, a very prominent industrialist from Louisville led their Committee on War Activities until mid-war when Mr. William J. Mulligan replaced him.

The two groups of wartime leaders representing authority and action worked together with little visible friction and no sign of major disagreement. Problems arose on occasion, as over some plans of the Knights, a few of the proposals of the field secretaries, and over strategies for approaching the government; but discussion flowed freely, and the open communication and sharing prevented the differences from detouring the programs. This style might be attributed to the overwhelming pressure for agreement exerted by the war, or to the persuasiveness of Catholic structure. Beyond these circumstances, however, lay the character and quality of the leadership. The style of Gibbons and Burke and Muldoon fixed the style of the Council. Gibbons found in Burke and Muldoon his kind of leaders, and the persons they in turn gathered around them adopted their ways and sought cooperation and consultation at every turn. They overcame some differences in taste and desires for independent action in order to develop the wartime ministry to its fullest.

The two-year career of the National Catholic War Council fell into three somewhat unequal but distinct periods. The initial one, characterized by frustration and confusion, lasted four months and ended in January, 1918. Important organizational steps established a foundation for the future, but the structure planned in August never rose on it. Instead, the Council underwent reorganization in January and spent the spring months working into the new structure. The final period of intensive and cooperative ministry lasted from April, 1918, until September of the following year.

Although Council structure changed in mid-course, the style and operating procedures established in the initial period did not. The Council reflected Burke's own views in almost every way, even after Bishop Muldoon came into the picture. The heart of its functioning was what he called its spirit. From the outset: "It was established not to control, but to direct; not to hinder or curtail, but to coordinate and to promote; not to rule with a master hand but to facilitate by conference and mutually accepted divisions of work."[4] Burke, Hooke, Muldoon, and a few others spent endless hours in consultation. They never tried to block the work of any group and always sought to bring separate activities into coordination. They introduced few new programs in the early months, but gradually came to realize that they alone had the centralized machinery and, after reorganization, the authority, to do some of the work. In the final period they began to use their own committees to direct more programs, including the collecting of historical records, the recruitment of workers for reconstruction activities, and participation in the United War Work Campaign.

The style of personal diplomacy foreclosed the need for an extensive committee system. The six committees set up at the August meeting proved adequate with only one addition and some slight name changes. The Committee on Legislation became the Committee on National Catholic Interests with special attention to national legislation affecting the Church. The Committee on Recreation and Recreation Halls became the Committee on Men's Activities, but with the same sphere of concern. The only new committee appeared in the spring of 1918 when post-war issues began to emerge. This Committee on Reconstruction developed one of the most active programs.

The primary leaders volunteered their time and energy, taking on their assignments in addition to other life-sustaining tasks. Burke continued his editorship, Kerby his professorship, Muldoon his episcopacy, and others their several duties. The hired staff consisted of Hooke and a small number of office personnel until the Council began to run some projects, and then it began to employ field secretaries. By the spring of 1919 it had become the administrative center of a large number of persons engaged in a complex variety of tasks. Burke had specifically denied any intention of creating a bureaucracy, but it came to look peculiarly like one.

Vexing problems accompanied this growth, not the least of which were the selection and management of the personnel. Hooke served well until near the very end when Burke and others became unhappy with his work. The problems lay in the area of financial mismanagement and are not very clear. Whatever they were, he resigned in August, 1919, and the Council hired Michael Slattery to replace him. The field secretaries became very numerous from the Armistice until the following summer and created some difficulties. The Executive Secretary wrote memos concerning their employment and their behavior while on assignment. A directive to them in January, 1919, cautioned them to be "very careful not to create the impression that the War Council has a large sum of money to distribute lavisly (sic). This has been the impression created by the field secretaries as a whole and has produced unfortunate results."[5] The leaders of the Council did not seem unduly concerned about the number of employees and even tried to secure a full-time chairman. The issue came alive during the reorganization and attention focused on Father Burke. The weakness of the Council, Kerby told Bishop Muldoon, was the "imperative need of consecutive thinking, of uninterrupted attention to the work as a whole and to the larger features of its several parts." Kerby suggested that the Bishop approach Burke's superiors in the Paulist Order requesting his release for full-time work, for he believed that "if providence ever prepared a man for a work, it prepared Father Burke in temperament, consecration, spiritual insight, force and intelligence for this task."[6] Burke began to spend more time in Washington but he continued his regular duties. Bishop Muldoon himself became virtually full-time in the summer and fall of 1918.

Each of the three periods of Council work had its particular character; frustration and confusion definitely marked the early months. Burke set out to do several things at once, all necessary but all time consuming and largely frustrating. His work for chaplains progressed, but very slowly due to a serious recruitment problem and government policies. He spent more time trying to organize the Council as a representative body and things went poorly from the start. The plan outlined at the August meeting projected a series of representative councils from the local to the national level. A small group of representatives attended the organizational meeting in September, but their numbers did not increase as the vast majority of bishops failed to cooperate. Some local and diocesan war councils were set up, but most of them showed little or no interest in the national body. Burke and others tried to encourage organization by personal contact, by letters, and by publishing a small handbook describing in some detail the ways to organize local and diocesan councils and to work with the national one, but the response continued to be poor.

Bad news clearly outweighed good news, and Burke's Council was not getting very far from the starting gate even as wartime problems mounted. The archbishops, meeting in early November, 1917, as the Trustees of Catholic University of America, debated the situation and decided on a major reorganization. They were the only constituted body of the Hierarchy and with full authority they named themselves the new National Catholic War Council. Their decision marked the farthest they could go to centralize and nationalize war work. The bishops had not responded to a Council of priests and laymen, even with the support of the leading prelates, but now they stood on the front line.

The archbishops stated their reason for the change in terms of central authority, and reflection since then has not challenged their motive although it has revealed a variety of facets of the issue. One of their concerns was the need to lift up the sacramental ministry. While they applauded the work of the Knights of Columbus, some of them feared its primarily recreational work might be identified in the public mind as the only Catholic work. Burke's Council supported the Knights' work but had no direct involvement in it and no control over it. The reorganization embraced all Catholic work and defined the K. of C. as in charge of the recreational part of it.[7] The authors of the Council *Handbook* put the change in terms of the discovery of "the elementary truth that system and forethought are the weapons by which we overcome confusion and wasted effort . . ."[8] Cardinal Gibbons said that local councils had not stepped forward because of uncertainty, which the involvement of the bishops would quickly dispel.[9] The most direct way of stating the entire problem is in terms of ecclesiastical authority. Burke was a fine man and a brilliant organizer, but he was not a bishop. Authority in the Church flowed from the top and although Burke, Kerby, and others tried to educate leaders on the need for unity and cooperation, they resisted. They guarded their autonomy and refused to cooperate until reorganization placed the problem squarely in front of them. The new proposal meant, Burke quickly saw, that "the entire Catholic Church of the country from the lowest to the highest of its members, . . ." was now organized for ministry and service.[10]

The politically astute Gibbons did not finalize the decision without extensive consultation, and set about the task of getting all the major parties to agree. He wrote to the bishops and set forth the wartime problems very much as Burke had done at the August meeting, and added that he was concerned for the "mental and moral preparation of our people for the war."[11] He asked them to send him some indication of their feelings, and by mid-December enough had responded positively for him to announce the matter settled. He had not, however, overlooked the Knights of Columbus. At a special consultation with their leaders in New York City his representatives had sought and obtained their agreement to the new program.[12] With reorganization agreed upon, he turned to the creation of a new operating structure. Since the archbishops did not have time to oversee the work personally, he summoned Bishops Muldoon, Schrembs, Hayes, and Russell to the work. Bishop Muldoon recorded that he "would serve both as a patriotic duty and as a Catholic duty. I hope we may be able to do something for God and country."[13] Gibbons exercised much wisdom in his selection. Bishops Muldoon and Schrembs were well recognized for their work with the American Federation, and Bishop Hayes had just been appointed Chaplain Bishop. Muldoon had a particularly wide reputation within the Church and has been described as "a truly progressive prelate who for many years was the Hierarchy's official spokesman on social questions."[14]

The Administrative Committee met from January 16 to 18, 1918, on the campus of Catholic University of America and established the new Council. Cardinal Gibbons told them that the archbishops had "delegated their authority to Your Lordships, as a committee to act in their name."[15] They interviewed the leaders of Burke's Council and of the Knights. Tensions existed and it was not easy to encompass all interests, but Muldoon found the groups cooperative.[16] The new structure included first the Hierarchy, in the persons of the archbishops; second, the Administrative Committee of the four bishops with full power to act; third, sub-committees consisting of the former Council, now named the Committee on Special War Activities and chaired by Burke, and the K. of C. War Activities Committee; and fourth, the large national representative assembly. The Knights continued their camp work, and all other war work became the province of Burke's Committee. The changes brought the bishops directly into power and the Knights immediately under their control. It added the impressive skills of Muldoon to the work and enlarged and enhanced the programs Burke's group had already initiated. The Administrative Committee met almost monthly and occasionally alone, but usually in connection with the leaders of the two sub-committees. Wartime programs developed and progressed with no further major disruptions to the end of Council service.

Creating the new organization took only a few days, but setting it in working order took several months. The Council adjusted to the new situation during the transition period. The Administrative Committee communicated the changes to the bishops and the Catholic press. It also notified the heads of religious orders, calling their particular attention to the increasing need for chaplains. Bishop Muldoon began to acquaint himself with the work. Since the Knights ran their own programs, the Bishop worked primarily with Burke and his Committee. The committees of the former Council, except for the one on chaplains, had never moved far beyond initial organization. With the one exception none of them had functioned as more than the work of the chairmen. They now organized in earnest and most of them met regularly until their work was completed.

Cardinal Gibbons had asked the Administrative Committee for a full report at the spring meeting of the archbishops, and that report outlining the reorganization moved the Council into the final period of intensive ministry. The archbishops fully endorsed the new structure and heard reports from the sub-committees. They noted that adequate funds seemed to be on hand, but voted to support a large fund drive should it prove necessary. Burke's most distressing problem, the general absence of local and diocesan councils, received considerable attention. Cardinals O'Connell and Farley acted together to move "that these councils should be formed in every diocese and the need and utility of them be strongly impressed upon the ordinaries."[17] They also received reports that alerted them to the possibility of an overseas ministry beyond that performed by the chaplains.

In the months after this key meeting Bishop Muldoon found himself drawn further and further into Council affairs, from writing letters to the Hierarchy urging their fullest cooperation to reviewing a draft of a constitution. In early June he noted that "the work is becoming very heavy and requires much time," and by the end of that month he was totally immersed in it.[18] Many issues attracted his attention, but the one that demanded so much time involved fund raising and the questions it brought up about the relationship between Catholic war work and the government.

Money had never been a serious problem for the Council, despite Burke's secretary's memory that in the early days it operated on a shoestring from a rat-infested office.[19] As dioceses and societies began to join the effort, they contributed and better offices were soon secured. After reorganization the Hierarchy supplied needed funds, both directly and through major financial drives. Cardinal Farley launched the first effort, a New York Catholic War Fund, in March, 1918, with a goal of $2.5 million, and a portion designated for the Council. The Fund topped $5 million and dispelled doubts about finances. In April when Bishop Muldoon asked the archbishops about funds, they told him "there is in sight about $15,000,000, which will last us a year in the war work."[20] However, American involvement in the war accelerated that summer and new monies were needed. That need led to the United War Work Campaign.

The welfare agencies associated with the government's Commission on Training Camp Activities had conducted separate and large financial campaigns during the first year of the war. By late spring of 1918 most of the agencies had decided to seek additional funding. Initial projections involved a united national campaign for a huge sum of money, but specific details remained very vague, and each of the organizations went about establishing preliminary budgets and in some cases plans for its own campaign. The Y.M.C.A. developed the most extensive ones, including dates, organizational charts, and specific budgets. The Council hired H. J. Hill of New York as its campaign consultant. He had worked with the New York Catholic War Fund and prepared a general prospectus for the new drive.[21] The Commission called representatives of the agencies to a meeting in late June to consider the nature of the united effort. Discussion immediately revolved around John R. Mott's surprising announcement that the Y.M.C.A. could not join such a campaign. He argued that Association financial plans were well developed and that many of its members would hesitate to contribute to a drive where their money might go to a religious program other than their own. Callahan, present on behalf of the K. of C., tried to meet one of these objections when he agreed to a drive in which donors could designate the use of their contributions.[22] Representatives of the Jewish Welfare Board and the American Library Association also argued for a joint drive, but said they were ready to go on their own if necessary. The meeting adjourned without a final decision. In the absence of a negative decision, most Catholic leaders continued to assume that a united campaign was still going to happen. Secretary of War Baker had the authority to announce all financial drives and the groups awaited his decision.

Mid-summer passed with no action from Baker but with considerable contact between his Department through Raymond Fosdick and the Council through Bishop Muldoon. The problem Fosdick faced was that many Americans regarded the K. of C. as a fraternal group and wanted equal status with it in the coming drive. At a conference on July 30 Fosdick proposed to Muldoon that the Council accept government recognition as the official Catholic wartime agency for all war work and then the drive could be made in its name. Muldoon wanted to know how Fosdick would deal with the charge that the government was recognizing the Catholic Church, and Fosdick replied that he would say to any challenging Protestant denomination that if it could show that 35% of the men in the army belonged to its group, as the Catholics could do, he would recognize it. Muldoon recalled that the discussion explicitly referred to a united fund drive. The members of the Council debated this proposal and finally decided to accept it, subject to the response of the Knights. Bishop Muldoon consulted with their Supreme Board and discovered some hostility and a strong feeling that they were being pushed aside. The Bishop reassured them and won their support by agreeing to get a clause in the agreement stipulating that the Knights would continue to be the agents of the Council in the camps and would therefore receive whatever funds were designated for Catholic camp work. At a meeting with Fosdick on August 7 to work out the final wording of the agreement, Muldoon again raised the issue of a united drive and Fosdick said flatly that he favored it.[23] The agreement did not mention the Knights, but it did say that "The National Catholic War Council will be responsible for all Catholic work in connection with the leisure time of the troops at home and abroad, . . ." and added that "This organization is free to choose such agents to carry on the work as it may deem wise, . . ."[24]

Bishop Muldoon took a short and well earned trip to visit his family in Rhode Island. Burke reached him by telephone on the fifteenth with the news of Baker's decision for a divided drive. The largely Protestant groups, the Y.M.C.A., the Y.W.C.A., the American Library Association, and the War Camp Community Service would present their appeal in November, and the other three groups—the Council, the Jewish Welfare Board, and the Salvation Army—would go before the public in February. The news discouraged Muldoon, but he decided to try to change the decision despite the difficulty of doing so now that it had been announced.[25]

Although they had able support from other groups, Catholics led the battle to change the Department's plans. Bishops Muldoon and Hayes telegraphed Fosdick and urged reconsideration. They told him: "For unity, economy and Americanization, let us have only one drive which without doubt would be an immense success from every viewpoint. One drive prevents any possible misinterpretation."[26] Supreme Knight Flaherty wrote Baker and painted a clear picture of how he and many Catholics saw the decision. Separating the groups in the proposed way "would be drawing a religious line in a time of war that cannot fail to cause great criticism and disturbance throughout the country."[27] The Knights released their statement to the press. Muldoon telephoned Burke in Washington on the nineteenth and discovered that the Knights' sharp and public protest had angered Baker and Fosdick. Burke felt it had harmed lobbying, but Muldoon responded that it showed "that the protest is strong and to the point."[28] Monsignor Splaine, on a field trip, wrote that the two-headed drive created opposition and resentment everywhere he went.[29] Pressure mounted and finally a break came. Baker called a conference of interested parties for Monday, August 26, at the War Department.

The Council seized the opportunity. Father Burke and Bishops Schrembs and Russell accompanied Muldoon. Baker invited Fosdick and Assistant Secretary Frederick Keppel. Muldoon presented the arguments for a united drive "from every angle possible."[30] He doubtless invoked national unity, the fostering of religious cooperation, and the financial advantages. Baker pronounced the arguments "sane" and intimated that there was hope for a united drive. It is not clear whether Muldoon persuaded Baker to negotiate or whether Baker came to the conference prepared to do so, but he proceeded to set forth conditions which might result in a united campaign. The two essential terms were far from easy and both concerned the K. of C. The War Department had not worked well with the Knights and had sought the new agreement with the Council in order to channel all Catholic concerns through it. One long-standing point of contention was their slogan: "Everyone Welcome, Everything Free." Earlier in the year the Department had asked them to drop the second part of this slogan because it aroused ill feeling among other welfare groups, particularly the Y.M.C.A., which were not in a position to give away things. The Knights pointed out that the objectionable part of the slogan referred only to items given to men at the front, but the Department insisted that they drop it anyway. They hesitated, for their program had given them strong favorable responses among the troops in France, who had developed considerable resentment over prices charged at Association canteens. Baker now voiced the request as a demand. Moreover, they would have to eliminate the $9,000,000 budget item for their free program. Muldoon resisted. He finally agreed to cut the budget item but not the slogan. He told Baker that the free program would continue until the Secretary issued a direct order to stop it, and added that he did not think he would have the courage to issue such an order.[31]

Baker's second qualification referred to the size and make-up of the Knight's proposed budget. Each agency had submitted a budget, outlining the major line items and the total funds needed. Baker regarded their request for $58,000,000 as much too high, even with the free item eliminated. Muldoon asked for time to consult with the Knights and the conference adjourned with agreement in sight if Council leaders could find a dollar figure acceptable to both the Knights and Baker. Muldoon took the lead, with the other two Bishops at his side, and served as arbitrators between the two parties. The final days of August were filled with conferences. Officials of the Knights agreed on $30,000,000, but Fosdick told Muldoon the Y.M.C.A. would agree to a united drive only when the figure fell to $20,000,000. Muldoon, now angry, told him "we would go out independently before we would take less."[32] Fosdick finally agreed to thirty million and drew up a proposal for a combined drive, subject to Baker's signature. The next day, August 30, Muldoon received word from Fosdick's office that politics might destroy the entire arrangement. Politicians, particularly from the South, were raising objections on nativist, anti-Catholic lines, and Secretary Baker's position had become vulnerable. The Department planned to ask President Wilson to announce the settlement, but the issue remained in doubt.

Knowing it was out of his hands, the Bishop returned to Rockford to await the outcome. The days had been "worrying" and full of uncertainties.[33] Shortly after he had come to the leadership of the Council he had visited Washington and met numerous government officials, including Baker. He had praised him highly and said he found him earnest in his efforts to do everything possible for the fighting men.[34] The debates of August left him less euphoric and more aware of the hard realities of dealing with the government. When the President announced, on September 5 through a public letter to Fosdick, the United War Work Campaign, Muldoon recorded: "Deo Gratias. Hurrah."[35] The President, using a political maneuver best understood by those directly involved, told Fosdick that it was his judgment that the seven societies ought "to unite their forthcoming appeals for funds, in order that the spirit of the country in this matter may be expressed without distinction of race or religious opinion in support of what is in reality a common service," and asked him to approach the societies for their concurrence.[36] The suggestion disguised the already settled arrangements and lifted the Campaign to the level of a national priority beyond politics. Muldoon played the political game and announced: "In this common drive for war funds we will follow the lead of the government with unqualified approval and enthusiasm."[37] Cardinal Gibbons thanked Fosdick for "securing the opportunity of a single united drive," without even a hint of irony in his words.[38] Yet he clearly knew about the difficult struggle and understood that his own Bishop Muldoon had turned the situation around. After the Campaign he told him: "The credit belongs to you, and I congratulate you most heartily. You were the live wire all the time."[39]

The United War Work Campaign must have seemed like an anticlimax to those Council leaders involved in the intense lobbying to secure it, but they turned their attention to it with great energy and efficiency. Muldoon assumed command, essentially moving to New York City for the months of September, October, and November. The Council faced substantial initial disadvantages. While it waited through August for approval, the Y.M.C.A. and Y.W.C.A. had forged ahead, setting dates, ordering printed materials, and refining their organizations. When the government announced the united drive, the Associations graciously acquiesced. Mott, named general campaign director, took down Association signs in his office and put up United Campaign ones. He offered the Council free office space at Association headquarters. Muldoon accepted. But general plans had solidified and Catholics, as well as Jews and the Salvation Army, simply had to accept them. Campaign officials invited Muldoon to "gear-in" and mobilize in six weeks what they had organized in three months.

The Council produced a blizzard of paper in the form of letters, a Campaign *Manual*, parish bulletins, and posters. The letters went out from Cardinal Gibbons, Bishop Muldoon, and Council officers, and were directed to bishops and priests, diocesan leaders, lay groups, and others. Gibbons stressed to both bishops and priests that the Campaign presented one more opportunity for the Church to prove its loyalty, for "while it remains true, that there will be a merging of forces, and no mention made of Catholic, non-Catholic, or Hebrew activity, a magnificent opportunity is here presented of adding glory to the Church."[40] Their Campaign *Manual* laid down the formal agreement among the agencies and described the organization that should be developed in each local parish. Bishops initiated action by appointing ministerial and lay leaders in their dioceses and encouraging every parish to follow suit, with local emphasis on lay leadership. Each pastor served as honorary parish chairman and was advised to "make suitable references to the campaign from his pulpit from time to time . . . realizing that the whole welfare of Catholic War Work at home and abroad is involved with the successful outcome of the United Drive."[41] The structure of the Campaign presented the most serious organizational problem, since the Association had decided on a state and county plan, which did not conform to local and diocesan boundaries. The Council adjusted as much as possible and decided to hold leadership conferences in the fourteen archdioceses. The influenza epidemic dealt the entire Campaign a serious blow and especially the late-starting Catholic component, forcing cancellation of almost half of these major meetings. Moreover, by the time they were scheduled, rumors of armistice had raced across the country. Nevertheless, Council leaders who spoke at the meetings urged the people on. Muldoon told the New York gathering that "if peace is signed within a month we will have to turn the trend of this stream of gold to social service."[42]

The Campaign proceeded without friction or major disagreement. Mott worked for a careful equilibrium of forces, and Catholic leaders felt embraced, not swallowed. The policy-making Committee of

Eleven, a sub-committee of the Commission on Training Camp Activities, had a well-balanced and very prestigious membership. Fosdick chaired it, with Mott his assistant, joined by such well known figures as John D. Rockefeller, Jr., and Cleveland Dodge. James Phelan of Boston and John Agar of New York represented the Council. The Campaign sought $170,500,000; the Council share, including K. of C. work, amounted to thirty million. The massive public effort began November 11 and ran head-on into the formal Armistice. Undaunted, workers solicited gifts until November 20. Pledges amounted to $205 million. When Campaign leaders finally closed the books, they had collected and distributed $188 million. The Committee of Eleven continued into 1919 to supervise use of the monies. A major problem in the post-war discussions was free distributions.[43]

From a practical point of view the agreement between the Council and the government, which made the Campaign possible, represented a vehicle to permit participation of the Knights of Columbus. In this sense it amounted to nothing more than public recognition of the subordination of the Knights' work to national Catholic management, a fact already fully understood in Catholic circles. In a more technical sense, the agreement changed the status of the Council, largely for the convenience of the government, and made it, in the view of some, an official agent of the government. The government did not control it in any way, but the altered status carried that risk. The issues of church and state came very near the surface during this time, although they never really broke through into public debate. It is doubtful that the Protestants in the General War-Time Commission would have accepted such a status had it been offered. Of course, with the largely Protestant Y.M.C.A. and Y.W.C.A. already closely identified with war work, they did not need it. In fact, Protestant prejudices were strong among the motives behind the government's proposal of the agreement. The Protestant Interchurch Emergency Campaign sought funds for church-oriented as distinct from welfare-related programs.

Even though the Council spent much time on the Campaign, it did not allow that project to interfere with its other programs. The major share of its work fell to Father Burke and the chairmen and committees under his supervision. This work involved ministry through the chaplains, various kinds of social welfare service, and the development of reconstruction ideas and projects and is considered separately under those headings.[44] Two of its more general ventures were in the areas of publishing and record keeping.

The Council early initiated a publicity and publishing campaign. It hired Larkin G. Mead of New York City as its publicity agent. Its *Handbook* described its history and program and solicited support from readers. It included an extensive listing of government and religious agencies involved in war work and encouraged Catholics to cooperate when and where possible. Burke projected the establishment of some kind of permanent national news bureau. One form this took appeared as the National Catholic War Council *Bulletin,* issued for the first time in June, 1919, under Michael Williams' editorship. It survived as the Welfare Council *Bulletin* and later as *Catholic Action.* A summary of the service of the Committee on Special War Activities appeared in 1920 titled *The Promise Fulfilled.* The Council produced a number of smaller publications and also a film record of its work, which it distributed widely both inside and out of the Catholic community.

The Committee on Historical Records, directed by Monsignor Henry T. Drumgoole, served a more general function encompassing the entire work of the Council. Burke first mentioned the need for such a group at the August meeting, when he suggested a committee which would collect records of all Catholics in the armed forces. The data would serve a dual purpose: (1) to help determine the proper number of Catholic chaplains since they were based on the proportion of Catholics in the armed forces; and (2) to serve as an "effective answer to the bigots' charge that American Catholics are not patriotic. . . ."[45] The Historical Committee maintained such Service Lists, renamed the Catholic Honor Roll, but greatly widened its scope. Drumgoole and his secretary, Peter Guilday, were both historians and they set about gathering materials to write a complete history. They issued detailed directives to local and diocesan councils, describing all important war materials and how they should be collected and preserved. Dioceses were encouraged to open War Museums, War Libraries, and War Archives. Guilday collected and filed virtually everything and anything that related to war work.[46] In the spring of 1919 they renamed the effort of accumulation The Peace Programme, largely as a publicity technique to urge people to send in their materials. They used the *Bulletin* to begin to set this record into print and wrote regular appeals for more information as well as reviews of histories written by local parishes and colleges. The Committee founded the Council Archives which continue to testify to the skilled work it performed. Michael Williams completed the projected history which remains the primary analysis of Catholic wartime service.

The widespread activities of the Council raised the question in the minds of many leaders about the long term future of the work. War work began to diminish in 1919, although it was not to disappear completely until well into 1920, and in its place national social and welfare work began to emerge. The situation of the Women's Committee was typical. It recruited and trained women for welfare work, established community centers, and started a social work school. Much of this activity simply could not be dropped. The Committee told Bishop Muldoon that its work "as we understood it was to create no new organization, but the vital need now is that definite measures should be taken to have some national body or committee of women that will be able to keep up and develop the national coordination of Catholic women's organizations."[47] The Committee fervently believed something had to be done and others agreed. The problem was different from what it was for the Protestants. Their General War-Time Commission was subordinate to the Federal Council and when it finished its work, it simply turned concerns that needed continuing attention back to appropriate Council commissions. But the War Council was a special, temporary group cut out of whole cloth. The concerns it discovered and bureaucracy it created could be turned over only to the Hierarchy itself, and that body had no means of handling either.

The National Catholic War Council served the Church well, so well, in fact, that as the agenda for its final meeting in September, 1919, was drawn up, plans were developed to continue its basic organization and some of its programs. These plans were realized when the Hierarchy voted to transform the Council into the National Catholic Welfare Council, as the vehicle to maintain a national Catholic ministry in peacetime.[48] The War Council was unique in American Catholicism. It mobilized the entire Church, including the Hierarchy, the clergy, the religious, and the laity in one vast effort to sustain and extend ministry in wartime. Behind the organization stood its leaders, who projected a national and united Catholic ministry at every opportunity.

1. The archbishops were Archbishop John Ireland of St. Paul; Archbishop Alexander Christie of Portland, Oregon; Archbishop John J. Glennon of St. Louis; Archbishop Sebastian G. Messmer of Milwaukee; Archbishop Henry Moeller of Cincinnati; Archbishop John B. Pitaval of Santa Fe; Archbishop Dennis J. Dougherty of Philadelphia; Archbishop James J. Keane of Dubuque; Archbishop Edward J. Hanna of San Francisco; and Archbishop George W. Mundelein of Chicago. Several of these men and Cardinal Farley died during or just after the war and the See of New Orleans was vacant. Those who came to

leadership as a result of such circumstances were Archbishop John W. Shaw of New Orleans, Archbishop Patrick J. Hayes of New York, and Archbishop Austin Dowling of St. Paul.

2. Aaron I. Abell, *American Catholicism and Social Action* (Notre Dame, Indiana: University of Notre Dame Press, 1960), p. 188.

3. Sheerin, *Never Look Back*, pp. 28-29.

4. John J. Burke, "Special Catholic Activities in War Service," *The Annals of the American Academy of Political and Social Science* 79 (September, 1918): 216.

5. Memo on *Field Secretaries.* Addendum. January 25, 1919, NCWC Archives.

6. William J. Kerby to Bishop Muldoon, May 29, 1918. Copy in NCWC Archives.

7. Sheerin, *Never Look Back*, p. 43.

8. *Handbook of the National Catholic War Council* (Washington, D.C.: National Headquarters, 1918), p. 34.

9. J. Cardinal Gibbons to the Bishops' Committee, National Catholic War Council, January 12, 1918. Copy in NCWC Archives.

10. Burke, "Special Catholic Activities in War Service," p. 217.

11. Cardinal Gibbons to Hierarchy, November 21, 1917. Copy in NCWC Archives.

12. "Report of a Special Committee appointed at a conference between representatives of the National Catholic War Council and of the Knights of Columbus," December 17, 1917, NCWC Archives.

13. *The Diary of Bishop Muldoon*, December 26, 1917. Roll 3, Microfilm copy in NCWC Archives. Hereafter cited: *Muldoon's Diary.*

14. Aaron I. Abell, "The Catholic Church and Social Problems in the World War I Era," *Mid-America* 30 (July, 1948): 144.

15. J. Cardinal Gibbons to the Bishops' Committee.

16. *Muldoon's Diary*, January 16 and 17, 1918.

17. Minutes of "Administrative Committee," April 10-11, 1918, NCWC Archives.

18. *Muldoon's Diary*, July 1, 1918.

19. Sheerin, *Never Look Back*, p. 50.

20. *Muldoon's Diary*, April 11, 1918.

21. See the following series of letters: H. J. Hill to Walter Hooke and to John Agar, especially Hill to Agar, August 1, 1918, NCWC Archives.

22. P. H. Callahan, "Origin, Conduct and Culmination of the United War Work Campaign," n.d. Copy in NCWC Archives.

23. *Muldoon's Diary*, August 7, 1918.

24. Raymond B. Fosdick to Right Reverend Peter J. Muldoon, August 19, 1918, and P. J. Muldoon to Raymond B. Fosdick, September 5, 1918. Copies in NCWC Archives.

25. *Muldoon's Diary*, August 15, 1918.

26. Bishops Hayes and Muldoon to Raymond Fosdick, August 19, 1918. Copy of Telegram in NCWC Archives.

27. Quoted in James A. Flaherty to Bishop Muldoon, August 16, 1918, NCWC Archives.

28. *Muldoon's Diary*, August 19, 1918.

29. Monsignor M. J. Splaine, "Report of Visitation of Camps," n.d., NCWC Archives.

30. *Muldoon's Diary*, August 26, 1918.

31. *Ibid.*

32. *Ibid.*, August 28, 1918.

33. *Ibid.*, August 28 and 29, 1918.

34. "The Bishop's Scrapbook," in the Archives of the Diocese of Rockford, Rockford, Illinois.

35. *Muldoon's Diary*, September 5, 1918.

36. Williams, *American Catholics and the War*, p. 186.

37. *Ibid.*, p. 189.

38. James Cardinal Gibbons to Raymond Fosdick, September 12, 1918. Copy in NCWC Archives.

39. James Cardinal Gibbons to Bishop Muldoon, November 15, 1918, NCWC Archives.

40. James Cardinal Gibbons to Reverend and dear Father, September 17, 1918. Copy in NCWC Archives.

41. *Manual National Catholic War Council* (New York: Special Campaign Headquarters, 1918), p. 13. Copy in NCWC Archives.

42. Williams, *American Catholics and the War*, p. 201.

43. For another account of this United War Work Campaign see Elizabeth McKeown, "The National Bishops' Conference: An Analysis of Its Origins." *The Catholic Historical Review* 66, No. 4 (October, 1980), pp. 571-73.

44. Much of the work of the committees is described in other chapters: Chaplains and Chaplains' Aid Association, chap. 6; Men's and Women's Committees, chap. 7; and Reconstruction and Bishops' Program, chap. 9.

45. Williams, *American Catholics and the War*, pp. 128-29.

46. Peter Guilday, "American Catholics and the War," *The Historical Outlook* 9 (1918): 431-32.

47. To the Right Reverend P. J. Muldoon from the Women's Committee, May 1, 1919. Copy in NCWC Archives.

48. See Chapter IX for the story of the founding of the Welfare Council.

V

Catholic Leadership

The key leaders of the National Catholic War Council were an exceptionally able and thoughtful group. Cardinal Gibbons, as chief prelate, gave the Council authority and experience of the national ministry of the Church. The other central leaders were priests, who understood the primacy of the sacramental ministry, but who also had special ministries. Bishop Peter Muldoon brought to the Council his administrative experience; Father John Burke shared with it his missionary zeal and his ideas and ability to communicate them; and Father William Kerby contributed his experience as an educator. In addition, these three priests had given extensive service to the social ministry of the Church. Each had a vision of the unity of the Church and its mission and had shared in the excitement of its ministry. Their individual experiences were impressive; their collective ones provided truly remarkable leadership for the Council. However, they offered more than an understanding of ministry and experience. They were also, especially Burke and Kerby, thinkers as well as doers. Their thoughts during the war set them apart as the leaders of Catholic ministry. They did not work in isolation and their ideas were supported by the views of other Catholic social theorists, especially those of Father John Ryan.

Oversight of Catholic life during the war, while shared by the entire Hierarchy, became the particular duty of Cardinal Gibbons. The war erupted late in what had been a long and distinguished career in the ministry of the Church, already marked by numerous firsts and celebrated by Catholics and non-Catholics alike. Born in Baltimore on July 23, 1834, the third child of Irish immigrant parents, he spent most of his early years in Ireland. He returned to the United States in 1853 and two years later entered seminary to study for the priesthood. He graduated from St. Mary's Seminary in Baltimore and was ordained on June 30, 1861. After several years of parochial work he was chosen Vicar Apostolic of North Carolina and consecrated on August 16, 1868, at the time the youngest Catholic bishop in the world. In 1877 he became Archbishop of Baltimore, the oldest and most important See in the nation, and nine years later he became only the second American ever named a cardinal. His administrative work and his writings revealed him to be both a keen organizer and a deeply spiritual man and moved him quickly to the front of Catholic life. Endurance enhanced those assets and as the decades of leadership passed, more and more Catholics, in and out of official positions, turned to him for guidance. By the time the war came, he had commemorated his fiftieth anniversary as a priest and was approaching the golden jubilee of his episcopacy. Just before the war former President Theodore Roosevelt told him, "taking your life as a whole, I think you now occupy the position of being the most respected, and venerated, and useful citizen of our country."[1]

His war service took two forms: as organizer and as formal spokesman. The organizing activities included his authorization of the first War Council, his reorganization of it under Bishop Muldoon, and his leadership of the committee which created the post-war Welfare Council. The provision of clear and provocative agenda constituted one important aspect of this task. Although he did not always write them, he carefully supplied them. To the committee working to form a post-war council he said, "I am not yet prepared myself to endorse all these suggestions, but . . . I pass them on to you as topics to be considered in the formation of plans."[2] He set as his goal a united and cooperative ministry during and after the war and he gave close and careful attention to choosing his assistants and bringing his fellow members of the Hierarchy into agreement. He was the key organizer even though he was not often able to attend the actual organizational assemblies, with the notable exception of the large meeting in September, 1919, which he personally directed to its successful conclusion.

Some members of the war generation knew about these skilful and important efforts, but many more recognized him in his formal role as public spokesman. The policy pronouncements at the start of the war were only the first of a large number of related statements he issued. Few carried the general burden of the initial ones, for most of them were released in connection with a particular concern or emphasis. They were sent to Catholic and non-Catholic press alike, although some, like the one on behalf of War Savings Stamps, seem to have been primarily written for Catholic publications. The content of the statements, including those supporting the American Red Cross, the United States Food Administration, the Liberty Loan, the United War Work Campaign, and the Committee on Public Information, was not nearly so important as the endorsement itself. His role was clearly formal, on behalf of American Catholicism, and in support of phases of a war effort he had already determined to be just. The statements were nationalistic, but almost always carried some reference to Christian social responsibility or ministry. When he wrote on behalf of the Red Cross Christmas Membership Drive of 1917, he said, "There is in these times a veritable ocean of sorrow and suffering engulfing millions of souls, and a society with the membership and resources of the Red Cross, actuated as it is by Christian principles, can best undertake the tremendous burden of extending intelligent and efficient relief. . . . It is my earnest hope that all of our people will cheerfully and generously cooperate with the Red Cross Committee in their efforts towards reaping the fullest measure of charity that it may be possible for the society to maintain."[3] In support of the Food Administration's conservation program he wrote: "To the Catholic the practice of self-denial will not be a new experience. The Church teaches her children the necessity of mortification at all times, and she believes in the special efficacy of abstinence, fasting and prayer at stated seasons. . . . These are the arms with which she equips the faithful for the spiritual combat of life. These too are the weapons with which our beloved country would now furnish us in order that we may successfully contend for the salvation of its most cherished institutions."[4] On at least one occasion he agreed to serve as Honorary Chairman of an organization. The League of National Unity formed to combat those who opposed the war, and to arouse patriotic feelings among all creeds and classes. He informed President Wilson that the League worked "to the end that our countrymen may see the folly of grave disobedience of unjust and ill-tempered criticism of national policies. . . ."[5]

The formal role usually carried him into public affairs, but every now and then he assumed it in speaking to his own Church. Pope Benedict XV set aside June 29, 1918, the feast of S.S. Peter and Paul, as a day for all Catholics to turn their minds and souls to God, seeking His blessing and guidance. Gibbons, on this occasion joined by the other cardinals, issued a statement through the War Council. Reminding their brethren of the nation's high goals and the Church's service, they said: "Surely this raises our aims and purposes up to the noblest standard of action, and sets the soul of the nation above the meanness and pettiness of selfish conquest or unchristian hate." Calling for obedience to the Pope's wish, they urged: "If we fight like heroes and pray like saints soon will America overcome mere force by greater force, and conquer lust of power by the nobler power of sacrifice and faith." Petitions to the Lord and Saviour would speed the day when all nations saw the way to "mutual concord and understanding."[6]

Some critics have charged that the nationalistic tone of his formal statements represented a subordination of his faith to the goals of the nation.[7] The Cardinal would not have understood such criticism. His view of his faith compelled him to support properly elected civil authorities and a just war. In a small tract on Catholic loyalty he wrote for the Chaplains' Aid Association for distribution to the soldiers, he told them that "as soon as a man is chosen to a public office, . . . then he is clothed with power by the Almighty . . . and in obeying the civil ruler you are obeying God Himself." Citizens, then, owed "hearty and loyal obedience to the constituted authorities," and should be slow to criticize them. Such unstinted loyalty was easier for American citizens since "we live in a country where liberty is granted without license and authority is exercised without despotism, where the Government holds over us the aegis of its protection without interfering with the God-given rights of conscience."[8] In addition, he almost always carefully placed his statements in the context of Catholic faith and social thought. He repudiated the militancy espoused by some and defined hatred as unworthy of the Christian, but he saw no need to apologize for his love of the nation. Many years before the war in an essay on patriotism he had declared: "my rights as a citizen were not abdicated or abridged on becoming a Christian prelate, and the sacred character which I profess, far from lessening, rather increases, my obligations to my country."[9]

While the formal role did not worry him, at times its demands wearied him. He willingly accepted the responsibility and he appreciated the fact that others in the Hierarchy shared it to a degree, but he also knew the uniqueness of his position made a full sharing of the task impossible. Not only was he the elder statesman, but his archdiocese included Washington, D.C., and therefore thrust him into national affairs. These considerations, along with the valuable example of the War Council, helped convince him of the need for a post-war agency, centrally located, which "could accomplish more than any individual, however able or willing he might be." The American Church had a great opportunity but it suffered from "the lack of a unified force that might be directed to the furthering of those general policies which are vital to all."[10] Centralization was happening in almost every sphere of life, in the government and in education, and it had to happen in the Church too. To the bishops he charged with planning for such a central agency he said: "on your younger minds and stronger arms, devolves the duty of surveying the field and planning the great work."[11] The Welfare Council immediately began to fulfil the Cardinal's hopes and to share the load of leadership by speaking on behalf of Catholic social thought in national affairs.

Cardinal Gibbons provided the authority and the organizational initiative; Father John Burke had the vision and carried out the actual working arrangements. Burke combined the inner life of a contemplative man with the skills of a community organizer and diplomat. His parents were Irish immigrants, his father a horseshoer living in New York City, when John was born on June 6, 1875. The family resided for most of his early years in the parish of St. Paul the Apostle, under the ministry of the Paulist Fathers. There he came into contact with this relatively new American Order, founded in 1858 by Father Isaac Hecker and three other converts to Catholicism for the express purpose of winning converts to the faith. The Paulists early established an extensive missionary and publishing program as a means of furthering their goals. John did well in school and like a small but growing number of immigrant children decided to attend college. He graduated from Jesuit-run St. Francis Xavier in 1896 and entered the Community of St. Paul the Apostle. The next several years he lived in Washington, studying for the priesthood at the Paulist Seminary on the campus of Catholic University of America. Ordained a priest June 9, 1899, in the University Chapel, he stayed on for two more years of theological study. Sometime later he commented that Paulists Hecker and Walter Elliott were the greatest influences on his life, but during these years in the classroom Prof. William Kerby also made an impact in the areas of social action and reform. The teacher and student developed a strong friendship, vigorously renewed in their work on the War Council.

Young Father Burke began his ministry in various cities, giving missions and doing traditional pastoral work. He was tall, with unusually large hands, and with a warm, friendly, and gentle manner. Devoted to his priestly calling, he had already begun to show an inclination to develop the inner life to a degree not typical of his fellow priests. In 1903, while on assignment in Iowa, he received a call to join the staff of *The Catholic World*, and after a year of apprenticeship he became editor. The specific reasons that inspired his superiors to make the appointment are not known, but within a few years his success with the journal must have fulfilled their most ambitious expectations. The work required not only the exercise of literary talents and knowledge, which he possessed, but also the skills of office management which he rapidly acquired. Writing editorials, soliciting articles, and editing an occasional book filled his time, but did not exhaust his energies. In 1911 he helped found the Catholic Press Association and through it became involved in the American Federation of Catholic Societies. These forays into national life did not distract him from his assigned task. Even during the war he divided his time between war work and editing, spending several days each week at his New York office. He resisted pressure from Bishop Muldoon to leave the journal and expressed considerable reluctance, even some unhappiness, when called to full-time service with the Welfare Council. Prior to the formation of this new Council he had confided to Kerby that he had little inclination to continue in the work: "I have done my share and played my part. The motive of immediate service to country has gone. The motive of service to the Church would win my consent to further service if I were asked. But it wouldn't be what I liked."[12] He did not formally retire from the journal until 1922. For the rest of his career until his death in 1936 he led the Welfare Council, later Welfare Conference, as its chief executive officer. Despite his initial hesitancy, he found this work increasingly fulfilled his vision of a national voice and ministry for his Church.

Father Burke made two quite different but closely related contributions to the War Council and through it to Catholic life in America. First, and of lesser importance, was the actual organizing work, beginning with the Chaplains' Aid Association, through the August, 1917, meeting, culminating in the War Council and its successor. If Gibbons took on the mantle of commander in chief of the Church's forces, Burke led the men and women in the trenches. He made the key contacts, decided on the next moves, and worked with fellow officer Muldoon when he arrived with aid. He never aspired to the commander's job, accepting his sometimes distasteful task graciously and with a degree of self-depreciation. The work was a necessity, not a favorite choice, and if anything, that perspective heightened his commitment and desire to perform well. Commander Gibbons set the agenda; officer Burke followed and always with an eye on the future. His favorite Bible verse was this: "He that puts his hand to the plough and looks back is not worthy of the kingdom of God."[13] As he struggled to help his

Church exercise a vital wartime ministry, so also he tried to build a structure that would make an expanded ministry possible after the war. The bishops worried him because he feared they might hesitate to carry it on and he did not breathe easily until they voted to do so. The Welfare Council was his wartime structure adapted for peaceful service, and although many changes have been made in the decades since then, its successor continues to bear the imprint of his work.

Organization made wartime ministry possible and established long-term patterns, but his primary contribution lay in the realm of ideas, not institutions. He revealed this most succinctly in a letter he wrote his secretary shortly after Cardinal Gibbons succeeded in getting his reassignment to fulltime administrative work: "I don't want the Welfare Council work. I'm not fitted for it. I never went into the priesthood for it. I don't think I'm called in any way to direct the national work of the Catholic Church in the United States. . . . You say you knew it: you knew the national work must be done. Yes, I knew it and I saw it but while the vision may be for me, I don't think the achievement is. Or rather the achievement as a personal thing has no charm for me. It has no stimulation. The vision has, but whatever I do, the vision is beyond the achievement."[14] His outstanding gift to his Church was the idea, a vision of a national Church, of Catholic unity. It was his passion, consuming him and enveloping all his other ideas. It did not come to him just in the war years, but it was strongest then, literally controlling and shaping everything he had to say. His messages always took the same form, whether he talked about the American Federation or a possible war council or a women's or men's organization: the unity of Christ meant the unity of His Church, meant those called to serve Him and His Church should begin with that unity and seek to mirror it in themselves and their organizations.

Surely others had a similar vision and held the same theological convictions, but Burke was the man in the center, generating the energy, activating the vision and with quiet but intense persuasion evoking it in others. Unity was the heart of his message to the August meeting which gave birth to the War Council. Three years later he carried the same theme to a large and representative gathering of Catholic women, called to effect a national organization. "We ought to be united," he told them. "We should think of ourselves, not as individuals, not as particular groups, . . . but as members of that one Body of which Christ is the Head. We live in Him, Who lifted us out of ourselves and incorporated us into Himself: bound us together one with another, not in ourselves, but in Him."[15] Hardly practical advice for organization and yet his emphasis elicited precisely that. It helped people focus on one center, beyond their dioceses, parishes, and personal groups or programs. It was the word for the hour and became the vehicle of practical work. Commenting on the credit due him for helping create the Welfare Council he said: "The NCWC was not thought out by me: it was given to me. From the beginning it was like a self-evident proposition. Granting Christ and the Church, it is nothing but Himself living in the Church and we (sic) living in the Church and we (sic) living in Him and her. So far as I could, it was for me to work it out."[16] Like St. Bernard of Clairvaux centuries earlier, the vision led to action; the life of the spirit led to an active life in the world. He nurtured his spiritual life carefully, partly by editing books on Christian mystics like St. Teresa, and partly by editing and writing books on prayer and meditation. He sustained throughout his life his early pattern of combining an active ministry with the spirit of a mystic.

The language suggested ecumenism, but he was not ecumenical in the full meaning of that word. The vision of unity related to the Catholic Church, not to all Christians, and he emphasized it with those in his Church to make them aware of their own deficiencies. They were widely separated by parish and diocese and organizations and the divisions had seriously disrupted Catholic unity which he fervently believed had to be restored. Beyond that he did not venture. He knew that some Protestants, especially through the Federal Council, espoused a fuller ecumenism, but he showed little interest beyond the general assertion that the desire to discover the unity of Christ always deserved support.[17] At the outset of war he suggested that patriotic service by Catholics might help prove the truth of the Church's claims and then Americans "will recognize the Church as the teacher that is of God."[18] As Protestant hegemony disintegrated, the Catholic Church would take its place. The war taught him that this was not going to happen and helped him accept, gradually and reluctantly, religious pluralism.

Theological ecumenism was strictly Catholic, yet curiously, practical unity was inclusive. Perhaps he was simply pragmatic, aware that Catholics had to work with Protestants and Jews on specific social projects. However, his language betrayed something deeper, a kind of active faith partially separate from his dogmatic one, that led him to propose and create vehicles for ecumenical action. Reporting on the American Federation's annual meeting in 1916, he said delegates discussed not only the work of the Church, "but the close and happy relations that should exist between ourselves and our separated brethren." Those who differed in doctrine were not expected to agree in doctrine, "but we do say that the American Federation in its social activity stands on a platform thoroughly American and sufficiently broad to include men of all faiths and all beliefs."[19] The Committee of Six which he chaired during the war functioned on behalf of such broad-based religious ministry.[20]

Organizing and vision obviously intersected at many vital points, on behalf of both Catholic and practical ecumenical activity, and gave shape and substance to the War Council. They were Burke's major contributions but did not include all his war work. He was an editor and through his editorials and other writings an expositor on many important topics. The consequences of his ideas in terms of personal influence in committees and on the public mind cannot be pinpointed, but as the views of a key figure in the implementation of Catholic wartime ministry they carried considerable weight.

In the years between 1914 and 1917 he shared the opinions of most Catholics in official positions, supporting American neutrality and advocating closer and more serious attention to the Pope's peace initiatives. In 1915 he editorialized: "War is not a necessity of human nature. War is by no means a Christian tradition. Indeed our very profession of Christian means that we are pacifists."[21] Like the vast majority of churchmen, Protestant and Catholic, his views evolved toward accepting the possibility of war as it came closer home. The April, 1917, edition of his journal went to press before the declaration of war, and he told his readers that if war should come they should understand that it "has been literally forced upon our country, and she is compelled to take up arms for her own honor and for justice among men."[22] This set the stage for the final movement of his mind on the war, announced in the lead article of the following issue: "Not only has the decision of our Government done away with all difference, so that we stand a united people, determined to push this war to a successful issue with all our power, but the long months of patient waiting have shown more and more clearly, and now with a clearness that admits of no question, that we have set out on a war that is eminently just." The argument closely paralleled that of the archbishops and he quoted the statements of the three Cardinals and much of Wilson's war speech in further defining his views. The justness of the war did not lead to any celebration of it. Patriotic as he was, he never stepped across the line into militancy. The hour of war was "solemn, even tragic." The mission of the nation was high; and its goals could not be achieved without "the true Faith of our Lord Jesus Christ. Let our prayer be that the entry of our Country into war may sober the hearts and turn the minds of her children not only to the high mission to which she has set herself, but to the eternal truths of God, which alone will insure its fulfilment."[23]

The brief phrase "all difference" occupied one section of the border between the just war analysis and the views of the militants, and Burke came closer to crossing that line on this issue than on any other. Although he never advocated hating the enemy abroad or those who disagreed with the war at home, he did deplore the lack of unanimity and grouped those who refused to agree among the uninformed, the ignorant, the selfish, and the shirkers.[24] He highlighted Cardinal Gibbons' role in the League of National Unity. People had the right to oppose and even resist laws they believed to be unjust, but what those people did not grasp was that "however lawful such a protest might be in ordinary circumstances, it is absolutely criminal when, as now, the very life of the nation is endangered. Having entered the war it is a matter of life and death that our country should win. For such a victory the complete unity of the nation is absolutely necessary."[25] Since no names were named and no groups defined, it is a little difficult to determine exactly to whom he was referring, but his language left little room for any kind of dissent. And yet, almost always, he put such appeals for national unity in the context of Catholic unity. The dissidents were not so much pilloried as they were informed of the truth and invited to embrace it. What people did not understand was that the "basis of a nation's life is spiritual; that our Catholic faith, because it is the teaching of God and of His beloved Son Jesus Christ, is the only key that opens to man's vision the right principles of that national life, and to his heart the inspiration that yields fidelity, hope and loyalty. Of Catholicism patriots are born."[26] Dissenters were encouraged to accept, by the editor who was ever a missionary, the Catholic faith as the only sure basis of unity.

If he edged near the militants on national unity, he moved far away from them on repentance. The theme that aroused them against Speer did not evoke a similar outburst against him, but his views were, if anything, even more plainly stated. Repentance belonged to religion and was the desire to undo offences of the past and the determination not to do them again. Although it began with the individual, it extended to his participation in national sins. Just as personal repentance foreshadowed personal regeneration, so national repentance was a "forerunner of renewed national life." "We as a nation," he said, "know that we have ample cause to strike our heart and exclaim: *mea culpa.*"[27] Genuine national repentance would bring many gifts. It would

> free us from the unsafe boastfulness too characteristic
>   of our country . . .
> make clearer the way for a more united national spirit;
> show us how we have failed in our duty to thousands in
>   our own country who, because of injustice, have never
>   had reason to look upon her and love her as a mother;
> bring out in clear light the magnitude of the task before
>   us both during and after the war;
> sanctify our sacrifice, sober our imagination, restrain
>   our habits, and enlarge our trust;
> help us to realize our need for charity from others and
>   through this realization, to extend charity to others.[28]

Editor Burke greeted the peace with thanksgiving, joy, and caution. While everyone celebrated the end of the war, the return of the soldiers and sailors, and the victory of democratic institutions, he thought people should also be aware of the new duties and responsibilities that arrived with peace. Faithful readers were probably not surprised at the vigilant tone. He had printed numerous reminders of relief needs that would follow the war, including an analysis of the British Labor Party's reconstruction program. Catholics in particular, given the large number of foreign-born in their midst, were responsible for the "apostolate of Americanism," by which he meant a vigorous and extensive Americanization program.[29] Reconstruction would require tempering enthusiasm with wisdom, especially since many of those efforts were needed at home. Returning soldiers would see more clearly through the eyes of their sacrifices "the wrongs and injustices that afflict the body politic," and they would seek remedies. "All of us," he declared, "must be ruled and guided by those principles of justice which are not subjective but objective, which bespeak the common welfare, which execute justice and which are the immutable foundations of social well-being, of order and of progress."[30]

Jubilant Americans were unprepared for even these relatively mild words of restraint and were taken totally by surprise by the near total collapse of the idealistic spirit that occurred in the immediate post-war period. As the years unfolded, cynicism and despair captured an ever widening circle of people. Father Burke resisted that encirclement, but he did become increasingly unhappy about American participation in the war. The memory of war service did not sour; the absence of achievement of national goals left a bitter taste. He wrote about this on occasion, and often obliquely. In a long essay on the relation of the Church to nationalism he used remote historical examples to make what seemed to be a very contemporary point. The Church advocated patriotism, the genuine love of country, but it repudiated, indeed declared war on, nationalism, which was "the belief that only those of our own nation are our brothers."[31] Nationalism perverted patriotism. It placed one's nation above right and wrong, insisted on absolute uniformity, and demanded that the nation reign supreme over all other loyalties. The Church rejected this in favor of Christian brotherhood, which began at home with patriotism but did not reach its true end "until it has circumnavigated the globe."[32] The rigors of peace chastened him somewhat, but he had spoken just as clearly during the war, keeping close to traditional Catholic thinking, yet turning it to the terms of his own passion for unity.

Others associated with the War Council joined Gibbons and Burke in the leadership tasks, both within the organization and as public spokesmen. Their opinions formed part of the total fabric of Catholic thought of the time. Among those whose views were most influential were Bishop Muldoon, Father Ryan, and Professor Kerby. Peter Muldoon, like so many of the Catholic leaders of the era, was born into the Irish immigrant tradition, on October 10, 1863, in Columbia, California. Although his early education was in the West, he came East to finish it, attending St. Mary's College in Marion, Kentucky, and St. Mary's Seminary in Baltimore. Ordained in 1886 in Brooklyn, he spent some years in pastoral work in Chicago before his episcopal consecration in 1901. Appointed first Bishop of Rockford in 1908, he continued in that post until his death in 1927. His family were deeply committed to the Church, with one sister and an aunt in religious orders and an uncle and a cousin in the priesthood. By interest and conviction he moved beyond his diocese into national Catholic affairs, one of a relatively small number of bishops who did so, choosing as his area social action and reform. From his position as first Chairman of the Social Service Commission of the American Federation he gained a wide view of what the Church was doing and of new areas for ministry. Immigrants were one of his long term concerns—how to keep those who were Catholic faithful, and how to assimilate and Americanize them all. Settlement houses were one solution and the war offered another. In October, 1917, speaking at the dedication of the Knights of Columbus auditorium at Camp Grant he said: "This splendid hall is the best exemplification of the fusion of all nationalities that can be had in the United States today."[33]

Bishop Muldoon had an active diocesan war ministry before he received the call to lead the Council's Adminstrative Committee. In this work he was the typical bishop, although somewhat more involved than most, responding to special wartime ministries with little opportunity for reflection or analysis of the larger issues. As early as May, 1917, he had decided to help the Red Cross. When soldiers began arriving at nearby Camp Grant, he provided priests to hear confessions and say Mass. His diocese quickly joined the Chaplains' Aid Association, and he personally attended a conference in New York City to become informed about its program. Speeches to civic groups were part of every bishop's task and he turned his in the fall of 1917 into occasions to present the needs of ministry in wartime. After January, 1918, he had to shift some of his attention to the Council's work, but his *Diary* attests to continued active involvement in local affairs, particularly in sustaining the ministry at the Camp and in working with the local fund raising programs of the Knights.

On the national platform he demonstrated that he was primarily a doer, an organizer, a negotiator, and not a proposer of ideas. He had never published extensively and Council leadership did not change his style. The new War Council took shape under his direction, and so did the Welfare Council. He and Burke worked easily together, since he shared with his Paulist friend commitment to national Catholic unity and direct social action. His crowning achievement came in the months from August to December, 1918, when he negotiated the united financial campaign and then led the Church's participation in it. Only once did he step out of the role of facilitator to help shape public opinion, and the occasion did not arise until after the Armistice. The Bishop was deeply concerned with reconstruction problems. If nations had renewed their social orders, the war might have been unnecessary. One problem he saw with most proposals was their focus on physical rather than spiritual reconstruction. "It is necessary," he counselled, "to reconstruct the world on the Christian plan, . . . that all the nations do unto one another according to the teachings of Jesus Christ."[34] When he and the other bishops of the Administrative Committee received a proposed reconstruction statement prepared by Father Ryan, they studied, endorsed and issued it. The Bishops' Program of Reconstruction and his defense of it gave him a national public audience for the first time.[35]

The Bishops' Program quickly became the most striking restatement of Catholic social thought to appear in the war era and moved Father Ryan to center stage, although he had never been far from the spotlight, producing a number of thoughtful articles analyzing the impact of the war on society. His essay on freedom of speech and the press published in February, 1918, opened for discussion an area of social thought that related to the Council's work in more theoretical than practical terms. A model of reasoned analysis rooted in Catholic thought, it projected a basis for active support for Pope Benedict's peace proposals.

Like most Catholic social thinkers of this era, Ryan found the basis for his reflections in the writings of Pope Leo XIII. The Holy Father had taught that both freedom of speech and of the press were rights only if used in moderation and only if they did not exceed the ends of true liberty. Unfortunately, Ryan's fellow Americans held a "greatly exaggerated conception of these privileges," and tended to allow persons to say anything they pleased so long as it was neither obscene nor libelous.[36] Conflicts had quickly arisen in both the legal and moral spheres and he set out to define proper Catholic boundaries and behaviour.

The legal issues did not interest him greatly. Some citizens argued that the constitutional right of free speech had been abridged by the Espionage Act which prohibited written or spoken words disparaging the effort to recruit men for the war. Ryan pointed out that the Constitution also gave Congress the right to declare war and prosecute it to a successful end. The Espionage Act was not so much a violation of the First Amendment as it was a fulfilment of the First Article. Moreover, the Constitution provided that disputes over interpretation should be decided by the courts, and those engaged in the legal issues should seek that remedy.

The moral arguments were the crucial ones. People generally obeyed the law, but they did not always grasp the moral implications of their behaviour. Ryan believed a democracy, dependent as it was on free and open discussion and the exchange of opinions, had to provide a general guarantee of free speech in war as well as in peace. Government officials were never infallible. Of course, war made a difference, since loss in war could mean the loss of independence. Governments were within their rights, therefore, to restrict speech in wartime in those areas essential to the successful prosecution of the war. Individuals behaved morally when they focused their criticism on policies in the stages of formation and on issues not essential to the war. One could "criticize George Creel's Committee on Public Information without rendering oneself liable to the charge of obstructing the Government, or exercising an unreasonable freedom of speech."[37] However, criticism in the area of the unessential carried an additional responsibility and a risk. The moral individual always criticized in a proper, helpful, moderate spirit. Criticism based on lies was clearly unreasonable, but so was destructive criticism that made people feel discouraged and therefore indirectly hindered the war effort. All critical exercise of speech also carried the risk that the government might disagree with the individual over what was essential. Ryan believed strongly in the power of properly elected authority. He advised that "while the Government is no more infallible than the dissenting individual, it has on its side the presumption of truth that always accompanies the acts of authority."[38] The reasoning held for just or unjust wars and meant that unjust ones would be very difficult to stop by means of dissent. He appreciated that and said that happily the present war was a just one. To those who persisted in opposing policies the government judged essential, he offered silence or martyrdom.

The heart of the moral use of speech and of the press in wartime lay in the reasonable and helpful opinions, even critical ones, concerning those things not essential to the war effort. In a war as total as the Great War, that could amount to a rather severe limitation of basic rights. Ryan more or less admitted this by applying his principle to a very important specific case of particular concern to Catholics. What, he asked, is the moral situation in relation to peace proposals, which might involve negotiation with the enemy? Specifically, could Catholics advocate Pope Benedict's proposal of the previous August which President Wilson rejected? The general argument concerning the need for open exchange in a democracy led him to respond affirmatively: "I cannot see that such freedom of speech is unreasonable. It seems to me, that . . . men and women have a moral right to advocate Pope Benedict's or any other not palpably unreasonable programme of peace negotiations. After all, the President is not infallible. His rejection of the Pope's proposals may have been a mistake."[39] His answer included one qualification and two conditions. If the government should explicitly deny discussion of peace as Secretary McAdoo proposed, then even appeals for the Pope's plan would be silenced. Moreover, those who advocated it must do so with moderation and modesty and "should not tack on to them lying insinuations about our reasons for entering the War or our objects in prosecuting it."[40] In light of this second condition he proposed a formula for the peace advocate: "I believe that the United States ought to seek peace along such and such lines, but I recognize that until a truce has actually been declared, the warmaking forces of our country should be kept up to the highest possible mark of efficiency and activity. I do not want my views on peace to have any influence towards a relaxation of our capacity to fight."[41]

How many people reasoned their way along Ryan's path cannot be calculated. He was certain neither Senator LaFollette nor Morris Hillquit had. If pacifists ignored it, so did militants, who too readily used the press to limit speech, in some instances persuading periodicals that all discussion of peace was unpatriotic and immoral. No leader of the Council directly attributed his views on the issue to Ryan; however, Council policy on peace proposals and reconstruction plans reflected his views.

Father Kerby combined the organizing skills of Muldoon and the reflective abilities of Ryan. He had long exercised both talents on behalf of his Church, as one of the founders of the National Conference and as the leading American Catholic theoretician on socialism. Drawn into war work very early through the informal discussion group in the summer of 1917, he served not only as Chairman of the Women's Committee but also as close adviser to Father Burke. After the war Burke told him that his cooperation and sympathy had been of great support and comfort, and he might well have added that Kerby's ideas had helped fulfil the wartime ministry. Kerby wrote nothing comparable to the Bishops' Program; his contribution to the policy was more general. But he did maintain a heavy writing schedule and his essays found willing publishers. One article in particular, selected by Burke for his journal, reflected the widespread conviction among Catholic leaders, and others, too, that the war had changed the world more quickly and deeply than almost anyone could either calculate or assimilate. He believed that the war was re-educating society and forcing men to re-examine their fundamental presuppositions closely. The task overwhelmed most people who took government, morality and law as fixed realities. They simply were not prepared to evaluate current affairs in terms of "the reorganization of the world."[42]

The re-education by war took two forms and Kerby strongly favored both of them because he believed they brought the world closer to the Christian interpretation of life. First, the war revealed a vast reservoir of good will, capacity for sacrifice, and concern for the neighbors and the strangers in life. He marvelled to find such attitudes "in a civilization which has been frankly builded on an appeal to selfishness."[43] In terms of property and welfare, Americans typically defended their own rights against all comers, to the point of an extreme individualism. The war compelled a collective, communal view. Taxes invaded accumulated wealth, the draft limited personal freedom, and the "gospel of the clean plate" entered every dining room. Personal re-education had a corollary in national policies, and nationalists found themselves in a changed situation too. He claimed isolationism died with the war, and preferences and principles "as they affect international relations must be restated in the new political science where we shall find our guidance. At every point where international policies touch us or we touch them, words, emotions, policies, sentiment must be changed in consonance with the new position which the United States now takes in that larger world . . . There is no longer any dream of a nation at peace. There is vision now only of the world at peace."[44]

The second lesson of the war related directly to the nation. He saw the emergence of the American nation state as one embodiment of the unity of life, long taught by his faith. This unity bridged geographical regions and challenged personal prerogatives. The nation undertook a multitude of new functions including intervention in industry, the determination of consumer prices, and the regulation of interest on capital. It required patriotic service, not self-service, and it exercised its muscle to achieve its ends when and where citizens became reluctant to give willingly on their own. Predicting with some accuracy, he insisted "there will be motive in abundance long after peace is declared for maintaining the expanded function that the state has lately assumed."[45] He did not see quite so clearly the coming clash between this new sense of national unity and the requirements of international peace and good will.

Kerby wrote with the war still in progress and the re-education process in its early stages. The ultimate consequences of the war lay in the future and he perceived that a large part of the difficulty of the time lay in uncertainty. Americans, like most people, wanted immediate gratification and instant interpretation. Although he suggested some favorable outcomes, like the continuation of the changes in industry which improved the status of workers, he declined to predict too much. Instead, he counselled that the Christian faith, with its system of deferred compensation in terms of eternal goals, could help Americans understand what was happening and teach them to accept postponed fulfillment. At the end of his analysis the professor turned priest and invited his readers to turn their eyes to God and find the true path to the future and peace.

Catholic social thought during the war flowed directly out of Catholic theological and social tradition, and the views of individual leaders served to interpret rather than change that tradition. That fact in no way diminished the important role of the interpreters, all of whom were responsible for the creation and development of the War Council as the vehicle of the Church's ministry. If they contributed little new to its substance, they definitely charted a new course, down a path of united national ministry and social involvement and reform. Burke's vision of unity and Kerby's understanding of the demands of a newly conscious nation state, set the direction of the Council in wartime and in the subsequent peace. Gibbons, Burke, Muldoon, Ryan, and Kerby were not the only ones involved in Catholic war work, but they were the key figures, and their lives and thoughts demonstrate how, on the basis of the just war theory, they fulfilled their calling to a Catholic ministry in war.

1. John Tracy Ellis, "The Spirit of Cardinal Gibbons," *Records of the American Catholic Historical Society of Philadelphia* 76 (1965): 14–15.

2. James Cardinal Gibbons to The Committee on General Catholic Interests and Affairs, May 5, 1919. Copy in NCWC Archives.

3. James Cardinal Gibbons to Theodore N. Vail, n.d. Copy in NCWC Archives.

4. James Cardinal Gibbons to Reverend and dear Father, June 26, 1917. Copy of Form Letter in NCWC Archives.

5. Ellis, *The Life of James Cardinal Gibbons* 2:247.

6. *Fight and Pray.* A National Catholic War Council Pamphlet.

7. Dohen, *Nationalism and American Catholicism*, p. 155.

8. James Cardinal Gibbons, *Catholic Loyalty* (New York: The Paulist Press, 1917), pp. 3–7.

9. James Cardinal Gibbons, "Patriotism and Politics," *North American Review* 154 (April, 1892): 385.

10. Quoted in Ellis, *The Life of James Cardinal Gibbons* 2:300.

11. James Cardinal Gibbons to The Committee on General Catholic Interests.

12. John J. Burke to William Kerby, August 15, 1919, in the Papers of William J. Kerby, in the Archives of Catholic University of America, Washington, D.C. Hereafter cited: Kerby Papers.

13. Sheerin, *Never Look Back*, p. 23. The reference is Luke 9:62.

14. *Ibid.*, pp. 60–61.

15. *Address of Rev. John J. Burke, C.S.P. at The National Conference Catholic Women* (Washington, D.C.: National Catholic Welfare Council, 1920), pp. 3–4.

16. Quoted in Sheerin, *Never Look Back*, p. 40.

17. *Ibid.*, pp. 26, 193–94. See also "With Our Readers," *The Catholic World* 109 (May, 1919): 276–83.

18. Williams, *American Catholics and the War*, p. 119.

19. John J. Burke, "The Catholic Federation Convention," *The Outlook* 113 (August 30, 1916): 1031–32.

20. See Chapters VI and VII for the Committee of Six.

21. Quoted in Sheerin, *Never Look Back*, p. 29.

22. "With Our Readers," *The Catholic World* 105 (April, 1917): 138.

23. "The Call To Patriotism," *The Catholic World* 105 (May, 1917): 152.

24. "Recent Events," *The Catholic World* 105:276.

25. "Recent Events," *The Catholic World* 106 (November, 1917): 273.

26. Williams, *American Catholics and the War*, p. 117.

27. "With Our Readers," *The Catholic World* 106 (January, 1918): 571.

28. *Ibid.*, 572.

29. "With Our Readers," *The Catholic World* 107 (August, 1918): 717.

30. "With Our Readers," *The Catholic World* 108 (December, 1918): 426–27.

31. John J. Burke, "The Historical Attitude of the Church Toward Nationalism," *Catholic Historical Review* 14 (April, 1928): 69.

32. *Ibid.*, 79.

33. *Muldoon's Diary*, October 17, 1917.

34. "Bishop Declares Christ Must Sit at Peace Table," Rockford *Republic*, January 7, 1919. Cited in *Muldoon's Diary*.

35. See, for example, To the Editor of the *Nation* from Peter J. Muldoon, National Catholic War Council, April 11, 1919, in *The Nation* 108 (April 19, 1919): 608. See Chapter IX for the Reconstruction Program.

36. John Ryan, "Freedom of Speech in War Time," *The Catholic World* 106 (February, 1918): 577.

37. *Ibid.*, 580.

38. *Ibid.*, 581.

39. *Ibid.*, 584.

40. *Ibid.*

41. *Ibid.*, 585.

42. William J. Kerby, "Re-Education by War," *The Catholic World* 106 (January, 1918): 451.

43. *Ibid.*, 454.

44. *Ibid.*, 455–56.

45. *Ibid.*, 457.

VI

The Sacramental Ministry

The National Catholic War Council and the General War-Time Commission strongly affirmed that their task was the religious life of the soldiers and sailors,and that meant first and foremost a ministry to them defined by preaching the Gospel and administering the sacraments. The fighting men had other needs, too, including social and recreational ones. The churches developed a wide variety of social service programs. They turned the recreational aspects of ministry over to the Y.M.C.A., the Y.W.C.A., and the Knights of Columbus. The division of ministry into sacramental, social, and recreational was never so distinct in practice as it was in theory; the priority of the sacramental ministry was always clear. Father Burke said it as succinctly as it could be said when he told the representatives gathered at the August, 1917, meeting that "it is the Mass that matters. . . ."

Chaplains were the traditional agents of this ministry. They had a long and respected history in America, but unfortunately in the years immediately preceding World War I their reputation tarnished and they fell on hard times. In the decade after 1898 four chaplains were either courtmartialed or resigned to avoid trial, the largest proportion of the chaplaincy ever disciplined in such a short span of time.[1] Until 1913 appointments were largely a matter of political patronage, and politicians did not always choose the best men for the job. Older ministers and clergy who did not fit well into local church situations seemed to dominate the selections.[2] When the nation entered the war, a high percentage of the army chaplains were political appointees who were near retirement and unprepared to serve effectively in the crisis. Navy chaplains faced similar, though slightly less serious, circumstances. Pre-war difficulties went deeper than the spoils system and a few inept men. Morale had all but disappeared. The government paid little attention to them. No less a figure than General John Pershing characterized them as follows: "Custom in our army . . . had often relegated them to the status of handy men who were detailed to write up boards of survey or operate libraries."[3] Chaplain Paul D. Moody, son of evangelist Dwight L. Moody and a staff chaplain in France during the war, explained that facilities for ministering to the spiritual needs of the men were "utterly disorganized, if the word disorganized can be applied to the almost non-existent."[4] Discriminated against in rank, and consequently in pay, they were self-equipped, which usually meant ill-equipped. The government provided "virtually no items of a professional nature."[5] They had no corps and no chief. At every turn regulations told them they were an extra group, relatively unimportant in the military scheme of things.

The government's attitude, far from revealing some special hostility toward the chaplains, largely reflected the opinion of the churches. With very few exceptions the religious bodies had taken only perfunctory interest in the appointment process and no interest in their ministry. One historian encompassed in one brief paragraph the instances he could find of denominational action on behalf on chaplains between 1899 and 1917. The exceptions were the Protestant Episcopal Church, the Methodist Episcopal Church, the Roman Catholic Church, and the Federal Council of Churches.[6] The three churches had each appointed some one official or a committee to serve as a central board of review for all candidates. The Council was more extensively involved.

Catholic action typified that of the interested churches. In 1905, Archbishop John Ireland suggested at the annual meeting of the archbishops that they centralize procedures for chaplains. Candidates had to seek appointment through their own bishops and then had to obtain their faculties from the bishops where they were stationed. The procedures confused chaplains and the War Department alike. The archbishops created the Catholic Army and Navy Chaplains' Bureau to represent the Hierarchy in matters relating to the appointment of chaplains. Under its first director, the Rev. A. P. Doyle, C.S.P., Rector of the Apostolic Mission House, it became the liaison between the Church and the War Department. Father Lewis O'Hern became director when Father Doyle died in 1913, and continued Doyle's policies. O'Hern worked hard, but the peacetime army and navy made few places for chaplains and he had little leverage to urge more. When war broke out, there were sixteen Catholic army chaplains and eight Catholic navy ones, and ten others attached to various National Guard units.

The Federal Council first became interested in the chaplaincy in 1911 when a navy chaplain, very likely Livingston Bayard, visited General Secretary Macfarland and told him that there had not been an increase in the number of navy chaplains for fifty years.[7] Investigation showed the charge to be all too accurate, exposed morale problems, and revealed an absurdly low proportion of chaplains to men, with 21 for 53,375 men. A similar poor ratio existed in the army. The Council petitioned President Wilson, members of Congress, the Secretary of War, and the Secretary of the Navy for more chaplains, specifically requesting that one be stationed on each major ship and at each navy yard and at every occupied army post.[8] The petitions generated little more than polite replies from the officials, but they marked the beginning of a concentrated Council campaign on behalf of chaplains.

The turning point in this campaign came in 1913. Bayard pressed Council leaders for more concrete action and presented them a proposed bill which would, if adopted by Congress, improve the naval chaplaincy by creating new appointment procedures, by authorizing increased numbers, and by making other improvements. They endorsed it and decided to lobby for its passage. Unfortunately, they had relatively primitive machinery for active and sustained lobbying. They had, however, supported a Washington Committee, an informal contact group for their work in national affairs. Other Protestant agencies also were interested in establishing a Washington office. These factors encouraged the Council to turn its Washington Committee into a Washington Office, with the help and support of the Home Missions Council. The new outlet opened in January, 1914, under the able leadership of Henry K. Carroll, hired as an Associate Secretary for the job. He promptly visited congressional committees, buttonholed legislators, and wrote many letters to politicians appealing for support. When the bill became law, the Council rightfully claimed a major share in the victory. One historian has judged that "no law ever passed by Congress, following the establishment of the naval chaplaincy, has had such far-reaching consequences for the Corps itself and for the spiritual welfare of naval personnel as this Act of 1914."[9]

Initial success created new problems and needs. The navy discarded the spoils system and turned to the churches for nominees. The Catholic Church, through its Bureau, responded immediately, but Protestant churches had no similar agent. The multiplicity of Protestant groups often discouraged military officials and dictated some united procedure. Carroll first met the problem by helping several denominations establish commissions on the chaplaincy, and then by offering the Council Office as a central nominating headquarters for all Protestant chaplain candidates. This cooperative plan gradually took hold. By the winter of 1916 many denominations were channeling their nominees through the Office, which in turn passed them on to the proper government authorities.[10] As the churches began to nominate chaplains, the need developed to persuade them of the importance of this kind of ministry. At the 1914 encampment of the Grand Army of the Republic the Council shared in founding the Association for the Promotion of the Moral and Religious Welfare of Our Soldiers and Sailors. Reorganized in 1915 as the Religious Welfare League for the Army and Navy, its members consisted largely of residents of Washington who were willing to try to effect changes in army and navy regulations so chaplains could work more efficiently, and to see to it that the soldiers and sailors were "in the thought and on the heart of the Church. . . ."[11]

Just as the Washington Office reached its greatest level of coordination, things began to fall apart. The Home Missions Council discontinued its support in January, 1917, and Carroll resigned. Macfarland refused to let the hopeful work die. He spent February and March in Washington, joined by Worth Tippy when he needed more manpower. By the end of this period he succeeded in combining the functions of the Office and the Religious Welfare League and reorganized them into the General Committee on Army and Navy Chaplains which he located in the Office. With Tippy's assistance he secured an agreement with Secretary of War Baker and the Adjutant General, and with Secretary of the Navy Daniels, that the Council, through this Committee, would have the power both "to investigate and nominate all candidates for chaplains, and that applications already on file in the department should be sent over to the Washington office of the Federal Council."[12] The agreement included only Protestant candidates. Macfarland obtained it by using his executive authority and without a directive from the constituent denominations. They did not always support Council initiatives, but they readily backed the new Committee.

When war began, Catholics and Protestants had ready organizations for recruiting chaplains. Each group had accumulated some experience with the nominating procedures and had developed relationships with the War and Navy Departments. Prospects for successfully supplying the needed chaplains and providing a ministry to the armed forces looked very good. They were realized, too, but only after considerable struggle. Catholics found their structures inadequate and had to reorganize them before they could supply chaplains in the numbers needed. Protestants faced fewer internal difficulties. Both groups had their biggest disputes with the government, particularly with the War Department.

The War Department did not always act consistently in its relations with the churches. It seemed to respond best to suggestions regarding the moral and recreational life of the men under arms, and with considerable reluctance to ideas and programs relating to the sacramental ministry. Its relationship to the Committee of Six is an instance of this complex behavior. Early in the fall of 1917 Father Burke received reports about very poor moral conditions in camps and camp towns in France. He contacted several prominent religious leaders, Protestant and Jewish, and invited them to a meeting in early October. After the consultation they wrote Raymond Fosdick at the War Department, recommending that "the policy adopted and followed by our government in this country with reference to the reduction of immorality among American soliders, the suppression of disorderly houses, etc. should, if possible, be put into operation in those countries where men in the service of the United States may be located, so far as Americans are concerned, and to this end we recommend that our Government bring influence to bear upon any and all authorities concerned to accomplish this desired purpose."[13] The Department agreed to act in accord with this proposal and Fosdick suggested that the informal group might serve in a special advisory capacity on religious matters. After lengthy discussions on their potential usefulness, the group decided to accept the offer and become the Committee of Six, chaired by Father Burke, and including Harry Cutler of the Jewish Welfare Board, and William Adams Brown, Bishop James DeWolf Perry, John R. Mott, and Robert E. Speer, all of the General War-Time Commission. This Committee met more than a dozen times during the war, occasionally on very general matters but usually on some aspect of the chaplaincy. Although Fosdick and the Department helped create it, the Committee often found itself lobbying the Department with proposals relating to the sacramental ministry. Many leaders of ministry during the war, Catholics especially, discovered "there were officials high in the government service, and officers high in the military ranks, to whom the *Sacramental* meaning of the chaplaincy was a closed book—at least until that book was opened even for them by the actual vision of the Sacramental ministry manifesting its divine character on the field of battle."[14]

Father O'Hern realized very early in the war that he faced major internal problems, both in recruiting chaplains and supplying them.

His conversations with Burke, Kerby, and Neill led to the creation of the Chaplains' Aid Association and the War Council. These organizations definitely helped equip chaplains but did little to increase their numbers. Unfortunately, many of the bishops seemed to be among those who did not share Council priorities. They did not join the first Council, nor did they quickly nominate adequate numbers of chaplains.

The confusions of episcopal jurisdiction, troublesome enough in pre-war conditions, multiplied vastly during the war. The leaders of the Church were aware of this. At the same time the archbishops reorganized the Council, the Pope appointed Bishop Hayes, Chaplain Bishop, with spiritual authority over all Catholic chaplains in the armed forces of the United States. The soldiers and sailors became his diocese, or as he preferred to call it, his "wartime jurisdiction," and the chaplains his priests.[15] Whenever a priest entered the chaplaincy, he left his bishop's jurisdiction and entered that of the Chaplain Bishop. Bishop Hayes delayed acting on his new authority until he received official written notification and that did not arrive until the following spring. Once it came he moved rapidly, establishing five Vicars General, one for Overseas and four at home in the Eastern, Great Lakes, Gulf, and Pacific Coast regions, and appointing O'Hern Executive Secretary with power to continue his liaison work in Washington. He communicated these new arrangements to the chaplains and the Hierarchy, telling the chaplains they would shortly receive a canonical visitation and asking them to accept and work within the new system. "Almost everywhere and nearly by everybody," he concluded, "the highest possible value has been set upon the ministry of the Catholic chaplain."[16] Reorganization meant that the "whole, vast, complicated business of supplying spiritual ministry to the hundreds of thousands of Catholics, coming from all portions of the United States, from a hundred dioceses, fell into order and achieved true Catholic unity: unity of purpose, unity of authority, unity of method."[17] If jurisdictional complexities had been the bishops' main reason for hesitancy, then nominations should have picked up, but they did not.

Shortly after this reorganization Congress passed a bill the churches had supported for increasing the number of chaplains. The Church suddenly needed 200 additional regular chaplains plus some for special ministries. Bishop Hayes and the Council wrote the Hierarchy, soliciting their aid. The Council's May, 1918, letter informed the bishops of the new needs and asked them to accept hardships in their dioceses in order to provide the soldiers and sailors with proper spiritual care. The religious orders had responded well; now the bishops must match them. Appealing to their pride, the Council said: "Besides, we cannot tell the government that we the strong church of the United States cannot fill its quota."[18] Nominations failed to meet demand and the Council wrote again in early July. The tone of this letter was sharper, even accusative. "Every effort must be made," the Council argued, "to avoid the responsibility of allowing our soldiers to go to their death without the sacraments, without the help of a priest. If in the future it shall ever be said that the Catholic Church of America deserted her soldiers in the most critical period of the war, it can never be truthfully added that the Administrative Committee did not put the situation plainly and strongly enough before the bishops of the United States, nor can it be said that the United States Government has failed in giving us its cooperation and assistance."[19] Recruitment still did not improve and Council leaders became exasperated. Muldoon reported to the Hierarchy later in July: "All of us, in spite of the great need of priests at home, must acquiesce in the sacrifice of more and more priests for duty in the war." If necessary, the number of masses should be cut, because "the convenience of our people must give way to the spiritual necessities of our soldiers."[20] Finally, the Apostolic Delegate, Archbishop John Bonzano, appealed directly to the bishops. His prestige and authority broke through the resistance, and nominations began to flow freely. By the Armistice the Church had not only filled its quota, but had a substantial waiting list of approved candidates.

While the bishops were responsible for many of the recruitment headaches and delays, they faced some difficult circumstances which were often beyond their control. Different groups approached them for priests. The Knights recruited some for their work and the Red Cross drew off others for special hospital ministries, thus reducing the number available for the regular chaplaincy. The War Department did not count either of these kinds of chaplains in its system until very late in the war. Geography caused other problems. Those bishops who had large army camps in their dioceses often supplied them with volunteer camp pastors and were reluctant to eliminate a ministry nearby for one far away. This worked a special hardship, peculiar to the Church. Many of the largest training centers, needing the greatest number of local pastors, were located in the South and areas of the Mid-west where the Church was weakest and dioceses already short of pastors. The large northern urban areas with many big churches with staffs of priests easily met their diocesan quotas whereas some of the hard-pressed dioceses could not approach theirs. Adjustment of quotas to meet such local conditions helped relieve the pressures on the weaker dioceses and improved recruitment substantially. One other problem affected some dioceses. The Church had just faced the largest single influx of immigrants in its history and had developed a ministry to them involving priests with special language abilities. Some bishops had many priests they could not release, short of eliminating the work of local parishes, and they were justifiably reluctant to do that. Some bishops held back to protect their own prerogatives, but others faced some genuinely painful choices.

Securing chaplains did not seem to involve equipping them, but Church leaders discovered quite early in the war that the government was not going to supply them with the kind of materials they needed. Burke's Aid Association grew slowly but surely from a small New York City base to a national organization. By the time chaplains were called up in large numbers it was ready to meet the demand. The Association performed two related but somewhat different tasks. First, it provided the Catholic Chaplains with their basic kits, at a cost of over $100 each. The kit included "a well made bag, containing a folded mahogany altar, sets of vestments, full sets of altar linens, missal and missal stand, a silver chalice, candles, candle sticks, crucifix, altar cards and everything needed for the celebration of holy Mass, and the ordinary administration of the sacraments."[21] The Aid Association remained in constant touch with the chaplains and renewed supplies as they were needed. It provided some 1800 kits during the war. It also published a bulletin which it circulated to chaplains as well as other members, with stories of camp and front line experiences mixed in with accounts of the work of the local chapters. The government refused to accede to various proposals for an army chaplains' corps, and this periodic contact filled the need for comradeship in an informal way for the Catholic chaplains.

The Aid Association tackled a second and equally ambitious work when it decided to go beyond basic equipment to materials used in counselling and other pastoral situations. It provided over 6,000,000 religious articles, from New Testaments and prayer books, tracts and pamphlets, to rosaries, scapulars and medals. The idea was to place these items in the chaplains' hands so they could distribute them to best advantage. Late in the war the Association took the further step of outfitting some K. of C. and army hospitals with altar furnishings, statuary, confessionals, and other equipment.[22] It remained a voluntary agency, associated with the War Council as one of its committees. Father Burke was the driving force behind its highly successful ministry from start to finish.

Protestants mobilized for chaplains three weeks after the declaration of war. The General Committee on Army and Navy Chaplains held a two-day conference of denominational leaders to perfect its organizational structure and procedures. It invited each denomination to appoint a permanent representative and encouraged each one to select persons from the Washington area because of plans for frequent meetings. Government regulations required that candidates for the chaplaincy be ordained. It established a higher standard, agreeing to restrict nomination in most cases to those ordained clergy with college and preferably seminary training, who also had at least a year of pastoral experience. Candidates might differ in educational qualifications since denominational ordination requirements varied, but they should all have experience in ministry.[23] The details of the nomination procedure produced the major debate. The question turned on the locus of authority and therefore the degree of cooperation. Some argued that the denominations should present the General Committee with their nominations as they had done before the war. This reduced cooperation to a minimum, requiring little effort beyond collecting, filing, and disbursing information. Others wanted the Committee to nominate candidates, proposed by the denominations. They maintained their procedure would "tend to make each man more truly a chaplain of all the Protestant men."[24]

The plan which emerged from this discussion decidedly favored the cooperative arrangement. The nominating procedure involved three stages. First, denominational committees sought applicants and proposed them to the General Committee. Second, the General Committee nominated those who measured up to the qualifications and forwarded their papers to the appropriate government department. Third, the Secretary of the Committee had veto power over every candidate. When he exercised that power, the case could be appealed to the entire Committee. The denominations investigated their own candidates, but the Committee reserved the right to conduct its own inquiries. The denominational committees placed their files in the Washington Office.[25] The plan nationalized and centralized the Protestant chaplaincy for those groups who were associated with the Federal Council as well as for some others which cooperated in this particular venture. The delegates at the Special May Meeting of the Council were told this procedure should make every chaplain "feel not only that his own church is back of him but also every other church, and he should see in himself the pastor of the men of varied faiths who are under his care, and vividly realize the sacredness and responsibility of that relationship."[26] The General Committee became a standing committee of the

General War-Time Commission, but also continued to hold independent status as a special committee of the Federal Council.

The General Committee began to function in an effective manner in May, 1917. Most of the denominations exercised their right to be represented on it, but not all the representatives regularly attended its meetings. The more faithful who performed the routine work included the Rev. E. B. Bagby for the Disciples of Christ; the Rev. Samuel Z. Batten for the Northern Baptist Convention; the Rev. Andrew R. Bird for the Presbyterian Church in the U.S.; the Rev. E. O. Watson for the Methodist Episcopal Church, South; the Rev. Wallace Radcliffe and the Rev. Charles Wood for the Presbyterian Church in the U.S.A.; Bishop Alfred Harding of the Protestant Episcopal Church; the Rev. Charles F. Steck for the National Lutheran Commission for Soldiers' and Sailors' Welfare; the Rev. J. Frederick Wenchel for the Lutheran Church Board for Army and Navy, U.S.A.; and Bishop William F. McDowell for the Methodist Episcopal Church.[27]

The staff and budget of the General Committee were never large. Bishop McDowell served as Chairman as well as the representative of his church. When the Committee became concerned in the summer of 1918 with the government's constant opposition to its larger program, it secured the Bishop's release from his other duties for three months of full-time service. He exercised considerable influence in Washington, and the Committee needed his uninterrupted attention to its problems. Several secretaries worked with it. Macfarland and Tippy met with it in the summer and fall of 1917. Clyde Armitage joined it as Secretary from November, 1917, until October, 1918, when Gaylord S. White replaced him. The numerous changes in personnel did no apparent damage to the effectiveness or the continuity of its program. Its expenses were approximately $55,000 for the three years, 1917 to 1920, and the Washington Office spent some of this on matters not directly related to the chaplains. Money came through the General War-Time Commission, much of it raised by the Interchurch Emergency Campaign.

The Committee focused entirely on securing candidates for the regular chaplaincy. The agreement with the War Department stipulated that it would relinquish the applications which it had in its files. The transfer had not occurred by July 19, and the Committee authorized Bishops McDowell and Harding to go to the Department and "make sincere request that they submit to us, without necessary delay, the further papers. . . ."[28] The Bishops evidently failed, for Macfarland later reported that he had to drive a truck up to the proper building and threaten to take the papers by force before they were turned over to him. [29] The Committee used these applications as a point of departure but soon developed its own forms and procedures. It suggested that its members place the new forms in the hands of interested individuals and representative leaders of their churches. Denominations were advised to appoint sub-committees in the principal cities to circulate the application blanks and to do the initial interviewing. Most of the churches utilized Committee forms but developed their own set of procedures for distributing them and investigating the nominees. The Methodist Episcopal Church's Committee on Chaplains called on each bishop to make suggestions and then travelled across the country interviewing the men. Clyde Armitage travelled widely, interviewing many of the applicants and looking for others. These procedures worked satisfactorily, although they were criticized as prejudicial to groups not represented on the Committee, or as giving too much authority to the Secretary. The Committee seemed to have little difficulty recruiting an adequate number of men, but at times it faced special shortages. On occasion the army or navy would need a number of Methodists or Lutherans and the approved candidates all came from other churches. It also sought greater numbers of nominees from Negro denominations.

Protestant leaders, like their Catholic counterparts, discovered that they too had to equip chaplains. Several denominations established funds to purchase equipment for their own men, and the Y.M.C.A. provided it for others. The National Lutheran Commision for Soldiers' and Sailors' Welfare, for example, supplied what it described as the standard items "consisting of motorcycle side car, communion service, typewriter, hymn or prayer books and $100 emergency fund." [30] The Y.M.C.A. system worked reasonably well at home but not overseas, and men found themselves in Europe without adequate materials. In June, 1918, the General War-Time Commission offered to serve as a central equipping agency for all chaplains if the denominations wished to deposit money with it, and within six weeks eight of them accepted the offer. [31] By this time the War Department, awakened by the pleas of churchmen and chaplains, issued an order that all chaplains were to receive at least a typewriter and transportation assistance. The Commission continued to supply some equipment but the order greatly reduced the demands made on it.

The Christian churches recruited and equipped their chaplains, but they discovered they had little control over their final appointment or the kinds of ministry they were assigned to perform. These matters were as imortant as recruitment, if not more so, but were subject to government regulations as interpreted by government officials, both civilian and military. In domestic and even overseas social service, the churches enjoyed considerable freedom to work out their individual programs, giving them a Protestant or Catholic form without serious government interference, although Catholic leaders faced more problems than Protestant ones. No such leeway existed in the chaplaincy, and certainly not in the army chaplaincy. The churches quickly learned that ecumenical approaches often succeeded where separate efforts failed. Appeals to the government ranged from private consultations to public protests and nationwide lobbying. The churches did not always agree with one another, but they did find a remarkably broad common ground. As one commentator had said: "History is full of instances of lavish charity bestowed on chaplains, but the carefully and intelligently systemized assistance is a matter of the last eighteen months. Not the War Department, but rather the Christian Churches, have made it possible for the chaplains to act with freedom and with power."[32]

The War Department determined the number of chaplains, both the quota for each religious group and the total number appointed. The groups found themselves in disagreement with the Department and each other over the quota system. The Secretary of War set the quotas in an arbitrary manner, and pegged the Catholic percentage at roughly one-fourth, which it had been for some time. Catholics protested this as unrepresentative of their percentage of the total religious population of the nation, as calculated in a recent census. Catholic leaders, including O'Hern, created "considerable agitation" and finally persuaded Baker to move their ratio upwards to roughly one-third.[33] Protestants promptly protested, not so much because of the actual ratio, but because the Department had failed to consult with them before announcing the change. The General Committee pursued the question of percentage for the duration of the war, but never regarded the issue as too crucial and definitely did not allow it to interfere with its coordinated work with the Catholics over the larger question of the total number of chaplains.

Church leaders, particularly Protestant ones, had advocated increasing the number of chaplains prior to the war and had succeeded in doing so in the Navy Department. In May, 1917, Congress provided money to build up the armed forces and granted the President authority to appoint one chaplain for each regiment, which meant for each 1,200 men. Churchmen found this a reasonable decision since it was an improvement over previous conditions. During the summer the War Department reorganized the army in order to make its various units comparable in strength to those of the French. The changes involved reducing the number of regiments and increasing them in size to 3,600 men. Chaplains were neglected in the reorganization, which resulted in a reduction of their number by two-thirds. Church leaders became understandably disturbed for the action radically curtailed the ministry they had already begun.

The General Committee discussed the decision at its August meeting. Someone presented Father O'Hern's opinion that the churches should make a united request to Congress for a law increasing the number of chaplains to about one for each 1,000 men. A number of members agreed, but decided to wait until they had a better understanding of exactly what was needed.[34] At its initial meeting in September the General War-Time Commission passed resolutions in favor of one chaplain for every 1,200 men and of placing them on a par with the medical corps in rank, pay allowance, and promotion, and instructed the Committee to act on these resolutions in whatever way it deemed appropriate.[35] The Committee met the very next day and decided to take direct action. It drafted a proposed bill asking for the appointment of one chaplain for every 1,200 men, but not for a change in rank and pay, because it feared that if it asked for the whole loaf it might not get anything.[36] The proposal, written in the form of a petition "To the President of the United States; To the Secretary of War; To the Congress of the United States," reviewed the situation of the chaplains and underlined the need for an increase in their number so as to provide better "for the spiritual and moral welfare of the various units in the service." It went on to suggest this: "That the churches consider that any discrimination in rank, pay and allowance of chaplains, or in the appointment and assignment of chaplains, as compared with other branches of the service, becomes in effect a discrimination against religion in the Army and against the Church, which they are confident the government does not desire to make." The petition highlighted the proposed bill. Protestants prepared the actual document, but Catholics had shared their ideas and interest, and so it was presented as representing the opinion of "the Christian forces of America." Leaders of both groups signed it, including North and Macfarland for the Federal Council, Speer and Bishop Lawrence for the General War-Time Commission, the leading figures of a number of the major denominations for their respective churches, Bishop McDowell and the members of the General Committee, Cardinals Gibbons and Farley for the Hierarchy, O'Hern for the Chaplains Bureau, and P. H. Callahan for the Knights of Columbus.[37]

Representatives of this ecumenical group spent Thursday, September 27, in Washington presenting their petition to President Wilson, the Secretary of War, the Chief of Staff, the Adjutant General, several lesser officials, and legislators on Capitol Hill.[38] O'Hern found Wilson noncommital and Baker attentive but unsupportive. Secretary Baker believed three chaplains to a regiment "unnecessary and unwise," and argued for no more than two.[39] The churchmen met with the Senate Committee on Military Affairs in a pre-arranged hearing. This Committee considered all bills related to military affairs, sorting out those to send on for full Senate consideration. Bills for increasing the number of chaplains were already before Congress, including one for two chaplains per regiment. The churchmen wanted their proposal, designated the Chamberlain Bill S.2917, substituted for the others and passed. The atmosphere of the hearing was congenial. The five Senators present listened attentively as Bishop Lawrence, General Secretary Macfarland, Father O'Hern, Senate Chaplain Forest J. Prettyman, and Bishop McDowell presented their case. Bishop Lawrence maintained that he spoke for "practically the whole organized Christian church in America," and O'Hern said: "We have back of us the support of the entire hierarchy of the church, and also all of our Catholic people."[40] They emphasized the imperatives for more chaplains. O'Hern adopted an attacking style, arguing that if Congress did not act, his Church would supply the necessary number without government sanction. The Protestant leaders were not quite so forward, content to stress the great need. Together they argued that the proposed measure would really do what the Secretary of War and the Secretary of the Navy wanted done, which was to give a grant of power to appoint more chaplains to more places. Lawrence pointed out that under the present law the Secretary of War could appoint only one chaplain to a regiment of 3,600 men, even if half were Protestant and half Roman Catholic. The bill would solve his dilemma about which religious group should have the chaplain since he could assign two or three representing different churches. Throughout the hearing the churchmen shared their conviction that the separation of church and state did not prevent the cooperation of religious and governmental agencies to facilitate an adequate ministry for the men in the armed forces.

The Senators responded that they found the arguments persuasive, but warned that Congress was close to adjournment and that the bill might not get passed before then. They substituted the Chamberlain

Bill for others before the Senate and it passed very quickly. It immediately got bogged down in the House Committee on Military Affairs, where it was when adjournment came on October 6. When Macfarland reported on these events, he noted that "our bill was accepted" and said it would carry over to the next session, when he believed it would "receive the vote of nearly all the Representatives when it is reported by the Committee."[41] Congress reconvened on December 3, and Macfarland quickly learned about the difficulties of predicting legislative progress. It took six months and heavy lobbying to get the bill through Congress. The General Committee prepared and distributed a form letter which members of local churches could use in appealing to their Congressmen. In January, General Pershing cabled the War Department and asked that the number of chaplains be increased by the terms of the bill, and the Federal Council published his message to bring more pressure on the legislators.[42] Protestant and Catholic leaders stepped up their efforts in March and April, Catholics joining their requests for more chaplains with their concern for another bill to protect theological students from the draft. The Committee of Six joined the lobbying with a letter from Chairman Burke to all Congressmen. Congress finally passed a version of the bill in April, but Wilson vetoed it because of an ambiguous amendment which he thought would endanger the entire legislation.[43]

May arrived. Congress had dawdled over the bill for almost half a year while the ministry to service men went unfulfilled. Church leaders became upset. Speer wrote Burke requesting him to "renew all the pressures" he could. Burke responded that "the situation is most depressing and if something is not done in a very short time I think we ought to consider some public protest. I sincerely hope that this will not be necessary, but I will be better able to speak after I go to Washington."[44] Speer sent sharply worded letters to the Chairman of the House Committee on Rules; Speaker Champ Clark; and Joseph Tumulty, Secretary to the President. He said to Tumulty that the President might like to know how things were with the chaplains in France, and he included part of a letter from Bishop Charles Brent, recently appointed Senior Staff Chaplain of the A.E.F. describing their situation.

We are dreadfully shorthanded here. As far as statistics can advise we have not one chaplain to 5000 men. . . . Last Sunday I was with our 1st Division on the eve of their going into the greatest battle of the war. Men in the ranks were asking for spiritual ministrations which we were unable to provide. Roman Catholics, desirious (sic) of making their confessions before

going out to die, are left unshepherded through governmental tardiness.
. . . It is cruel beyond words to send our young men across the sea to live in
conditions of unwonted hardship and temptation, to encourage them to be
ready to die for the country, and then neglect to furnish them with those
spiritual ministrations which are at the door of every citizen in home life.[45]

Bishop Brent, Speer continued, did not speak too strongly. The
churches had done their best to get the bill passed, but failed. He appealed to Tumulty to apprise Wilson of this new request for action, a
request "endorsed by the 40,000,000 members of our Christian
Churches, Protestant and Catholic alike." Tumulty, perhaps sensing
the explosive potential of Brent's appeal, did just that. Wilson questioned Baker about the status of the bill and Baker informed him several days later that the revised bill had passed.[46] Wilson also asked
Baker if there really were a shortage of chaplains to which the Secretary replied: "General Pershing has presented to me very strongly his
needs of additional chaplains, and as soon as the bill is passed we will
expedite appointments as rapidly as possible."[47] Whatever Baker said
to the President at least some churchmen considered him to have been
the chief roadblock to the bill, and its passage a clear victory for their
efforts. Hooke sent Armitage a letter of mutual congratulations and
Tumulty a request for the pen the President used to sign the bill, telling him it was "of great moment to our people and many of our Hierarchy have labored most earnestly to secure its passage."[48]
From the beginning of the war churchmen urged the War Department, and especially Baker, to establish a training school for chaplains.
The idea emerged from early discussions within the General Committee for a conference of chaplains. Chaplain Bayard and Secretary
Tippy explored the suggestion and broadened it into a training conference. The plan, as originally presented to the Department, would have
permitted the Committee to work out specific details for the school,
including faculty and curriculum. It would cover expenses and already
had offers of free facilities in New York City and Boston.[49] Baker responded that such a school did not seem necessary. The Committee
accepted the decision but kept the idea alive. In the fall Secretary Armitage renewed the request and this time the Department commissioned
Chaplain Alfred A. Pruden to develop a detailed plan. In the meantime
a group of churchmen led by Henry B. Washburn prepared a proposal
too.
Washburn and Pruden presented their separate plans to the January, 1918, meeting of the Committee. Faculty members of the Episco-

pal Theological School and the Harvard Divinity School in Cambridge initiated what became the Washburn plan and then developed it in conjunction with representatives of the Baptist School at Newton and the Methodist one in Boston. It entailed use of the faculties and facilities of the several theological schools in the Cambridge-Boston area to train volunteer chaplains, camp pastors, and those candidates for the regular chaplaincy who wished to attend. Washburn mentioned that similar training sites could be established in Chicago and San Francisco, other theological education centers. The curriculum would emphasize the spiritual mission of the chaplain.[50] Chaplain Pruden outlined a government-run school, to be located at Fort Monroe, Virginia. The five-week sessions would be based on a curriculum of military matters unfamiliar to most ministers, but essential for the chaplain, including military law, international law, and army regulations. Pruden also had time in his schedule for worship, preaching, and discussion of the more spiritual aspects of the chaplaincy. The government school would accept only men in the regular chaplaincy or candidates for it.[51]

After reviewing both plans the Committee approved the one presented by Pruden, asked the Department to do likewise, and called for the school to begin immediately. It also expressed appreciation to Washburn and the schools he represented. Several years later Washburn accused the Committee of rejecting the school which would have given the strongest emphasis to spiritual life.[52] This criticism demonstrated a failure to understand the Committee's rationale. It rejected Washburn's proposal because it would emphasize those parts of the chaplain's task for which most ministers were presumably already prepared, and would not specifically prepare them for military life. Moreover, the Committee worked primarily with and for the regular chaplains, whereas Washburn's plan seemed aimed more at voluntary ones. Pruden secured Father O'Hern's approval before he submitted his final plan to the Department.

With favorable recommendations from Protestants and Catholics in hand, Baker approved the plan and placed Pruden in charge of bringing it to life.[53] The school began by March 1 and from the start ran into serious difficulties. It no sooner opened than the commandant at Fort Monroe asked the Department to move it, evidently because he saw little value in it and felt it took up facilities he needed. The Committee intervened, with support from O'Hern, and worked with Pruden to make certain that the school survived. It successfully relocated at Camp Taylor near Louisville, Kentucky. Committees of churchmen began visiting it, including members of the General War-Time Commission and the Committee of Six, and they did not always like what they saw. Visitors stressed in their reports that more time should be given for reflection and study and less to classroom work. They noted that the curriculum had too little spiritual thrust and too much military content.[54] The critics succeeded in modifying the curriculum in some respects.

A new crisis hit the school in the fall. General Pershing had recommended to the War Department that chaplains be required to remove their rank insignia and wear only the cross. Chaplains were to retain their rank but not wear it for he believed that the insignia of rank created a road block in the way of a fully effective ministry. When the Department complied with his request, chaplains and churchmen objected. Criticisms of the action became very vehement at the school, especially among the faculty. Chaplain Pruden and several of the faculty held an indignation meeting and inspired some of the students to mail protests to the Department. It could do little about the civilian protests, but it acted with speed once it received the letters of the candidates. After investigation it found Pruden, his fellow faculty members, and several students guilty of insubordination and dismissed them on October 24.[55] The school had a very short life after the incident. When the Armistice arrived, the Department summarily closed it. By that time there had been seven sessions, at which more than 1,000 men had been trained.[56] Problems and criticisms aside, the school played an important role helping train clergymen from a variety of backgrounds to become military chaplains.

The General Committee and the Chaplains' Bureau recruited, equipped and protected the interests of regular chaplains. They had very little to do with that multitude of clergymen known as camp pastors. Yet, those pastors were an important part of the whole question of the army chaplaincy. Protestants took the national lead on this issue; Catholics dealt with it primarily on a diocesan basis. The Federal Council announced in April, 1917, that the churches should appear as churches in the camps, not simply disguised as welfare agencies. Worth Tippy suggested that this could be accomplished in part if distinguished ministers of the several denominations visited the camps as camp pasters with, of course, the approval of the camp commandants.[57] Pastors fitting this description began to appear in the camps soon after they opened. Often self-appointed, they did not always adapt to the regular chaplains' programs and tended to focus solely on the men of their own churches. The delays in legislation increasing the number of chaplains intensified the need, and camp pastors of a bewildering variety descended on the camps.

Primarily because of the shortage of chaplains the Federal Council supported these men. Its Inter-Church Committee on War Work recruited some in the summer of 1917 and its General War-Time Commission undertook to organize them and help their ministry. The Committee on Camp Neighborhoods, under the leadership of Clarence A. Barbour and Roy B. Guild, sponsored conferences in Atlanta, Georgia, and Fort Worth, Texas, in January, 1918. They brought a good number of the camp pastors together and developed guidelines for the future performance of their work. The recommendations encouraged them to carry on their work in cooperation with that of the local chaplains and Y.M.C.A. Secretaries, and advised them to wear uniforms and secure credentials from their denominational war commissions.[58] Additional conferences were held through the spring. Things seemed to be going so well that the Committee began to prepare a manual or handbook for the pastors. Then in June, Chairman Barbour suggested that the manual might not be published in the near future. Rumblings of trouble between the pastors and the War Department had reached him. On July 24 he noted that in light of possible adverse action by the Department, denominational war commissions should be advised that a conference on the subject might be necessary in the near future. Ironically, that very day the Adjutant General issued an order cutting off the work of all camp pastors.

Evidence suggests the Department did some artful maneuvering preparing this order, using some churchmen as a foil. The Department called on the Committee of Six in June for an advisory opinion. The Committee passed two resolutions, both somewhat ambiguous if taken separately. It resolved that "volunteer chaplains be not withdrawn from the camps until, under provision of the recent act, a sufficient number of regular chaplains are commissioned to take their place," and that filling regular chaplaincies did not necessarily mean the end of the need for camp pastors.[59] Members of the Committee, including Speer and Brown for the General War-Time Commission, apparently did not know what use would be made of the resolutions. A month later they got some idea when the Adjutant General issued his order. The new law increasing the number of chaplains, the order said, eliminated the need for camp pastors. Camp commandants were instructed to inform, in as tactful a manner as possible, all pastors performing such functions in their camps that their services would be terminated within three months. The order suggested that to soften the blow the public should be informed that plans were being made to invite distinguished men, including clergymen, into the camps to give addresses on the moral and spiritual factors in the war. Chaplains were still free to invite clergymen into the camps to conduct services on special occasions.[60] Committee of Six resolutions were not mentioned by the Department, but word got out about them in such a way that it seemed as though they supported the order. Church groups, especially Protestant ones, began to raise questions about the nature of the Committee of Six and its authority to speak on behalf of the religious forces of the nation.

The General War-Time Commission and its Committee on Camp Neighborhoods reacted to the order with speed. Within a week Speer and Brown, now in their roles as Commission leaders, talked with Assistant Secretary Frederick Keppel in the Department and filed a protest with him. Keppel assured them that the order would not be carried out with haste, but they wanted it withdrawn. The Commission subsequently appointed Speer, Brown, and McDowell as a committee to arrange a formal appeal to the Department. The three men worked out a careful approach and a concrete proposal. They decided to appeal to the Department in an irenic spirit, praising the work it had done for chaplains and camp pastors, and stressing the value of the ministry which the latter had performed and could still perform among the men. They based their proposal on a provision of the Adjutant's order and outlined a way camp pastors could work under the authority of the chaplains.[61]

Conferences were held with Keppel at the Department on September 23 and October 3. All the major leaders of the Commission, the General Committee, and the Committee on Camp Neighborhoods attended the first one. Keppel and the churchmen agreed to a solution, based on the Commission's proposal, and appointed a small committee to work out the details. The second conference agreed to a specific plan and issued a nine-point settlement. It endorsed the regular chaplaincy and asked the churches to seek the best men for it. One Department concern had been that camp pastors had drained off many men who might otherwise have entered the chaplaincy. Men who for one reason or another did not qualify for the chaplaincy could have their names presented to the Department by the Commission or its agent. The Department would certify the names and turn them over to the chaplains in the various camps, who could, with the approval of the commanding officers, invite the clergymen into the camps for ministry. The clergymen were not designated camp pastors but they were to fulfil that function. The government agreed to the proposal because it put the camp pastors under military authority, and perhaps introduced enough qualifications to encourage some of them to enter the chaplaincy. The Commission signed it because camp pastors would continue to serve, albeit under different circumstances.[62] The end result was a compromise, particularly for the Department. The churches yielded some ground too, but they won a reversal of the Adjutant's order. They considered this a victory for their right to continue to minister to the men in the camps.

The churches were interested in the chaplains overseas as well as those at home, and that interest brought them into close and intimate contact with the work of the three chaplains, two Protestant and one Catholic, who were appointed to organize the chaplains in the A.E.F. Bishop Brent, the Senior Staff Chaplain, quickly came to be known as Chief of Chaplains, A.E.F. When General Pershing first asked him, a personal friend, to take the job, he hesitated. He knew there was no precedent for a chaplains' organization and he had little experience with military affairs. But he recognized the need and knew that he had the strong support of churchmen at home. Speer had written him filling him in on the work of the churches. He had told him the General War-Time Commission was keeping informed about overseas developments, "and if you should accept this position which has been offered, it would be the fulfilment in large measure of the plans which we have had at heart and which in any way whatsoever we shall rejoice to see developed and consummated."[63] After his appointment on May 1, 1918, he became an unofficial member of the Commission, receiving its reports and other frequent communications from Speer and Armitage. He understood the problems of recruitment and sent his associates home to visit church officials and elicit their continued support. Chaplain Francis B. Doherty, his Catholic associate, carried word of their activities to the Chaplains' Aid Association. Burke published an enthusiastic report of his visit, stressing the ecumenical character of front line ministry.[64] The leaders of the Commission saw in Brent one of their own in a position of authority to carry out their plans. When they found the War Department frustrating their efforts at home, as in the argument over the number of chaplains or in the camp pastor dispute, they took some comfort in his ability to form a corps of chaplains, equip them to some degree, and protect their welfare from within the military establishment.[65] The churches and Brent saw each other as partners in providing a ministry to the fighting men.

Differences of opinion between the churches and the War Department continued through the Armistice and into the post-war era. The Department closed the chaplains' school and commissioned only half its final class. Bishop McDowell protested the abruptness of these decisions and pointed out that men facing demobilization required ministry too. Baker responded that the troops would be released so fast that further appointments were unnecessary. Time proved the Bishop right, but being right gave him little comfort. Brent felt the pressure in Europe and filed a protest with Keppel over being left so shorthanded. By the end of the war, over 1,200 Protestant and over 600 Catholic clergy were serving in the army chaplaincy, with over 1,000 Protestant and a similar proportion of Catholic approved candidates waiting for appointments. Few of those on the waiting list received appointments and most of the active ones were out of military service in less than a year. The Department followed its Armistice cutbacks with a proposed bill to decrease the proportion of chaplains to men in the regular army to one for every 2,000. That move inspired the General Committee to formulate its own proposals for the post-war chaplaincy, and present them to Secretary Baker. He probably winced when he saw them, for they reflected the opinions he had frequently opposed during the war. The Committee desired the following: (1) a chaplains' corps with a chief of chaplains; (2) a policy toward promotion and pay in accord with the policy followed in other corps; and (3) the maintenance of the wartime proportion of chaplains to men.[66] The Committee subsequently published the proposal in pamphlet form and distributed it to chaplains, the religious press, and other news media. They achieved partial success. The government did not create a chaplains' corps until after World War II, but did appoint a chief of chaplains when it reorganized the army in 1920. Chaplain John T. Axton became the first Chief on July 15, 1920.

From the beginning of the war the Navy Department adopted toward the chaplains an official policy that differed remarkably from that of the army. Secretary of the Navy Daniels quickly understood the need for a chief chaplain and some kind of corps. He appointed Chaplain John B. Frazier to be his Chief and gave him authority to handle all affairs dealing with chaplains.[67] Frazier, formerly chaplain on Admiral Dewey's flagship in the Philippines, opened an office adjacent to the General Committee office and kept in close contact with the Protestant and Catholic recruiting programs. There were far fewer navy chaplains than army ones and the administrative tasks were simpler, yet Daniels and Frazier acted to meet as fully as possible the needs of their men. On occasion the work of the navy was held up as an example to the army. It was the absence, one commentator averred, "of even such an elementary form of organization in the Chaplains Service of the Army which has caused much of the difficulty in that branch of the service."[68]

The churches produced a major and stirring effort on behalf of the chaplains. The Federal Council and the Hierarchy, through their chosen agents, projected their goals for wartime ministry into the executive offices and legislative halls of the government, and were successful, despite opposition, in getting many of their ideas accepted. If Protestants often took the lead on these issues, it was in part because Catholics were involved in discussions with the same offices over social service questions. The protests were rarely bitter and always over policies, not personalities, and directed, as Speer told a correspondent "in helping those who will have authority to see just what the value and the necessity of the work is and to facilitate it in every way."[69] The churches definitely achieved their primary goal of providing a ministry of Word and sacraments to the men in the armed forces and in large measure won the right to do it on their terms. Those who have accused them of failure of ministry or of obediently accepting such opportunities as the government doled out to them have neglected to examine the story of the chaplaincy. They took the initiative to protest and to try to change those government attitudes which they believed detrimental to an effective ministry, and it was their policies that shaped and moulded the chaplains' service. Brown said in his concluding report as Secretary of the General War-Time Commission that he believed that the churches had effected a moral revolution in the nature and function of the chaplaincy. The Commission's most satisfying work had been to focus "the attention of the country and of the War Department on the needs of the chaplains."[70] And, of course, that meant on the needs of the men in the armed forces for appropriate and adequate ministry.

1. Clifford M. Drury, *The History of the Chaplain Corps, United States Navy* (Washington, D.C.: U.S. Government Printing Office, 1949), 1:143.

2. Worth M. Tippy, *The Church and the Great War* (New York: Fleming H. Revell Company, 1918), p. 39.

3. John J. Pershing, *My Experiences in the World War* (New York: Frederick A. Stokes Company, 1931), 1:283.

4. Paul D. Moody, "The Precedent of the First World War," in *Religion of*

Soldier and Sailor, Willard L. Sperry, ed., (Cambridge: Harvard University Press, 1945), p. 11.

5. Roy J. Honeywell, *Chaplains of the United States Army* (Washington, D.C.: United States Government Printing Office, 1958), p. 185.

6. Daniel B. Jorgensen, *The Service of Chaplains to Army Air Units, 1917-1946* ("Air Force Chaplains," vol. 1; Washington, D.C.: U.S. Government Printing Office, 1961), pp. 10-11.

7. Charles S. Macfarland, *Across the Years* (New York: The Macmillan Company, 1936), p. 175.

8. *Annual Reports of the Federal Council, 1913*, pp. 6-11.

9. Drury, *The History of the Chaplain Corps* 1:142.

10. Macfarland, *The Churches of Christ in Council*, pp. 245ff.

11. *Annual Reports of the Federal Council of the Churches of Christ in America, 1915* (New York: n.p., 1915), p. 39.

12. *Annual Reports of the Federal Council, 1917*, p. 77.

13. John J. Burke to Raymond Fosdick, October 11, 1917, CTCA Records.

14. Williams, *American Catholics and the War*, p. 238.

15. Bishop Patrick J. Hayes to My dearly beloved Chaplain in Christ, April 15, 1918. Copy of Form Letter in NCWC Archives.

16. *Ibid.*

17. Williams, *American Catholics and the War*, p. 240.

18. Bishops Schrembs, Russell, and Muldoon To the Hierarchy of the United States, May 1, 1918. Copy in NCWC Archives.

19. From Bishops Muldoon, Schrembs, Hayes, Russell, July 3, 1918. Copy in NCWC Archives.

20. The Administrative Council, National Catholic War Council to the Hierarchy of the United States, July 10, 1918. Copy in NCWC Archives.

21. "With Our Readers," *The Catholic World* 105 (September, 1917): 861.

22. Sara P. Murphy, "Lending a Hand to the Chaplains," *National Catholic War Council Bulletin* 1 (June-July, 1920): 3. Hereafter cited: *NCWC Bulletin*.

23. *Minutes of the General Committee on Army and Navy Chaplains*, March 30, 1917, in the Library of the General Commission on Chaplains and Armed Forces Personnel, Washington, D.C. Hereafter cited: *Minutes of Chaplains*.

24. "Agenda: Conference on Chaplains," *Minutes of Chaplains*, April 25, 1917.

25. *Minutes of Chaplains*, April 25-26, 1917.

26. Macfarland, *The Churches of Christ in Time of War*, p. 156.

27. Renton, *War-Time Agencies of the Churches*, p. 186.

28. *Minutes of Chaplains*, July 19, 1917.

29. Macfarland, *Across the Years*, p. 126.

30. J.A.O. Stub to Walter G. Hooke, June 21, 1918, NCWC Archives.

31. "A Depot for Supplying Chaplains' Equipment," *FC Bulletin* 1 (October, 1918): 7-8.

32. Henry B. Washburn, "The Army Chaplain," *Papers of the American Society of Church History*, Series 2, 7 (1923): 22.

33. Lewis J. O'Hern, C.S.P., to Right Reverend and dear Bishops, November 14, 1917. Copy in NCWC Archives.

34. *Minutes of Chaplains*, August 13, 1917.

35. *Commission Minutes*, September 20, 1917.

36. *Minutes of Chaplains*, September 21, and October 29, 1917.

37. *Ibid.*, October 29, 1917. Appendix.

38. See "Washington in War Time," *The Congregationalist and Christian World* 102 (October 11, 1917): 498-99.

39. O'Hern to Right Reverend and dear Bishops.

40. U.S. Congress, Senate, Committee on Military Affairs, *Increasing the Number of Chaplains in the Army*, Hearing on S. 2917, 65th Congress, 1st Session, 1917, p. 12. See also William Lawrence, *Memories of a Happy Life* (Boston and New York: Houghton, Mifflin Company, 1926), p. 391.

41. *Minutes of Chaplains*, October 29, 1917.

42. General Pershing to the War Department, January 18, 1918. Copy in Speer Papers. See also "A Cablegram from General Pershing," *FC Bulletin* 1 (March, 1918): 1.

43. U.S. Congress, Senate, *Army Chaplains—Veto Message*, Document No. 216, 65th Congress, 2nd Session, 1918, p. 1.

44. Robert E. Speer to John Burke, May 9, 1918. Copy in the Speer Papers, and Burke to Speer, May 14, 1918, Speer Papers.

45. Quoted in Robert E. Speer to Joseph P. Tumulty, May 9, 1918, in the Papers of Woodrow Wilson, in the Library of Congress, Washington, D.C. Hereafter cited: Wilson Papers. For Brent's entire letter see Bishop Charles Brent to Robert E. Speer, April 18, 1918. Copy in the Records of the Adjutant General's Office, in Record Group 94, in the National Archives, Washington, D.C. Hereafter cited: AGO Records.

46. See the following items in the Wilson Papers: Memo from the White House to the Secretary of War, May 10, 1918; Newton D. Baker to Woodrow Wilson, May 17, 1918; Note from Woodrow Wilson to Tumulty, (May, 1918).

47. Baker to Wilson, May 17, 1918, Wilson Papers.

48. Walter Hooke to Clyde Armitage, May 21, 1918, and Walter Hooke to Joseph P. Tumulty, May 21, 1918. Copies in NCWC Archives.

49. *Minutes of Chaplains*, July 19, 1918.

50. Arthur C. Piepkorn, *A Chronicle of the Training School for Newly Appointed Chaplains and Chaplain Candidates During the First World War*, n.d. Manuscript in the Records and Papers in the Office of the Chief of Chaplains, Washington, D.C., pp. 4-5. Hereafter cited: OCCh.

51. *Minutes of Chaplains*, January 31, 1918.

52. Washburn, "The Army Chaplain," p. 20.

53. Official documents relating to the establishment of the school are in the files in OCCh.

54. *Commission Minutes*, May 15, June 5, and September 4, 1918.

55. Official records of the episode are in AGO Records.

56. Honeywell, *Chaplains of the United States Army*, pp. 175-79. See also

"Training the Chaplains," *The Presbyterian* 88 (August 8, 1918): 22; Eric North, Training Chaplains for the Army," *The Homiletic Review* 76 (August, 1918): 107-08; Paul B. Rupp, "The Making of an Army Padre," *Reformed Church Messenger* 87 (August 8, 1918): 6-7.

57. "Minutes of a Joint Conference Between A Committee from the Administrative Committee of the Federal Council of the Churches of Christ in America, and A Committee from the War Work Council of the Y.M.C.A.," April 21, 1917, *Commission Minutes*.

58. "Camp Pastors and Camp Neighborhoods," *FC Bulletin* 1 (March, 1918): 13-14.

59. *Minutes of the Committee of Six*, June 17, 1918. Copy in Speer Papers.

60. See the following: From the Adjutant General of the Army to The Commanding General, Pt. of Embarkation, Hoboken, N.J., July 24, 1918, in the Records of the A.E.F., Chaplains' Office, Record Group 120, in the National Archives, Washington, D.C. Hereafter cited: Chaplains' Office.

61. *Commission Minutes*, September 4, 1918.

62. A copy of the agreement appears in *Commission Minutes*, October 16, 1918.

63. Robert E. Speer to Bishop Charles Brent, April 22, 1918, Chaplains' Office. See also "The Ranking Chaplain," *The Congregationalist and Advance* 103 (May 23, 1918): 646.

64. *Bulletin*, Chaplains' Aid Association 1 (July, 1918), pp. 9-10.

65. On Brent see Alexander C. Zabriskie, *Bishop Brent: Crusader for Christian Unity* (Philadelphia: The Westminster Press, 1948), pp. 122-32; and Charles H. Brent, *Soldiers of the Wooden Cross*, January 5, 1919. A General War-Time Commission Pamphlet.

66. *Minutes of Chaplains*, February 11, 1919.

67. For Daniels see Josephus Daniels, *The Wilson Years: Years of War and After*, 1917-1923 (Chapel Hill: The University of North Carolina Press, 1946), pp. 200-205, 278-82.

68. "Effective Work of the Committee on Chaplains," *FC Bulletin* 2 (January, 1919): 14-15.

69. Robert E. Speer to Bishop Charles Brent, May 27, 1918, Chaplains' Office.

70. William Adams Brown, "The Service of the General War-Time Commission," *FC Bulletin* 2 (June, 1919): 110.

VII

The Social Ministry

Protestants and Roman Catholics performed a multitude of social ministries during and immediately following the war. They both looked primarily to problems created by the war, although some of the needs they moved to meet had pre-war roots, particularly those dealt with by the Protestant Committee on the Welfare of Negro Troops and the Catholic Women's Committee.[1] They performed the majority of these ministries outside the boundaries of the camps and cantonments with, of course, the indirect needs of the troops a major source of many of them. Occasionally each group intervened directly in camp life, the Protestants to build places for worship and the Catholics to challenge government social hygiene programs.

Much of the attention and the energy of the General War-Time Commission and the National Catholic War Council focused on the local churches and parishes, not only in camp communities but in general, the Protestants urging cooperative local ministries and the Catholics encouraging parochial war councils on the model of the national one. Division ruled when the war began, in Protestantism a separation of the churches and in Catholicism a conflict of local interest groups. The government had an analogous experience in trying to rely on voluntary efforts of local groups to mobilize the nation's resources and gradually abandoned voluntarism in favor of direct control of various sectors of the economy, including new industrial regulations and the nationalization of the railroads. Church leaders were either unable or reluctant to exercise such authority and had to rely on persuasion. United action increased immensely during the war, although successful service sometimes happened even as cooperation and coordination failed. The Commission and the Council also discovered that some so-

cial ministry was too complex or too expensive or both to occur without their intervention and direction. Reluctantly each group moved to
fill that role and assumed more and more program responsibility as the
war went on. The larger projects usually involved consultation with
appropriate local or national government agencies and were often carried out in cooperation with them. They also required field agents,
social workers, and a number of other employees. Protestants and
Catholics approached the war in similar ways, formulating special
wartime policies and calling leaders experienced in social ministry,
but at the point of implementing these ministries they developed their
own distinct programs.

The General War-Time Commission served as the major Protestant
clearinghouse for information on possibilities for ministry and social
service. It partially fulfilled this role by sponsoring a large number of
committees, but the information vital to cooperative efforts was so
scattered and so voluminous that no number of meetings would suffice
to share it all. Each denomination had some kind of research bureau at
work collecting data on soldiers, camps, and other important items;
but, as William Adams Brown pointed out, "there was no one whose
business it was to know the field as a whole, no one who was studying
what each was doing in its relation to all the others and collating that
information in such a form as to make it equally available for all."[2] In
the fall of 1917 the Commission appointed a Committee on Survey
of the Field and Work. It had five members and never grew in size
although it early had one important personnel change. In November,
Samuel McCrea Cavert replaced its original secretary and so began his
illustrious career in the movement for church federation in America.

The Committee on Survey had already begun an investigation of
the social and religious conditions of the cantonments and camps
when Cavert took up his job. The cantonments were largely tent cities,
located in the South; whereas, the camps consisted of wooden barracks
and other permanent structures, located mainly in the North.[3] Material for this appraisal had been accumulated by members of the denominational war commissions, by members of the Inter-Church Committee on War Work, and by Commission members. Cavert sifted through
the mass of collected data, organized it, and had it mimeographed, all
in about one month.

Preliminary in nature, the *Survey* contained information designed
to help either a visitor or a permanent religious worker.[4] Cavert listed
each installation on a separate page with such specific data as the size
and location of the camp, the religious forces in and near it, and the

work of the Commission on Training Camp Activities. A visitor to Camp Lewis at American Lake, Washington, for example, could discover that it was a National Army Cantonment of about 47,000 men under the command of General H. A. Greene, that two Protestant and three Roman Catholic chaplains were stationed there, and that the eight churches in Tacoma "are keeping open house for soldiers, and are working hard to meet the new situation."[5] Copies of the study were sent to denominational wartime commissions and to selected officials in the various places surveyed. Raymond Fosdick received a copy with a note attached suggesting that he might like to see "what we are doing in this line." He replied that he had read it through and found it not only interesting but extremely useful.[6]

The Committee immediately began another survey, reviewing the large locations and investigating the numerous smaller military posts and naval stations, in order to provide a comprehensive analysis of the religious and social work under way or planned for all men in the armed forces. Cavert worked on this with characteristic vigor. He had certain basic materials at hand, including an independent study of many of the smaller camps, prepared by the War Commission of the Northern Baptist Convention. Proceeding primarily by correspondence he gathered data on 241 installations. He asked the chaplain at the Naval Station at Seattle, Washington, for example, if he would please inform him about "the approximate number of men now stationed there, the general moral and religious environment and what the churches are doing to help meet the needs of the enlisted men."[7] Cavert concluded his collecting by May, 1918, and within the month reported that 2,500 copies of the new study were off the press and many of them already distributed.

The May *Survey* included the largest and most of the smallest military and naval bases in the United States. In addition to the basic kind of information presented in the first survey, this one contained a more forthright, if often epigrammatic evaluation of the moral and religious conditions in and near each location. El Paso, Texas, which enjoyed the presence of some 7,000 soldiers, reported: "Liquor and vice situation very bad." Salem, New Jersey, near Fort Mott on the Delaware River, reported: "Salem is wet; moral conditions fairly good." Cavert warned that although the information was incomplete, it was sufficiently correct to serve not only as a manual for those working to provide religious services to the men, but also as a source of enlightenment to those who wanted some concrete examples of the services which the churches and other religious forces of the country were rendering during the war.[8] In August the Committee produced its final survey describing the work in and around military and naval hospitals.[9]

The various surveys encouraged churches near military installations to initiate special ministries, but the vast majority of churches were located far from any camp and their ministries were vital too. Recognizing that mobilization extended to all the churches, the Commission established in October, 1917, the Committee on War-Time Work in the Local Church and Cooperation with the American Red Cross, to focus on churches in cities and urban areas distant from military bases. Like so many of the committees of the Commission this one had important roots in the Federal Council. The deepest and most influential of these drew sustenance from the Commission on the Church and Social Service, which early in the war had promoted, through a widely distributed pamphlet, a plan to win local churches to the support of the Red Cross. It had also joined in advertising the Red Cross's campaign for $100,000,000 and issued a poster linking that organization's work to that of the Federal Council.[10] The new Committee chose Worth Tippy to be its Secretary. He was then serving as Executive Secretary of the Social Service Commission. He had left a prestigious New York City pulpit the previous February to work for cooperative Christian social programs, partly because he fervently believed that the "social applications of the teaching of Christ are the test of the genuineness and power of the religious forces of the nation."[11] The other roots lay in the Commission on Interchurch Federations, which had already produced two useful handbooks on cooperative work for local churches.

The Committee on War-Time Work accomplished the bulk of its work by the summer of 1918. It extended earlier efforts on behalf of the Red Cross by encouraging that organization to mail a circular to 135,000 pastors, priests, and rabbis, asking them to observe Red Cross Sunday. In the early spring of 1918 it helped promote the Red Cross Home Service program, an effort to provide care for the families and dependents of soldiers. It also enlisted clergymen as Red Cross speakers. Services for the Red Cross were important, but hardly encompassed or exhausted local church wartime ministry possibilities. Under Tippy's leadership the Committee prepared and distributed a pastor's manual describing an extensive Wartime Program. Heavy demand required two new editions in four months. The editor of one major religious periodical found that "the committee has achieved in its Wartime Program a substantial foundation for the building up, to a maximum influence, of the active agencies within the church for service to the nation."[12]

The manual told pastors and local churches that they had important parts to play in the war.[13] Pastors who believed that they had to enlist in the chaplaincy in order to get to the heart of the action were cautioned to reflect on the total situation. In fact, pastors held key leadership roles in most local communities, and on their shoulders rested the task of sustaining the moral and spiritual life of the people. First, they should create special wartime committees representing all the groups in their churches; and second, they should develop new programs in relation to local needs. Every local committee should not only support the Red Cross, but also cooperate with other government programs, such as those for the conservation of food and fuel and for the purchase of War Savings Stamps and Liberty Bonds. They should raise money for these Loans "as an offering from the soul of the people." They should also speak out against fault-finders and seek to silence criticism of any kind.

Pastors had a special responsibility for ministry to the soldiers and their families. Their churches should have honor rolls and at least one service flag, and should keep in touch with their men through committees of correspondence. They could render special service by meeting with draftees before they were called to active duty in order to interpret to them the real aims of the war. They were also charged with the cares and needs of those families who had sons overseas, and with the coming ministry of consolation. Local committees were encouraged to keep a sharp eye on social conditions in their communities. They should see to it that the children of the poor were adequately fed and that working mothers were not overworked in the name of efficiency. Those living in industrial areas should give attention to the needs of the growing masses of workers, particularly the Negroes, who often had very inadequate living conditions.

The supreme task of the local churches was to provide moral support and guidance to the people, and leaders should relate their programs to that task. The times challenged them "to awaken a deeper religious life within the people by a strong, tender, passionate preaching of the Gospel of God's grace, and by calling the nation to prayer." They should keep the ethical issues of the war from being distorted by material values, for "the fires of altruism must be kept burning lest we ourselves become Prussianized." The suggested tasks were great enough to require cooperation among Christians, and the spiritual ones, which could lead to a great religious reawakening of the people, should inspire it.

In the spring of 1918 the Committee shifted its focus to the problems of rural churches. The change took place in April when it established a Rural Church Section and secured the Rev. Edmund deS. Brunner from the Moravian Church Extension Society to direct its activities. Tippy turned his attention to another committee. Under Brunner's guidance the Committee published a partially rewritten version of its basic pamphlet with an emphasis on rural life. It followed this with another publication describing ways rural churches could help those who participated in the Boys' Working Reserve, a program to use city boys to help resolve the farm labor shortage.[14] It distributed over 50,000 copies of the first pamphlet and over 80,000 of the second, circulation figures boosted by the help of the United States Department of Agriculture. Brunner participated in a number of state conferences sponsored by that Department aimed at interpreting wartime work to rural people, and directed an extensive publicity campaign on behalf of programs vital to rural churches. In the fall of 1918 and the following spring he helped develop and promote the idea of Rural Liberty Churches, which were defined as country churches which conformed "to certain standards of patriotic and social activity."[15] The approach of the Committee on War-Time Work to most of its programs involved a mixture of enthusiasm for government work with a strong commitment to cooperative ministry.

Before the Committee on Survey had completed its initial study, the General War-Time Commission could see that a great need in some camps would be for a place of worship. They were cities of 30,000 to 50,000 men without the normal complement of buildings or services found in a city of similar size. The only non-military buildings in most camps were the structures erected by the Y.M.C.A., the Knights of Columbus, and the Jewish Welfare Board. The government did not build chapels or churches, and chaplains and camp pastors had to use the facilities of the welfare organizations or hold services outdoors.[16] These facilities were inadequate and many soldiers stationed at camps near large cities attended the local churches. Those camps which had no neighborhoods nearby simply had no suitable place of worship available. The Inter-Church Committee on War Work voted "to approve and undertake the erection of suitable buildings for interdenominational work outside the camps and cantonments, wherever the local churches are inadequate to meet the war situation; the proposed building to be available for the use of the denominations erecting and maintaining the same."[17] The Commission subsequently appointed a committee to investigate the erection of such interdenominational centers at Camp Upton, Long Island, and at Camp Dix, New Jersey. Within several months it had sorted out the problems in the half dozen locations which needed buildings and had various projects underway. Although no one situation was typical, the initial venture at Camp Upton faced and solved most of the problems which confronted the other projects.

By early October, 1917, the committee working on the Camp Upton project reported success in several areas and the Commission adopted its plan. The Camp contained 40,000 to 45,000 men and was six miles from the nearest village. General J. Franklin Bell, Camp Commandant, had offered a plot of land inside the Camp as a site for the building. The Commission voted to accept the site and construct a Church Headquarters on it, "the cost of the erection to be paid for by the denominations cooperatively, the building to be used as headquarters and centre for church work for the chaplains, both regular and voluntary, and for other religious workers properly admitted into the Camp."[18] The Y.M.C.A. official at the Camp approved of these plans and agreed to share administration of the building with representatives of the chaplains and local leaders of the cooperating denominations. The Commission needed one final authorization, that of the Commission on Training Camp Activities. Its relations with Fosdick's Commission had been cordial. Worth Tippy had offered Fosdick the services of the Federal Council the previous May and had made several useful suggestions for improving welfare work for the soldiers during the summer. Fosdick had responded graciously on these occasions.[19] When he was approached about the Upton project, he quickly approved it.

Once over these initial hurdles, the Commission called a meeting of interested denominational executives to define in explicit terms their commitment to the plan. The Northern Baptist Convention, the Methodist Episcopal Church, the Congregational Church, the Presbyterian Church in the U.S.A., and the Protestant Episcopal Church, formed a cooperative committee and agreed to unite in erecting the building. They also voted to look with favor on the application of any other denominations which might at a later date wish to join them.[20] Within a month the five churches had hired architects, approved their plans, and let the contracts for the construction of the building. The builders broke ground before Thanksgiving, 1917.

Quite understandably some confusion accompanied such an innovative cooperative effort. Unfortunately, the denominations created the major problem when they failed to fulfil their agreement to keep in close touch with the officials of the Y.M.C.A. Soon after construction began, William Hirsch, Association Camp Secretary at Upton, asked that it be halted. An immediate conference between representatives of the Commission and the Association revealed that Hirsch had not been shown any plans for the building and that the Association at Upton had no voice in the final decisions. Moreover, Hirsch, who had once been "very cordial in his attitude toward the proposition," no longer saw a need for the kind of building proposed.[21] His ruffled feathers were smoothed and an agreement to continue construction was reached only after long discussions and the attendant delays.

No other significant interruption occurred in the construction of the building. Indeed, its erection, furnishing, and policy decisions about its use were accelerated when the Commission created the Committee on Interchurch Buildings to oversee the work. The denominations, already committed to paying an estimated $23,000 for the building, agreed to spend several thousand more dollars to furnish it. They also voted to open the chapel for the purposes of worship "on equal terms to all men or groups of men of whatever faith."[22] Catholics and Jews joined the Protestants in the services which marked the formal opening on Sunday, February 24, 1918, and later both of those groups used it for some of their services.[23] The completion of the Upton Church Headquarters cleared the Committee agenda for more serious attention to projects at Camps Dix, Sherman, Cody, Dodge, and Meade. In most of these camps two or more denominations cooperated in the work. A sceptic looking at this interdenominational venture might conclude that pragmatic considerations and government limitations dominated the projects. While these were doubtless elements in the decision of the churches to unite, the cooperative spirit dominated the program. They could have chosen to erect no chapel or to erect individual ones just outside camp limits. Their decision "to carry on the work without jealousy among themselves or toward any other agency" revealed a genuine commitment to cooperation.[24]

The Federal Council had charged the Commission with sustaining its commitments to justice in the industrial order. Many of the abuses specified in the Social Creed of the Churches had been attacked and modified, but the leaders of the Council feared that the patriotic sentiments engendered by the war could lead to new abuses in the interest of victory at any cost. Tippy, in a report to the initial meeting of the Commission, called on it to develop programs which would preserve industrial and social standards. He referred to the nation's labor troubles, especially those involving the International Workers of the World, and asked for the creation of an impartial commission to study "the industrial conditions which make men discontented and so ready to be misled by self-interested or lawless agitators." He was most concerned with the sense of injustice which existed among many working people, for he believed this was at the heart of the industrial unrest. The Commission established a Committee on Industrial Conditions in response to his appeal.[25]

The Committee concerned itself with two basic types of wartime industrial communities. One type was the old established center which experienced tremendous growth immediately after the declaration of war. A factory in Waterbury, Connecticut, for example, had an increase of 10,000 workers. Businesses in the Bethlehem, Allentown, and Easton area of Pennsylvania expanded in similar proportion. The other type was the entirely new industrial location. Among these were twenty-four Ordnance Reservations.[26] Samuel Batten proposed a survey of these industrial centers and Tippy undertook it, using questionnaires and visitations to gather data on the social and religious conditions. While he was working on this he discovered that the Home Missions Council was carrying on a similar investigation. Commission leaders, always interested in cooperating with other agencies, directed him to place his findings and recommendations for action before the Annual Meeting of the Home Missions Council in January, 1918.

Tippy painted a discouraging picture. Problems in the industrial centers were extremely large and complex. It was not just a matter of a few hundred or even a few thousand people moving into a community unprepared for them, but of ten thousand or tens of thousands moving into completely new communities. The lack of adequate housing constituted the biggest single problem. Almost equally important were the increase of Sunday work and the use of a seven-day work week. The only positive thing about the extended work week was that most areas retained the eight-hour day. These problems were complicated by the influx of great numbers of Negroes from the South and the rise of racial tensions in some areas. Finally, he reported "that the churches are not acting concertedly except in a few instances; also that they are not taking an organized part in what is being done by chambers of commerce in cooperation with industrial concerns and the government." He concluded his presentation with a proposal for united action by a joint committee of the Home Missions Council and the General War-Time Commission. He believed that together they could complete the

survey and formulate and carry out a plan to meet the needs he had
outlined.[27] When the Council declined a joint effort, the Commission
encouraged Tippy to proceed. Each of his reports in the spring of 1918
indicated more areas surveyed and more denominational social service
commissions engaged in the study. By April, five denominations had
agreed to release capable men and pay their salaries for three months
in order to organize religious work in industrial centers. A month later
the number of workers doubled. In June, his study largely finished,
Tippy told the Commission that the maintenance of the religious life of
the people in the industrial centers had emerged as one of the truly
great needs of the war.[28]

The urgency of conditions finally moved the Home Missions Council to join with the Commission in a cooperative program. Representatives of the two agencies met and created a Joint Committee on War
Production Communities. They directed it to continue updating the
survey of the areas, to take a religious census of their populations, to
seek to organize local churches wherever needed, to study rural industrial relations, and to undertake welfare work for the increasing
number of Negroes in the centers. They defined war industry as
"shipyards, munition plants, mining and lumber camps, food production, and all other industries essential to the conduct of the war."[29]
The Joint Committee met for the first time on July 15 and elected John
M. Glenn, Chairman, and Tippy, Executive Secretary. The Home Missions Council agreed to underwrite its budget. The staff of the new
committee included representatives of the Commission on the Church
and Social Service and the denominational home mission and social
service commissions. It met almost weekly until December and then
occasionally until it disbanded the following April. Its work covered a
wide field. Concern for the welfare of Negro workers led to the employment of the Rev. Harold M. Kingsley as Secretary for Negro Welfare. It joined with the Committee on War-Time Work in the Local
Church in issuing two pamphlets relating the work of rural churches
to industrial concerns. Failure of the churches to provide a ministry
for the men who toiled in the remote lumbering areas of the nation led
to a study of these areas and an outline for a possible ministry in them.
It also supervised the work of as many as twenty-six community organizers, who sought to create a cooperative ministry among local
churches in the well-established industrial centers.[30]

One of the more interesting projects of the Joint Committee was the
establishment of local churches on the government-owned Ordnance
Reservations. The Reservations were really cities, built primarily for

making nitrates, constructing ships, and generating electricity. The government built them from the ground up, including the manufacturing plants, the homes for the workers and their families, the schools, and the Liberty Theaters. It proposed to build a place of worship in each center, but several Protestant denominations objected that such action would be a violation of the principle of the separation of church and state. Instead, it granted permission to Catholics, Jews, and Protestants to establish one place of worship each in each center. Tippy had recommended to the Home Missions Council in January that the churches erect in each center "a common church of a temporary character like those at Yaphank and Camp Dix." He suggested the buildings be open all day and late into the night because of shift work, and that they should be social centers as well as places for worship and should be open to "Jewish rabbis for services and to Catholic priests for masses." Soon after the Joint Committee organized, it picked up this recommendation and began to plan a Liberty Church for the new city of Nitro, West Virginia.[31]

Nitro was a particularly needy community. The government located a large munitions plant there, operated by the Hercules Powder Company, and erected temporary housing for some 10,000 workers and their families. They worked in three shifts, seven days a week. The town had two schools and two Y.M.C.A. huts, one for whites and one for Negroes. Investigations by the Joint Committee revealed a desperate need for a Protestant church. It held a conference with church leaders of nearby Charleston and won their complete support for a plan to erect a cooperative Protestant church. The church would be a united one, but it would be the responsibility of a given denomination to provide funds to erect the building and to supply a pastor. The Joint Committee would provide cooperative funds for current expenses. The main reason for putting the title of the building in the name of one denomination, the Presbyterian Church in the U.S.A. in this case, was that the Joint Committee was neither incorporated nor permanent. It hoped that this church and similar ones elsewhere would flourish and continue their ministries after the war. They could do this best if related to a single, permanent denomination. The Liberty Church would be open to all Protestants and would have no denominational name publicly attached to it. Since some persons might not want to become Presbyterians, as they presumably would if they joined, the church arranged to enroll members on separate denominational rolls.[32]

Plans for the Nitro Liberty Church did not proceed smoothly. Tippy held a conference with the Ordnance Department and informed them of the proposal. The Department approved it but denied permission to erect a building, arguing scarcity of materials and labor. The Joint Committee resolved to go ahead under a modified plan. They made an arrangement with the Y.M.C.A. whereby the Liberty Church could use the Association's auditorium for worship and its other facilities for educational and social work. The Presbyterian Board of Church Extension promptly assigned a pastor. Nitro Liberty Church held its first services on November 9. The cessation of hostilities lessened the need for munitions, and the plant immediately cut back production. The pastor resigned in January because of illness. The Liberty Church survived, however, under a new pastor and on a less active basis. Liberty Churches were also established at Ancor, Ohio; Belcoville and Amatol, New Jersey; Penniman and Seven Pines, Virginia; and Muscle Shoals, Alabama. Several of these, including the one at Nitro, outlived the Joint Committee.

According to Tippy, the Liberty Churches took a disproportionate amount of the Joint Committee's time and effort. Arrangements with the government were especially difficult. And yet, the time was well spent since the churches proved useful. They were few in number and were scattered around the eastern part of the nation in unlikely places; however, their number was not too important. They were the concrete result of the response of the Commission to the needs of a special segment of society in wartime. These churches won little public notice and very little reference in history books, but they did exhibit the cooperative as well as the ministerial aspect of the wartime policy of the Federal Council.[33]

The Commission experienced considerable success implementing Federal Council commitment to ministry in terms of social service. The vision of Christian cooperation, aided by the spirit of national unity, helped facilitate most of the projects. At the same time that spirit occasionally encouraged activities which violated the wartime policy. Some of the materials published by the Committee on War-Time Work in the Local Church appealed to attitudes narrower than those outlined at the Special Meeting in 1917. The Commission also failed to be as forthright and as outspoken as it should have been on the issue of conscientious objection to war.

The wartime policy directed the Commission thus: "To protect the rights of conscience against every attempt to invade them." Some men chose to become conscientious objectors very early in the war, and the Administrative Committee of the Federal Council appointed a small committee in the summer of 1917 to investigate the situation, but took no new public stand. The Commission continued to circulate the May statement. It also regularly received the pamphlets and other publications of the National Civil Liberties Bureau, and from the summer of 1917 until late the following summer, the Bureau cautioned restraint on the part of those who would agitate publicly for justice for conscientious objectors. In July, 1917, it praised the "open-minded consideration" which the War Department had given its suggestions for treatment of the objectors. It also cited the supportive position of the Council's May statement and encouraged objectors to turn there for help.[34] One year later it reported that little public agitation had been undertaken because supportors of the objectors believed "they had more to gain relying upon the understanding and liberalism of the Administration than upon the exceedingly hazardous attempt to convert public opinion through the press.[35]

In the fall of 1918 reports circulated that some imprisoned objectors were being seriously mistreated. The Bureau immediately sought redress through the War Department, and when it failed to get it, turned to public protest.[36] In mid-October the Commission received its first formal request for action for objectors when it was asked to act on behalf of those who were being mistreated. It appointed a committee which received letters and personal testimonies about the matter, and finally drew up a statement. The Commission recognized the sensitive character of the issue, and its Executive Committee carefully reviewed the proposed document before releasing it in March, 1919. The statement generally praised the way the War Department had handled the objectors and reflected quite closely the Bureau's earlier favorable judgments about the government's efforts on behalf of the approximately 5,000 men involved. However, it concluded that the charges that "a considerable number of men have been treated with undue severity, in a few cases even with brutality, by certain of the military authorities" were substantially true. Such treatment failed to measure up to the nation's standards and the interests of democracy would be served best by releasing all those who were beyond question sincere.[37]

The statement did not go so far nor was it so frank as Council policy warranted. The failure of the Council and Commission on this issue was not, however, what most critics thought it was. They have charged that the Commission should have been as enthusiastic and as involved in the problems of the objectors as was the Civil Liberties Bureau.[38] That critique failed to distinguish between the attitude possible for a group such as the Bureau, with a small base of support and a single purpose, and a group like the Commission which represented large national organizations and many purposes and a multitude of programs. John Haynes Holmes presented the more accurate and potent criticism. He took public notice of the March statement and said it was heartening to find the churches on the right side of the issue. Why, however, had they taken so long to make their stand? The answer appeared all too plain: their leaders were playing safe. They were, he claimed, "guilty of the final indecency—that of doing late and in security, as though of their own accord, what they refused to do at some cost, when the honor and the lives of men were hanging in the balance."[39] This analysis properly challenged the five-month gap between the request for action and the public statement. The Commission should have acted with greater speed than it did once it became aware of the gravity of the situation. It should have sought more conscientiously to guard "the rights of conscience."

The National Catholic War Council launched its social ministry very much after the manner of the General War-Time Commission, by surveying the situation. The accumulation of data began in September, 1917, in the form of reports solicited from welfare agencies already at work, like the Society of St. Vincent de Paul. During Council reorganization its committees initiated a systematic effort to obtain enough information to project specific programs and budgets. Several of them mailed out carefully constructed questionnaires, directed to diocesan offices, men's and women's groups, and the welfare agencies. The Women's Committee wanted correspondents to provide membership data, an account of war service already performed or planned, and suggestions for improving Catholic women's work in their own communities. Because returns came in slowly and were often incomplete for any given region, various committee leaders undertook fact finding tours. Drs. Kerby and Guilday, joined by Michael Slattery, were the first to go. Their five-day trip in late May, 1918, through the dioceses of Pittsburgh, Erie, Buffalo, Rochester, Syracuse, and Albany showed much willingness to serve but woefully little cooperation. Women, for example, were everywhere active, but in very parochial and often isolated groups, like the Catholic Women's Saturday Afternoon Club in Buffalo and the Catholic Women's Service League in Albany. They made personal contact with the several bishops and other leaders and gathered a fund of knowledge. Charles Denechaud took a trip in August. Burke encouraged him to "take a good survey of the needs of the dioceses and all that concerns our field of work, and offer to help in meeting them."[40] The committees never seemed to get so much information as they wanted, for requests for additional reports continued to stream from the main office, even after the war ended.

No one field of service dominated Council work, but the investigations highlighted women's work as perhaps the greatest area of need. It responded with its largest single commitment of time and energy. The accomplishments of the Women's Committee can easily be reduced to statistics because it maintained very complete and accurate records. It opened twelve Visitors' Houses which served 572,600 meals and received approximately 1,400,000 guests. It operated 28 Community Houses in the United States, employing 65 trained field secretaries and attended by an average of 1,638 people monthly, and ran almost two dozen similar establishments in Europe. The Women's Committee gathered data on over 4,600 local and diocesan women's groups. It encouraged them to join in local war work and recruited their members for its own programs. It served as the connecting link between the Association of American Colleges and Catholic women's schools to provide 87 scholarships for two groups of French women who were invited to America to study in 1918 and 1919. Since the war revealed a serious shortage of trained Catholic women social workers, the Committee founded a National Catholic Service School for Women in Washington, D.C. It also established a directory of Catholic social workers and women who had gained skills through volunteer welfare work. The Committee discovered among some of the most active groups a definite interest in national affiliation. It proceeded slowly but purposely in this area, charging its field secretaries to promote national unity in quiet ways, and calling together a Women's Advisory Committee in December, 1918.[41] To make certain these efforts bore fruit it spearheaded the call for a national meeting of the largest and most representative of the women's groups in March, 1920, and presided over the formation of the National Council of Catholic Women.[42]

The Women's Committee, charged with coordinating national work, faced an almost overwhelming task. The immediate problem involved locating and identifying the large number of separate national and local groups and encouraging them to share in a variety of kinds of war work. It invited them to participate in general national programs like those on behalf of the Red Cross and the Food Administration, and also in much more specific local projects, such as protective work for girls through the formation of girls' clubs, care of children made dependent by the war, special education classes for the foreign-born, and recreation programs for women war workers.[43] The absence of a genuinely national Catholic women's organization was and remained an immovable roadblock in the way of Catholic women's work at the camps for most of the war. The Y.W.C.A. had, like the Y.M.C.A., early secured a monopoly of war work. When Catholics challenged this, the government relented in the face of the proposal of the Knights of Columbus, a well prepared and national Catholic men's organization, but held firm against any program involving many different local groups. Catholic women yielded by default; and the Y.W.C.A. proceeded to establish numerous Hostess Houses at camps and cantonments where families could meet their men, relax in a pleasant atmosphere, and arrange for overnight lodgings. It had the national resources and the trained personnel to create and staff such establishments quickly. Although it was without question a Protestant agency, it included some Catholic women and made sincere efforts to avoid sectarianism.

Council leaders, particularly Father Burke, continued to believe in the principle of Catholic women's work at the camps and frequently approached the government seeking permission for it. Finally, in the summer of 1918, the War Department granted special permission for Catholic guest houses at the great centers of embarkation and debarkation, Camp Merritt at Hoboken, New Jersey, and Camp Upton on Long Island. At about this same time Fosdick entered negotiations with the Council in connection with the United War Work Campaign and the role of the Knights of Columbus. The agreement they reached included women's work for it made the Council responsible "for all Catholic work in connection with the leisure time of the troops at home and abroad." Burke promptly set plans in motion for women's camp work, only to meet with further delay, this time caused by the bureaucracy set up to organize the financial campaign and disburse the funds. The Committee of Eleven established to oversee the fund formed a subcommittee to deal with expenses relating to women's work. Burke served on this small committee, with representatives of the Y.W.C.A. and the Jewish Welfare Board, for about eight months when its work ended as a result of camp closures. The meetings were friendly gatherings to sort out requests for guest houses and assign the work to one of the three groups. The crucial decisions that launched the Council in women's work were made at the beginning of these sessions. Each group obtained access to the camps for welfare work in relation to women visitors. Since existing sites were retained, the Y.W.C.A. did not have to surrender any of its work. A camp could have one service building for each 3,000 men, and each agency would be granted an equal share of the new buildings. Small camps could have a service building at the discretion of the agencies, and all one-building units would have lists of volunteers of the groups which did not run them. All buildings would be open to all guests regardless of religious affiliation. Representatives of the Council and the Jewish Welfare Board preferred a common designation for all centers, whereas the Y.W.C.A. argued to retain its own name. The position of the Association came as no surprise to Council leaders because Mabel Cratty, General Secretary of the Association, had earlier informed the Council that it wished "to reserve the use of the words 'Hostess Houses' for its houses." The Association sustained its point of view before the Committee of Eleven and the Council called its centers "Visitors' Houses."[44]

The Women's Committee established a dozen of these Houses, including two in Europe, one in Paris and one at Lourdes. Relatively large and expensive buildings, they were purchased, or in the case of most of those in camps, built, with funds raised in the United War Work Campaign. The majority of them opened shortly after the Armistice and closed in the following November when the government shut down most camps. The overseas units were like service clubs with reading and writing rooms, cafeterias and large recreation and entertainment programs. Those at home had similar facilities but with primary emphasis on visitors to the camps, and their short term housing needs. All the Houses were staffed by field secretaries, recruited and trained by the Women's Committee. They wore a specially designed blue uniform and agreed to a strict code of conduct. Fosdick, after visiting the Paris center, wrote that he had "no hesitation in saying that it is one of the best single pieces of work in Paris, and it is being carried on in a spirit of service that could well serve as a model."[45] Every House, including those in Europe, depended on a large number of local volunteers. The Committee realized from the start that the Houses had a lifespan limited by the length of the war. Some began very late, and the one at Walter Reed Hospital was so long in construction that the Committee had to surrender it to the government before it opened.

As the war moved toward armistice, leaders of the Women's Committee began to turn their attention from the Visitors' Houses toward other, non-camp oriented centers for social ministry. Committee Chairman Cooper, accompanied by Dr. Frederick Rice, made an extended tour of major cities in the Midwest, including Cleveland, Columbus, Detroit, Chicago, and East St. Louis. They visited bishops, social workers, hospital directors, and the leaders of men's and women's groups, investigating the possibilities for opening health clinics, community centers, and other welfare projects, and generating volunteers to serve in such potential work. Charles Denechaud went abroad about the same time as the Council's official Overseas Commissioner to carry out similar investigations there. The Community House developed as one result of these surveys. Greater in number and much longer in duration than Visitors' Houses, the centers served a large variety of functions. Many in the United States were founded in immigrant areas, Polish and Italian in particular, and were social centers with an emphasis on the English language and Americanization classes. The latter were run by the Reconstruction Committee as part of its program. The Women's Committee built these projects around local organizations and leadership, supplying some funds and trained workers as stimulants. The long term goal was local control and the development of a permanent program, like those that emerged at Merrick House in Cleveland and at the Catholic Community House in Baltimore.[46]

The most ambitious project occurred in East St. Louis. Substantial immigrant populations, the severe race riot of 1917, and immediate post-war economic problems left this town's citizens in despair and its economy in near ruin, and made it a choice target for a massive renewal effort. The social welfare agencies that had cooperated with the Commission on Training Camp Activities, including the Council, agreed to such a large scale program, under the general supervision of a government sponsored, locally run War Civics Committee. The agencies poured large amounts of money and staff time into the community. The Council built a $275,000 Community House and launched an extensive program with a focus on education for citizenship. At the laying of the cornerstone Cooper maintained that the House represented "the old spirit of Christian love."[47] Bishop Muldoon, Father Burke, and Michael Slattery attended the dedication of the House in May, 1920, marking its significance for their work. Muldoon said on the occasion: "You must follow in the footsteps of Christ, the greatest social worker in the world, since he went about doing good. This place must be the center of mercy, it must be a place where newcomers to America will be welcomed, it must be a factory of American citizens."[48]

Overseas Community Houses, while not so large or so numerous as those at home, constituted an important component of the work. Twenty-one Houses and 112 social workers were involved in projects in France, Belgium and Italy. Almost all centers were opened in areas of devastation or industrial dislocation and attended to the needs of native young women. Girls' homes, hostels, clubs, and playgrounds for workers' children were founded in places like St. Mihiel, Verdun, and Billancourt, and were named Maison Mary Burke, Maison Ste. Delphine, and Maison Marie-Louise. One account described the Houses "as a professional home for the French working woman and girl whether she toiled all day in the motor factory or made fancy garments in the nearby dressmaking shop. Courses in English, stenography, typewriting, music, dramatics and gymnastics were given gratuitously. Athletic, social and study clubs were opened to her and an inviting canteen offered her a palatable, well-planned luncheon at cost price."[49] Arrangements included the transfer of this work to local supervision and control as soon as possible.

One of the most enduring projects of the Committee stemmed from the decision to erect these various places of social ministry, especially the Visitors' Houses. Surveys had turned up few trained Catholic women social workers and even fewer Catholic centers where they could learn the skills. The Council charged Cooper and Kerby to propose a feasible solution to the problem. Their plan, approved by the Council in October, 1918, committed it to open its own school as soon as possible in the Washington area. Within six weeks the Committee secured a local estate, Clifton, hired a small permanent staff led by Miss Maude Cavanaugh and Miss Helen Cronin, engaged a larger part-time faculty mostly from nearby Catholic University of America, and recruited enough students to open its National Catholic Service School for Women. The initial curriculum stressed domestic arts and friendly counseling, mixed with concentrated lecture sessions on topics like "Catholic Principles in Social Work," and "Relief of Poverty."[50] Applicants flooded the admissions committee, assuring a plentiful supply of students and demonstrating wide interest in such work. The sessions during the first two years became longer, eventually reaching six months, and more academic, with time given to studying as well as attending lectures. The School moved steadily in the direction of professional training. Several people helped found it, but from the start Father Burke took a strong personal interest. He conducted the retreat for the first overseas unit, wrote the School's "Act of Consecration," and shared in its curriculum. Clifton graduates were known as "Father Burke's girls."[51] The School became the National Catholic School of Social Service in 1921 and merged with the School of Social Service of the Catholic University in 1947.

The Men's Committee faced substantially different problems from those which confronted the Women's Committee, although it adopted almost identical initial procedures for gathering data and developing a comprehensive list of organizations. One difference lay in the size of the surveying task, since men's groups far outnumbered those for women. By January, 1919, the Committee had on file the names and addresses of 9,714 men's organizations in over 3,300 towns and cities, almost twice the number of women's groups, and that did not include the Knights of Columbus. Many of these were local branches of large national bodies, like the St. Vincent de Paul Society, the Catholic Total Abstinence Union, the Ancient Order of Hibernians, and the Holy Name Society. Two of the largest groups worked through local and diocesan units, kept no national records at all and had no comprehensive mailing lists until the Committee developed them. The more profound difference lay in the fact that the largest and most distinctly national men's group was already deeply involved in war work under the Council's direction.

Information collecting began seriously in April, 1918, and almost immediately the Committee received mixed responses. Many groups welcomed the contact and proposals and cooperated immediately, seeing the new suggestions as helping their local work; however, quite a substantial number expressed either surprise or hostility at the inquires. Chairman Denechaud reported that their letters revealed that the leaders of many of the groups had attended the August meeting and helped create the Council, expecting to be part of the coordinated effort. They had gone home disappointed because "one national organization was singled out to do all the work, and all other national bodies had to coordinate with it. No matter what the claims of the ability of that particular organization were to do the work, others felt that their organization also had ability, and were capable of doing big things." He felt these attitudes would never have arisen had the Council been more successful in its early career.[52]

The Men's Committee overcame these feelings, potentially crippling to its program, in a direct and straightforward manner, without in any way criticizing the Knights of Columbus or upsetting its relationship with them. Denechaud's explanation rested on the distinction between camp and non-camp work. The Knights supervised camp work and received government as well as Catholic authorization for it. But wartime social ministry clearly extended beyond camp borders and he faced the immediate problem that no one in the Catholic community either comprehended or coordinated the work there. Gradually, the honesty and logic of the argument as well as the vision of the need persuaded many of the leaders to join their groups to the national effort. Some accepted Committee membership and by mid-summer

Denechaud and Slattery had recruited Dr. Gaudin of the Catholic Knights of America; F. W. Heckencamp of the Western Catholic Union; John J. Hynes of the Catholic Mutual Beneficial Association; Rev. E. F. Garesche, S. J., of the Sodalities of the Blessed Virgin; Thomas Flynn of the Catholic Federation of the United States; Ignatius D. Dwyer of the Young Men's Institute, Pacific Jurisdiction; and Rev. John G. Beane of the Catholic Total Abstinence Union. Others joined as the program grew. The Central Verein cooperated indirectly, accepting copies of Committee material and distributing them to its local groups.

The Committee served a truly coordinating function, stimulating and uniting the work of others and initiating relatively little of its own. The two exceptions to this were the Service Clubs and the Everyman's Clubs, and in the case of the former it directly ran only a small number of those it helped start. Service Clubs provided men in uniform a place for relaxation and entertainment in camp towns and in major urban centers as an alternative to the kinds of entertainment typically offered them. The Commission on Training Camp Activities kept trying to clean up areas frequented by troops, but fought a difficult and often losing battle. The Committee urged local men's groups to open their club doors to soldiers and sailors, to send representatives to meet troop trains, and to use camp bulletin boards to make their availability known.[53] Many local groups responded, but with few if any full-time staff and limited resources, they struggled to meet the demand. Moreover, many of the youngest and most vigorous members of the clubs had either enlisted or been drafted. Surveys in the fall of 1918 showed many men's groups depleted in membership and finances. The Committee hired field secretaries and offered funds to support local groups, and in some large camps and urban areas opened its own Clubs. The end of the war increased rather than diminished the need as the troops from overseas poured home and the sudden transitions depressed morale. At their peak of operation in the spring and summer of 1919 almost 400 Service Clubs existed, most of them local meeting places of the Young Men's National Union or Young Men's Institutes, transformed for the occasion with a temporary name and Council funds. The Committee ran only twenty-two, including the Benedict and Philopatria in Philadelphia, the Cardinal Farley in New York City, the Admiral Benson in Hoboken, the Victory in Norfolk, and the Pershing in Baltimore. Its only overseas ventures were a Club in Paris run in cooperation with the Women's Committee, and another one in the Canal Zone.

Everyman's Clubs opened in the summer of 1919 as the Committee response to serious labor unrest. Founded primarily in the central and far west regions of the nation in places like Butte, Montana, and Tacoma, Washington, they were the only project it totally controlled. The first one, named a Workmen's Club, consisted of little more than a building with rooms for meetings and relaxation and a moving picture machine. Under the name Everyman's Clubs they grew in number to fifteen and in services to include education programs, citizenship training, and information centers for matters like war service insurance and employment. Late in 1919 the Reconstruction Committee established Employment Bureaus in many of them. Male versions of the Community Houses, they were far more temporary, most of them closing in the spring of 1920.

All the other work of the Men's Committee took the form of coordination. Men's national and diocesan organizations had developed very extensively and the challenge lay in bringing them and their programs together. It encouraged them to participate in the United War Work Campaign and in the government sponsored convalescent work at base hospitals. It urged Catholic Colleges to support the government's program for Student Army Training Corps and solicited from them scholarships for a small number of wounded French soldiers who wanted to study in America. In one case the Committee demonstrated the value of an organization keeping close contact with government projects. Near the end of the war the government created the War Waste Reclamation Service in cooperation with the Council and other welfare groups to direct a campaign to collect waste paper, cloth and metals. Local agencies which joined the program received payments for materials reclaimed. The Committee immediately realized this would affect the St. Vincent de Paul Society which performed the same work, and secured the appointment of fifty-two local Societies to the new program. Then the Red Cross moved to have all revenue from the project directed to its program. The Committee successfully argued against this, protecting some revenue for the Society.

One area of coordination became very time consuming by the summer of 1919, to the surprise of some War Council leaders. After the war the Boy Scout Movement launched a nation-wide campaign for new members. The war inspired aura of uniforms, added to the urgent need for boys' work in large urban areas, challenged the scouting movement. They turned to many groups, including the Catholic Church, creating a new Catholic Bureau under the sponsorship of Archbishop Hayes of New York. When their appeal reached the Council, Burke initially reported: "A careful investigation of the Boy Scout Movement shows a strange desire on the part of this organization to encourage the work of Catholic Boy Scout organizations. In fact, their handbook specifically certifies that Catholic Boy Scouts shall be under the direction of Catholic auspices."[54] His discovery and that of many Catholics was that the Scouts recognized religious pluralism. The Council approved participation and the Committee launched an aggressive campaign, including extensive use of its new mailing lists and many articles in the Catholic press. Within six months it assisted in the establishment of 719 new Catholic Boy Scout Troops, and had preliminary data on another 428 in the process of formation. Secretary Slattery took the lead in this effort, urging men's organizations to help with finances and leadership. He saw it as a major reconstruction project. Young men had borne the brunt of the war: their younger brothers and sons must now be given a special opportunity and scouting offered it.[55]

From time to time Council speakers hinted at their desire for a national laymen's organization to carry on the coordination stimulated by the war. Burke, for example, suggested that the Church needed a school for men social workers as much as one for women. He saw trained Y.M.C.A. Secretaries and asked why the Church could not match them. The Men's Committee held a meeting in December, 1918, of the executive heads of the large national organizations to discuss reconstruction programs. Slattery reported "that this was the first time in the history of Catholic Organizations, when every one of our Catholic bodies was present. This surely marks an epoch in Catholic Societies and speaks hopefully for a united Catholic laity in all great problems of the future:"[56] The issue did not disappear. Under Bishop Schrembs' guidance, with Burke and Slattery present as speakers, a national meeting of men's organizations took place in Chicago on May 6, 1920. The representatives created the National Catholic Layman's Council. Careful to protect the autonomy of individual groups, it purposed to coordinate "all existing Catholic Laymen's organizations so that their united action may be more effective."[57] At its first annual meeting the following September this new group became the National Council of Catholic Men. Father Burke keynoted this assembly, just as he had the one called earlier which had resulted in the National Council of Catholic Women. Ever faithful to his vision of unity he called the men to organize so that the whole social order might be remade on the principles of Christ. Catholics were in welfare work, not just to fight evil, but "as Christian men possessing the truth of Jesus Christ and determined to make Christ known by our visible unity with all the souls of America with whom we come in contact by human speech or human action."[58]

The work of the Men's and Women's Committees consumed much of the time and more than half of the budget of the Council and related to almost all the rest of its work. Through the Hierarchy the Council had direct contact with the ordained ministry of the Church; through these two Committees it developed direct access to the lay ministry. It used this on a variety of different occasions, but never more extensively or successfully than in its protest campaign against the social hygiene films produced by the Commission on Training Camp Activities and endorsed after the war by the United States Public Health Service.

Publicly the War Council and Fosdick's Commission worked together without disagreement until the fall of 1918. Privately, Muldoon, Burke, and Hooke often questioned the policies of Baker and Fosdick. The disputes almost always involved the Commission's "Protestant" bias. Baker and Fosdick were not personally prejudiced, but the culture reflected Protestant power and they seemed reluctant to help speed the arrival of religious pluralism. The Commission admitted the Knights of Columbus to the camps only after private reminders of the usefulness and fairness of such decision. Catholic women's groups stood in line a long time waiting to serve. Even after the Commission formally recognized the Council for all Catholic work it supported a divided financial campaign. The strategy of consultation worked, however slowly, in all these areas of organizational adjustment but did not get very far when the issue involved a matter of belief.

The Commission had oversight of all camp and camp community activities which related to the free time of the men in the armed forces. Outside the camps it often assumed the role of a vice squad, aiding local law enforcement agencies in their fight to maintain wholesome recreation facilities. It solicited the Council's help in this program and Muldoon had encouraged bishops and local groups to support it.[59] Inside the camps it reached the men through the welfare agencies and its own Social Hygiene Division, recruited from the American Social Hygiene Association. That Division produced pamphlets, lectures, and films on proper sexual behavior for distribution to the soldiers and sailors. Their work, especially the sex education film "Fit to Fight," brought immediate protests from many groups. Burke and Hooke led the Catholic critics, with support from Bishop Russell and other prominent clergy. The controversy effected some modifications in the film and remained private until the fall of 1918 when Burke opened the issue to the public and took the first step in what became a national campaign against the entire social hygiene project. He did so without knowing the war was almost over and therefore decided to challenge the Commission in an area of wartime policy.

Two factors motivated Burke. First, the Commission produced two new hygiene items, a pamphlet on venereal disease and a new film titled "The End of the Road." Hooke, after seeing them, wrote: "The entire program of the Social Hygiene section of the commission is damnable."[60] Burke spelled this out as determined opposition to Catholic social teaching. He said the Commission had a good charter and many constructive programs, but with the films it had "departed into paths that for the most part lead downward, . . ." and are marked by a "pessimistic obsession of the chronic inability of men and women to be true to virtuous and noble ideals." The films showed the horrors of venereal disease and warned men and women to beware. But, Burke counselled, "Out of negation nothing can come. Out of fear simply of physically evil consequences nothing can come when the danger of such consequences are (sic) removed. Purity is not simply abstinence from sexual indulgence: purity is the moral life of the soul."[61] The second reason for Burke's movement lay in the projected audience of the new materials. Unlike "Fit to Fight," the new film would be shown to girls and young women in local communities, and the pamphlets would be distributed widely. Burke went public only when the Commission decided to do so.

The end of the war quickly altered the Commission's program, and supervision of its social hygiene work became the responsibility of the United States Public Health Service. The American Social Hygiene Association revised the title of "Fit to Fight" to "Fit to Win" and sold distribution rights to a film company. However, advertisements for the film continued to carry the endorsement of the Public Health Service. The New York Commissioner of Licenses refused to license it, and a court battle ensued. The film began to appear in other states. The Council joined other groups, including the Federal Council, and declared the film unfit for public viewing. When the Public Health Service refused to respond to this pressure, the Council launched a massive grass roots campaign to get the film endorsement withdrawn. Beginning in June, 1919, and using its large mailing lists, it sent letters signed by Slattery and Cooper to all Catholic lay leaders. It argued that "The film must be squelched. . . . We are calling upon our Catholic Men's and Women's Societies of the country to respond as a unit, and make their protests so vigorous that even the most callous will hear a voice that when it speaks will receive attention." Correspondents were urged to write the Surgeon General in Washington and the health departments in their home states: "immediate action is necessary. . . . Let the Catholic laity speak. Let it be prompt and vigorous and by its forcible expression demonstrate to those in charge that, although we are a patient people, we shall not tolerate any violation of the standards for which Catholic manhood and womanhood stand."[62] Letters poured into Washington and the Public Health Service responded by disclaiming sponsorship of the film or responsibility for it. The Council did not agree. It sent its correspondents a follow-up letter and enclosed a pamphlet detailing the faults of the film. The point of the protest was not the distribution of the film, which was indeed in private, commercial hands, but the government's endorsement which could be withdrawn. "So long as such public and explicit endorsement remains unrevoked," the Council advised, "the United States Public Health Service is and must be held responsible for the grave harm done to public morals."[63] Pressure continued to mount and finally late in the summer the Public Health Service announced withdrawal of its support from "Fit to Win" and all other similar films.

The Committee on National Catholic Interests, charged with monitoring national legislation for laws affecting particular Catholic concerns, might have turned to public campaigns on several occasions, but did not. Council leaders found it necessary to intervene in only three legislative debates during the war. One of these, the bill to extend the number of chaplains, became an issue before the Committee was fully prepared to act; and most of the required lobbying fell to Cardinal Gibbons, Father Burke and Secretary Hooke. The other issues, exemption for seminarians from the draft and provisions for sacramental wine in the wartime prohibition law, primarily concerned the ordained ministry. Moreover, the lists of lay leaders were not ready until after all these matters had been settled.

Whether Executive Secretary Hooke or Committee Chairman Kelly did the lobbying, the procedures were the same and the results uniformly successful for the Church's interests. Of course, the Church had lobbied on behalf of its interests before the war. The new phenomenon was the presence in Washington of an officially sanctioned Catholic lobby. Summing up his Committee's work, Kelly said: "It has at least prevented the Federal Council of Churches from monopolizing the field as the sole representative of religious opinion of the country and has succeeded in presenting Catholic standards and wishes in an effective manner."[64] In the spring of 1918 when modifications in the Selective Service Law were proposed which would have changed the status of theological students and made them eligible for the draft, the Council moved promptly to meet the challenge. If passed the amended law would have threatened the future of the ordained ministry, shut off a major source of new chaplains, and forced at least some of the seminaries to close. Hooke took the lead, writing and making personal contact with a number of key congressional leaders, including Senator George E. Chamberlain, Chairman of the Senate Committee on Military Affairs. Some congressmen supported the amendments because they felt seminary enrolments had increased since the beginning of the war, making the exemption a resort of slackers. Hooke gathered information from Catholic seminaries and demonstrated that the small increases in enrolments were fewer than the average peacetime increases. Monsignor Drumgoole of St. Charles Seminary, Phildelphia, and Monsignor Peters of St. John's Seminary, Brighton, Massachusetts, supplied the key data. Cardinal Gibbons expressed his concern to Speaker of the House Champ Clark. The effort to maintain the exemption was successful and might well have been without Council intervention, since Protestants were at work, too, but Council work demonstrated an ability to bring useful information and pressure to bear on an issue important to the whole Church. Chairman Kelly engaged two seminarians for the summer of 1918 in order to compile a list of legislators who could, on the basis of their interests and records, be expected to support the Church's interests. Lobbying takes time and the cultivation of personal relationships, and the Council's short lifespan provided only a foundation for the more extensive efforts of the Welfare Council.

The Protestant Commission and the Catholic Council engaged in a variety of social ministries during the war. Each group had ministered in many of these ways in peacetime, Protestants practicing comity in home missions and Catholics running settlement houses in industrial and immigrant areas. But the war intensified the needs and led the churches to nationalize increasingly their approaches to them. The rapid growth of bureaucracy surprised many of the leaders; the postwar discovery that they needed to continue it startled them even more. The realization came most strongly to the Catholic leaders, but affected the Protestant ones as well. The social ministries had another major feature in the large degree to which they depended on the direction as well as the participation of the laity. This was hardly news to Protestants who had chosen a layman to lead their wartime work, but it came as a pleasant revelation to Catholics. The women's and men's groups, once given united and national direction, provided a new source of identity and strength. Father Burke, ever with a keen eye on the future, was at the heart of the post-war movement to consolidate these gains in lay life and work.

1. See Chapter VIII for the Committee on the Welfare of Negro Troops. See below for the Women's Committee.

2. *Annual Reports of the Federal Council, 1917*, p. 238.

3. A map of the major camps and cantonments appears in Frederick L. Paxson, *America at War, 1917-1918* (Boston: Houghton, Mifflin Company, 1939), p. 104.

4. The full title was *General War-Time Commission of the Churches: Survey of National Army Cantonments and National Guard Camps, November 20, 1917*. A General War-Time Commission Pamphlet.

5. *Ibid.*, pp. 2-5.

6. Gaylord S. White to Raymond Fosdick, December 12, 1917, and Fosdick to White, December 14, 1917. Copies in CTCA Records.

7. Samuel McCrea Cavert to Lt. O. T. James, March 5, 1918. Records of the Bureau of Naval Personnel, in Record Group 24, in the National Archives, Washington, D.C. Hereafter cited: Naval Records.

8. *Survey of the Moral and Religious Forces in the Military Camps and Naval Stations in the United States*, May 1, 1918. A General War-Time Commission Pamphlet.

9. *Moral and Religious Forces in the Military and Naval Hospitals in the United States*, August 1, 1918. A General War-Time Commission Pamphlet.

10. *Annual Reports of the Federal Council, 1917*, pp. 152-53. The poster appeared in many periodicals, including *The Christian Advocate* (New York), 92 (November 1, 1917): 1134. On the work of the Red Cross during the war see Foster Rhea Dulles, *The American Red Cross: A History* (New York: Harper and Brothers, 1950), pp. 138-72.

11. Quoted in The *Times*, February 19, 1917.

12. "A War Time Program," *The Congregationalist and Advance* 103 (February 7, 1918): 184.

13. *A Wartime Program for Local Churches with Emphasis upon Churches Distant from Training Camps*. A General War-Time Commission Pamphlet. The following analysis is based on the Third Edition.

14. *A Wartime Program for Country Churches*, and *The Country Church and the City Boy*. General War-Time Commission Pamphlets.

15. Edmund deS. Brunner, "A year of Cooperative Work in the Rural Church Field," *FC Bulletin* 2 (February, 1919): 30-31. See Renton, *War-Time Agencies of the Churches*, p. 197.

16. The government did not undertake to erect fully adequate places of

worship at army camps until World War II. See "Army Chapels to be Built," *FC Bulletin* 24 (May, 1941): 11.

17. "Minutes of the Meeting of the Sub-Committee on Cantonments," *Commission Minutes*, September 10, 1917.

18. *Commission Minutes*, October 5, 1917.

19. See Worth Tippy to Raymond Fosdick, May 11, 1917, and Fosdick to Tippy, May 17, 1917; and Tippy to Fosdick, August 25, 1917, and Fosdick to Tippy, September 10, 1917. Copies in CTCA Records.

20. "Minutes of the Interdenominational Comity Committee on Religious Work Around the Camps," October 16, 1917, *Minutes of Committees*.

21. "Joint Conference between the Representatives of the War Work Council of the Y.M.C.A. and of the General War-Time Commission of the Churches," September 25, 1917, and "Minutes of a Meeting of Conference on the Church Headquarters at Yaphank," November 27, 1917, *Minutes of Committees*.

22. "Minutes of Conference," December 27, 1917, *Minutes of Committees*.

23. "Minutes of the meeting of the Committee Appointed on the Formal Opening of Camp Upton Church Headquarters," February 13, 1918, *Minutes of Committees*. The opening service was reported in The *Times*, February 25, 1918. See also "Religious Unity Serving the Soldiers," *The Homiletic Review* 75 (April, 1918): 298.

24. "War Status of Protestant Churches," *The Presbyterian* 87 (October 25, 1917): 5.

25. *Commission Minutes*, September 20, 1917.

26. *Miscellaneous War Production Centers*. Appended to "Minutes of the Meeting of the Committee on Field and Assignments of the Joint Committee," August 20, 1918, *Minutes of Committees*.

27. *Home Missions Council*. Eleventh Annual Meeting (New York: Home Missions Council, 1918), pp. 172–77.

28. *Commission Minutes*, June 5, 1918.

29. "Minutes of the Meeting of Representatives of the General War-Time Commission of the Churches and the Home Missions Council," June 29, 1918, *Minutes of Committees*.

30. The pamphlets on rural work were Elmer J. Bouher, *100% American: The War Story of a Country Church* (New York: The Joint Committee on War Production Communities, 1918); and *A Reconstruction Program for Country Churches* (New York: Joint Committee on War Production Communities, 1919). See also Worth Tippy, *Documentary Report on the Logging Camps of the Pacific North West. With Recommendations* (New York: Joint Committee on War Production Communities, 1919).

31. *Home Missions Council* (1918), p. 178.

32. "Recommendations as to Procedure at Nitro, West Virginia and Similar Communities," Appended to "Minutes of the Meeting of the Joint Committee on War Production Communities," August 19, 1918, *Minutes of Committees*. See also *Commission Minutes*, October 2, 1918.

33. *Annual Reports of the Federal Council of the Churches of Christ in America, 1918* (New York: Missionary Education Movement, 1918), pp. 96–103; *Home Missions Council.* Twelfth Annual Meeting (New York: Home Missions Council, 1919), pp. 58–83.

34. *Conscription and the Conscientious Objector* (New York: The Civil Liberties Bureau of the American Union Against Militarism, 1917), pp. 8–9.

35. *The Facts About Conscientious Objectors in the United States* (New York: National Civil Liberties Bureau, 1918), p. 27. See also Donald Johnson, *The Challenge to American Freedom: World War I and the Rise of the American Civil Liberties Union* (Lexington, Kentucky: University of Kentucky Press, 1963), pp. 26–54.

36. *Report of Treatment of Conscientious Objectors at the Camp Funston Guard House* (New York: Relatives and Friends of Conscientious Objectors, 1918). See also: "Conscientious Objectors in Prison," *The Survey* 41 (November 23, 1918): 224; and Norman Thomas, "War's Heretics," *ibid.*, (December 7, 1918): 319–23.

37. "Treatment of Conscientious Objectors Reviewed by the War-Time Commission of the Churches," *FC Bulletin* 2 (March, 1919): 52–53.

38. Abrams, *Preachers Present Arms*, p. 148.

39. John Haynes Holmes, "Belated Aid for Objectors," *The New Republic* 18 (March 15, 1919): 217–18.

40. John J. Burke to Charles Denechaud, August 10, 1918. Copy in NCWC Archives.

41. "Report of the Committee on Women's Activities," From April 1918 to February 10, 1919, NCWC Archives.

42. *The Promise Fulfilled* (January, 1920), pp. 4–6. A National Catholic War Council Pamphlet.

43. *Handbook of the National Catholic War Council*, pp. 17–18.

44. "Meeting of the Committee of Four," October 31, 1918, Attached to "Minutes of the Committee of Eleven," November 6, 1918. See also Mabel Cratty to Walter Hooke, July 22, 1918, in NCWC Archives.

45. *The Promise Fulfilled*, p. 9.

46. John O'Grady, *Catholic Charities in the United States* (Washington, D.C.: National Conference of Catholic Charities, 1930), pp. 299–301.

47. "Opening of East St. Louis Community House," *NCWC Bulletin* 1 (September, 1919): 14.

48. "Our House in East St. Louis," *NCWC Bulletin* 1 (May, 1920): 22.

49. "National Catholic War Council in Europe," *NCWC Bulletin* 1 (May, 1920): 12.

50. May M. Murphy, "The National Service School for Women," *NCWC Bulletin* 1 (June, 1919): 12.

51. Sheerin, *Never Look Back*, p. 45.

52. "Report of Committee on Men's Activities," August 1, 1918, NCWC Archives.

53. *The Catholic Soldier In Camp and Out of Camp*, pp. 13–14.

54. "National Catholic War Council," Report to the Administrative Committee by Father John Burke," May 9, 1919, NCWC Archives.

55. "Scouting Under Catholic Leadership," *NCWC Bulletin* 1 (August, 1919): 7-8.

56. "Report of the Committee on Men's Activities," January 23, 1919, NCWC Archives.

57. "National Catholic Laymen's Council," *NCWC Bulletin* 1 (May, 1920): 27.

58. "Lay Apostolate Accepts Its Mission," *NCWC Bulletin* 2 (October, 1920): 5.

59. Williams, *American Catholics and the War*, pp. 173-75.

60. Walter Hooke to Dr. Peters, October 14, 1918, NCWC Archives.

61. "With Our Readers," *The Catholic World* 108 (October, 1918): 137-38. See also Francis P. Schiavone, *The Honor Legion* (New York: The Chaplains' Aid Association, 1917).

62. "Our Fight Against Unclean Films," *NCWC Bulletin* 1 (July, 1919): 19.

63. "Our Fight on Evil Films is Succeeding," *NCWC Bulletin* 1 (August, 1919): 14. See also *"Fit to Win"* (Washington: National Catholic War Council, 1919). A National Catholic War Council Pamphlet.

64. Edward A. Kelly to John J. Burke, C.S.P., Chairman of the Committee on Special War Activities, February 12, 1919, NCWC Archives.

VIII

A Special Ministry

Negroes have always had a special place in American culture, carefully set aside for them by a comprehensive pattern of racial segregation, most apparent in the South, but not without its outlines in every section of the nation.[1] This remained true during World War I despite the promotion of that war by Wilson and others as a struggle for self-determination and democracy. Segregation actually increased during his first term as President, partly due to the policies of his own administration.[2] Most white Americans experienced little if any incongruity of wartime practices and goals. However, some citizens and organizations, including some of the churches and the Federal Council, perceived that the nation that fought to make the world safe for democracy had not yet determined to make itself safe for Negroes. The Federal Council developed a special ministry to meet the needs of Negro soldiers.

The Selective Service Act, passed on May 18, 1917, was perfectly democratic. It required all men between the ages of twenty-one and thirty-one to register, and over 700,000 Negroes complied. A few days prior to the passage of this law over 40,000 men entered the various camps set up to train men to be officers, but that exercise turned out to be less democratic, for all of those men were white. Rumors had circulated for some time that the government intended to offer commissions to white men only and a few Negro and white leaders protested quite vigorously the exclusion of Negroes. Participants in the protest included Robert R. Moton, Principal of the Tuskegee Institute, and Joel Spingarn, President of the National Association for the Advancement of Colored People. The religious press also criticized the government's plan, one editor arguing: "Instead of bringing forward new methods of humiliating and repressing colored Americans in this hour of national crisis, now is the time to practice the democracy which we profess as a nation and for which we enter the war, and encourage the fullest loyalty and the most enthusiastic devotion to our country by absolute justice and equal opportunity for all citizens eligible for enlistment."[3] The raised voices resulted in the establishment of a segregated officers' training camp at Fort Des Moines, Iowa. It opened a month later than the camps for white men, and as a consequence the first Negro officers were commissioned a month later than the initial group of white officers.[4]

Racial turmoil made the first summer of the war long and hot. The increased pressures of the northward migration of large numbers of Negroes, the escalating contest for jobs, and the continuing harshness of segregation produced a series of confrontations, including the devastating one in East St. Louis, Illinois. That town erupted in mob violence on July 2. When the holocaust passed, at least nine whites and thirty-nine Negroes lay dead and a record for brutality in a civil disorder had been established that has almost no equal in the nation's history.[5] *The Christian Advocate* called it "a tragedy belonging in the same bloody category with the merciless act of which we have thought only the Turk and the Hun were capable."[6] Other editors also raised the theme of brutality, one of them noting that the riot looked like the rape of Belgium. One account described the following scene at the riot: "In one case, for instance, a ten-year-old boy whose mother had been shot down was running around sobbing, looking for his mother, when some members of the mob shot the boy, and before his life had passed they picked him up and threw him into the flames. A colored woman with a two-year-old baby in her arms was trying to protect the child, and they shot her and also shot the child, and threw them into the flames."[7] The N.A.A.C.P. responded to the violence with a Silent Parade in New York City. The marchers carried signs proclaiming: "THOU SHALT NOT KILL," and "MR. PRESIDENT, WHY NOT MAKE AMERICA SAFE FOR DEMOCRACY."[8] The editor of the Congregational weekly approved of the march and called on the nation "to suppress and promptly punish all outbursts of barbarism."[9] Barbarism involving Negro soldiers and white townspeople broke out at the end of the summer in Houston, Texas.

While many citizens protested racial injustice and violence, they rarely tied their protests to the war effort. Negro leaders in particular drew a careful line between anger at the way their people were treated and their support for the war. W. E. B. DuBois articulated one position in a widely circulated and instantly famous editorial in *Crisis*, the journal of the N.A.A.C.P., in which he admonished his fellow Negroes: "Let us not hesitate. Let us, while this war lasts, forget our special grievances and close our ranks shoulder to shoulder with our own white fellow citizens and the allied nations that are fighting for democracy."[10] Many leaders concurred, at least in part, because they believed that a victory for world-wide democracy would lead to distinct improvements in American democracy. President Moton joined his protests with the suggestion, made to President Wilson and Secretary Baker, that a Negro be related to the government in an official capacity, perhaps in the War Department, "who could advise the Secretary in such matters as concerned the relation of Negroes to the various measures set in operation for winning of the war."[11] When Wilson agreed, Moton proposed Emmett J. Scott, Booker T. Washington's private secretary for eighteen years and the acting Secretary of Tuskegee Institute, for the position. Baker announced Scott's appointment as a special assistant in charge of Negro affairs on October 5 and the decision met with widespread approval among the Negro leadership of the nation.[12] These events directly affected the ministry of the churches through the Federal Council.

The Council had on several occasions since its founding acted in a general way against segregation and some of its attendant evils, and a few months prior to the war it had created a permanent Committee on Negro Churches. At its Special Meeting in May the Council pledged "to hold our own nation true to its professed aims of justice, liberty, and brotherhood."[13] The Committee did nothing spectacular in the summer of 1917 to fulfil this pledge: however, it provided an organizational structure in which Negro and white religious leaders could together study the problems of Negroes and to which various commissions of the Council could refer inquiries about ministries related to them. The General War-Time Commission made such a referral in September when John R. Hawkins, Financial Secretary of the African Methodist Episcopal Church requested that it study the needs of Negro troops.

The Committee met under the direction of its Chairman, Bishop Wilbur P. Thirkield, and with Hawkins present by invitation, to consider what might be done. The lack of Negro chaplains stood out as the crucial initial issue for it meant, given segregated camps, a very limited sacramental ministry. The War Department's provision for Negro officers failed to include chaplains. The Committee recommended that the Commission approach the Secretary of War and clarify the need for Negro chaplains and the justice of equal status. It also suggested that the General Committee on Army and Navy Chaplains work with accredited representatives of Negro denominations in recruiting chaplains. Welfare work among Negro troops constituted a second important concern. Realistically appraising the kinds of things which could be done given the prevailing pattern of segregation, the Committee advised the Commission: "(1) It is understood that the negroes are to be trained separately and apart from the whites. It naturally follows that their religious and social activities will be managed or conducted separate and apart from the whites. (2) The direction of religious and social activities among the negro soldiers can be managed most successfully by negroes." The kinds of ministries needed by the troops seemed to call for "a special field agent or secretary whose duty it shall be to make special visits to these various camps or cantonments and make recommendations for the successful organization of religious and social activities in and around each and all camps where negroes are quartered and make a report of the same to the Executive Committee of the General War-Time Commission of the Churches."[14]

The Commission accepted the Committee report and realized that extensive work needed to be done. Negro troops clearly constituted a special ministry. It therefore arranged to reorganize the Committee as its own special Committee on the Welfare of Negro Troops, keeping most of its members and retaining Thirkield as Chairman. It added other well known white and Negro leaders including George Foster Peabody, the Rev. Thomas Jesse Jones, and President Moton. It adopted the former Committee's welfare work recommendations but only after modifying the second one. Always concerned for cooperative work, it added that work done by Negroes for Negroes should, if possible, also be "in cooperation with the local and general commissions for work among the white societies."[15] Hawkins agreed to serve as voluntary field secretary until a permanent appointment could be made, and he quickly began investigations in the Washington, D.C., area. Thirkield approached Scott concerning War Department welfare plans, but Scott had not had time to calculate the dimensions of his work. The Bishop decided to withhold Committee action until Scott could explore the needs and project the extent of the government's programs.

The new Committee met in February, 1918, and Scott presented his plans. He explained that his assignment directed him to oversee the general welfare of Negro soldiers and not specifically their religious welfare. He gave a detailed account of the work being done in the communities near camps containing significant numbers of them. When Thirkield asked for recommendations about work the Committee could do, Scott suggested that the churches in camp communities needed to be made more fully aware of their responsibilities for the religious life of the soldiers, and that the allotment of chaplains for these soldiers be filled immediately.[16] This review of the situation convinced the Committee that the time had come to act. On March 1 it hired Charles Williams, the Physical Director at Hampton Institute, as its Field Secretary, and directed him to survey moral conditions in the camps and the nearby communities, and more particularly to investigate the religious work those communities were doing for the soldiers. The Committee reiterated the need for the General Committee on Army and Navy Chaplains to devote itself to finding and urging Negro pastors to enter the chaplaincy. It also added Scott to its membership.

During the spring and summer months Williams visited in a systematic manner thirteen of the major camps and studied the moral and religious conditions surrounding them. He wrote detailed reports on his findings and sent copies not only to members of the Committee but also to the War Department. This coordination provided Scott a constant flow of fresh information and hence added leverage in his requests for action. Although Williams served as the designated Field Secretary, several other Committee members participated in the work. Bishop Thirkield, for example, visited a number of camps and their communities, investigating conditions and making addresses on the moral aims of the war.[17]

Williams' findings and those of the others who helped him surprised no one on the Committee, since they were well aware of the pervasiveness of racial prejudice, but the reports did reveal some of the special ways prejudice manifested itself in wartime. Segregation existed in many forms in the communities adjacent to the camps. Recreation facilities, such as movie theaters, were almost always segregated in the South. Moreover, the places open to Negroes, such as ice cream parlors and public dance halls, were rarely supervised and consequently were frequented by prostitutes and other undesirable persons. Williams found that the efforts of the Commission on Training Camp Activities to abolish prostitution in cities near camps had actually led to "a scattering of prostitutes to all sections inhabited by colored people."[18] Even the Negro prostitutes faced a serious plight, for few cities had Negro women workers or police women to deal with them. Still fewer localities had detention homes for these persons, and strong opposition existed to establishing them. He discovered this: "Money appropriated by the Government for the establishment of detention homes in cantonment cities was seldom used for Negro girls. Instead they were usually placed in jail, or sent to the prison farm or the 'stockade,' the home of the chain gang. . . . The inmates lived in dirt and disease, sleeping on ragged, greasy mattresses on concrete floors and eating food prepared in the most unsanitary manner."[19] Negro churches in camp communities were doing almost as little as the welfare groups and seemed to lack any sense of a special ministry for the soldiers. In some localities he found one or more local churches provided rooms and recreation facilities and in a few instances leading churches gave special programs for the men. The churches in Atlanta, Georgia, were among the few examples of cooperative ministry. They supported trained workers and a recreation program and held special united services Sunday afternoons. However, such programs were rare and cooperative action almost non-existent.[20] The overall picture of care for the social and religious life of the Negro troops looked bleak.[21]

Life inside the camps did not seem much better than life outside them. Williams reported many traces of both segregation and lack of organization. Negro troops in camps in the North and Negro officers stationed in both the North and the South generally received fair treatment and the respect due them. Most of the camps had adequate food, barracks, and clothing. However, he discovered notable exceptions to this, one of which he described after the war: "In Camp Humphrey, Virginia, through which 40,000 Negro soldiers passed, not until after the Armistice and until the white soldiers were discharged did the Negro men have such conveniences as barracks, comfortable mess halls, and sanitary facilities; and their "Y" tent was especially leaky. Such conditions in different places easily gave the Negro people the impression that their sons were being mistreated and were suffering in the camps, and this accounted for considerable unrest."[22]

Everywhere, the main problem consisted of the lack of a "proper atmosphere."[23] The existing atmosphere destroyed morale and stifled patriotism. Several factors contributed to this. More than 350,000 Negroes served the nation in the war and almost half of them were assigned to non-combatant units, most of them in the capacity of stevedores. The War Department did not see fit to provide any military training for these men. In addition, the commissioned and non-commissioned officers for these units were almost invariably white. The men found special dissatisfaction "in the attitude of the white 'non-coms,' who, in many instances, were promoted to such positions because of previous knowledge of Negroes, usually gotten on plantations, public works, turpentine farms and the like. The great trouble is that many times white officers, 'non-coms' and colored soldiers bring into the army civil customs and attitudes which are not in keeping with the spirit and principles of the National Army."[24] Williams reported that the places of amusement erected for the use of troops in the South, meaning on the camp grounds, were often closed to all Negro troops. Negro chaplains were very few in number and poorly distributed. Ineptness as well as prejudice characterized the handling of the soldiers' problems. One of the many examples of this related to the application of the law that authorized the founding of schools for all non-English speaking foreigners in the camps. The War Department interpreted the law to exclude illiterate Negroes, on the basis that military circumstances, meaning their non-combatant assignments, did not require that they learn to read.

Williams presented the Committee two sets of recommendations. In the first he suggested that public agencies and churches be encouraged to furnish recreation centers and supervised dance halls, to suppress vice in Negro sections of camp communities, and to provide women workers and detention homes for wayward girls. He also proposed that the Federal Council organize churches in camp communites. The Committee voted to bring these matters to the attention of agencies which were in a position to take immediate action, including the churches, the Commission on Training Camp Activities, the War Camp Community Service, and the Y.M.C.A. It also decided "to secure a field secretary to give his time and efforts in organizing colored churches for more effective service to the colored troops."[25]

The second set of recommendations covered the things Williams believed needed to be done to give Negro troops recognition and status as first-class soldiers. He urged that there should be Negro non-commissioned officers in the stevedore units, more Negroes in officers' training schools, an increased number of Negro chaplains, and an educational program for troops who were illiterate. The Committee prepared resolutions on these and several related topics but realized that most of the recommendations concerned things beyond the immediate jurisdiction of the churches. In order to get these matters before the proper authorities it decided to seek a consultation with the War Department. The Committee worked closely with its parent Commission in setting up the meeting and selecting the delegation. The appointees included the members of the Committee and representative leaders of the Commission and the Federal Council, including Bishops Lawrence and McDowell, and William Adams Brown. They set the conference for September 25, with Assistant Secretary Frederick Keppel. They made some effort to gain the support of a wider circle of church members for their appeal by releasing their recommendations to the religious press. At least one denominational periodical printed an exact copy of them two weeks before the conference and commented that they deserved Baker's closest attention. "They are not," the editor said, "the captious criticisms of political opponents, or the expression of racial self-assertiveness. They are based upon the principles of human equality which lie at the basis of America's participation in the War for Freedom."[26]

The conference with Keppel marked the high point of the Committee's service. It took the form of a public protest by churchmen who had studied the situation thoroughly and who believed that Negro troops were being mistreated, both as soldiers and as human beings. The Rev. M. Ashby Jones, the pastor of a white Baptist church in Atlanta and the son of Robert E. Lee's chaplain, made the presentation. The statement contained two parts, the first a summary of the actual conditions of the troops, and the second a series of seven recommendations for action.[27] The latter, largely identical to those proposed by Williams, clearly showed that the churchmen believed that the nation, through the Department, had fallen far short of decent, acceptable practice in its treatment of Negro troops. They also projected a clear picture of what needed to be done in order for the troops to receive justice in the armed forces of the nation. The generally defensive replies of Keppel and the other Department official who sat in on the conference indicated that the recommendations touched sensitive spots in government policy. The official, a general in the army, responded to the request for education of illiterate Negroes with a simple reiteration of the military need to educate foreigners so that orders could be understood. He evidently did not grasp the irony of training foreigners to read English when many Americans who could not read were not included in the training. Reports of the conference carried no indication that Keppel opposed any of the proposals but his concluding remarks contained the traditional excuse for positive action against segregation. Keppel is reported to have said that "the time element entered into most of the difficulties. These difficulties . . . could be solved in time, but in the meantime it is necessary to organize an army rapidly."[28] The Committee recognized the need for rapid mobilization, but questioned whether the way in which most of the Negroes were mobilized measured up to the nation's professed ideals. The Department acted on some of the recommendations, but Scott reported after the war in a speech made to the Association for the Study of Negro Life and History that despite the reduction of segregation the Department accomplished, Negro soldiers had not received a square deal.[29]

After the conference the Committee devoted its main energies to organizing the work of the local churches in camp communities. To this end it hired the Rev. G. Lake Imes, Dean of the Bible Training School of Tuskegee Institute, as Field Secretary. Imes travelled fairly extensively, visiting many of the camp neighborhoods. In December, the Committee issued a pamphlet assuring Negro churches and their members that it had taken pains "to insure that every provision that the Government and the various welfare agencies are making for the comfort and welfare of our fighting forces is enjoyed by our colored soldiers and sailors." The pamphlet also outlined some programs which local churches could use in ministering to the troops."[30] When the General War-Time Commission concluded its work in the spring of 1919, the Committee reverted to its status as the Committee on Negro Churches and continued its program directly under the Federal Council.

The summer of 1919 proved to be longer and hotter racially than the first summer of the war. The violence of Chicago almost equalled that of East St. Louis two years earlier, and in addition major riots occurred in places like Longview, Texas; Knoxville, Tennessee; Omaha, Nebraska; and Washington, D.C. Bishop Thirkield chaired a conference on racism held under the auspices of the Home Missions Council. One consequence of this meeting was a formal statement, *A Race Crisis*, issued jointly by that Council, the Federal Council, and its Committee on Negro Churches. The churches admitted their implication in the prevailing racism and announced their responsibility for its resolution. They outlined a constructive program, including economic justice, equal opportunity, and adequate educational facilities. The authors of the statement then went to the heart of the matter, which was "the failure to recognize the Negro as a man." "Respect for Negro manhood and womanhood," they continued, "is the only basis for amicable race adjustment, for race integrity and for permanent racial peace. If we talk democracy, let us act democracy. If we propose a democratic program for the protection and self-determination of the weak and oppressed people of Europe as a means of permanent peace and goodwill abroad, let us apply the same program at home."[31] The Federal Council followed this verbal commitment with an organizational one when it created a permanent Commission on Church and Race

Relations in 1921. This marked the real start of the yet unfinished struggle by the united churches against racism in America.

The Catholic Church did not share with the Protestant ones the awakening to the racial crisis in this period. It had, through its Hierarchy and several of its religious orders, spoken and acted for racial justice in the years prior to the war. The work of the Oblate Sisters of Providence, the Sisters of the Holy Family, the Society of Saint Joseph, and the Sisters of the Blessed Sacrament, on behalf of Negroes, merited attention, but did not represent a national Catholic commitment. The Hierarchy made such a commitment at the Second Plenary Council in Baltimore in 1866, when it said: "By the bowels of the mercy of God, we beg and implore priests as far as they can, to consecrate their thoughts, their time, and themselves wholly and entirely, if possible, to the service of the colored people."[32] The Third Plenary Council of 1884 added nothing to this plea except the formation of a Commission for Catholic Missions among the Colored People and the Indians. The Commission's task involved administration of the proceeds of an annual collection taken in all parishes.[33] In 1907, the Hierarchy through Cardinal Gibbons, established the Catholic Board for Mission Work among the Colored People. The new Board sought funds in addition to those collected by the Commission, and tried "to create and foster the missionary spirit among Catholics and others in favor of the colored people."[34]

The war introduced nothing new into the Hierarchy's thinking on this subject. The *Handbook* of the War Council made no specific reference to work for Negroes, and the Archives contain very few references to work done on their behalf. The K. of C. ran some huts for Negro troops and had Negro secretaries in charge of them.[35] The post-war "Pastoral Letter" contained some reflections on them grouped under the rubric of Negro and Indian Missions, and pointed out that the "lot of the Negro and Indians, though latterly much improved, is far from being what the Church would desire." It went on to declare: "In the name of justice and charity, we deprecate most earnestly all attempts at stirring up racial hatred; for this, while it hinders the progress of all our people, and especially of the Negro, in the sphere of temporal welfare, places serious obstacles to the advance of religion among them."[36] Little if any concrete action seemed to follow these words. The War Council did little to refute the judgment of one historian, that between Appomattox and the close of World War II, the Church's relations with the Negro have been a failure of both mission and ministry.[37]

World War I confronted the nation with a new racial situation and provoked widespread awareness of a genuine racial crisis. Migration, urban violence, and large numbers of Negro soldiers alerted many citizens to the national character of racism and the clear hypocrisy of the American way in race relations. Some churches, especially those related to the Federal Council, became involved in the crisis and determined to bring a word of reconciliation and ministry to it. The war ended their complacency on the issue of race. The Council switched from its traditional social gospel stance of nonchalance about racism to a clear involvement in its present realities. The Catholic Church, occupied with other issues, primarily those concerning the immigrant and economic life, did not experience a similar discovery. Its full commitment to racial justice, in deeds as well as words, lay several decades in the future.

1. The terminology used in this chapter reflects the usage of the World War I era. Direct quotations are unaltered.

2. Kathleen L. Wolgemuth, "Woodrow Wilson and Federal Segregation," *The Journal of Negro History* 44 (April, 1959): 158-73.

3. "Racial Justice in the War," *The Congregationalist and Christian World* 102 (May 17, 1917): 627.

4. Emmett J. Scott, *Scott's Official History of The American Negro in the World War* (Chicago: Homewood Press, 1919), pp. 82-91.

5. Elliott M. Rudwick, *Race Riot at East St. Louis, July 2, 1917* (Cleveland and New York: The World Publishing Company, 1964).

6. "Democracy Disgraced," *The Christian Advocate* (New York), 92 (July 12, 1917): 691.

7. Channing H. Tobias, "Shall America Be Made Safe for Black Men?" *The North American Student* 6 (March, 1918): 266.

8. Lerone Bennett, Jr., *Before the Mayflower: A History of The Negro in America, 1619-1964* (Revised Edition; Baltimore, Maryland: Penguin Books, 1968), p. 293.

9. "The Negro's Appeal for Justice," *The Congregationalist and Christian World* 102 (August 9, 1917): 166.

10. June, 1917. Quoted in Kenneth B. Clark, "Morale of the Negro on the Home Front: World Wars I and II," *The Journal of Negro Education* 12 (Summer, 1943): 423.

11. Robert R. Moton, *Finding a Way Out* (Garden City, New York: Doubleday, Page and Company, 1921), p. 241.

12. See, for example, the letter of John R. Hawkins to Secretary of War Baker, reprinted in Scott, *Scott's Official History*, p. 48.

13. Macfarland, *The Churches of Christ in Time of War*, p. 131.

14. "Minutes of the Meeting of the Committee on Negro Churches," October 18, 1917, *Minutes of Committees.*

15. *Commission Minutes,* October 19, 1917.

16. "Resumé by Mr. Emmett J. Scott of War Camp Community Work Among Negroes Accomplished up to February 16, 1918," Appended to "Minutes of the Meeting of the Committee on the Welfare of Negro Troops," February 16, 1918, *Minutes of Committees.*

17. "New Orleans," *The Christian Advocate* (New York), 93 (July 25, 1918): 944.

18. Charles H. Williams, "Resumé of Conditions Surrounding Negro Troops," Appended to "Minutes of the Meeting of the Committee on the Welfare of Negro Troops," August 5, 1918, *Minutes of Committees.*

19. Charles H. Williams, *Sidelights on Negro Soldiers* (Boston: B. J. Brimmer Company, 1923), p. 83.

20. Williams, "Resumé of Conditions Surrounding Negro Troops."

21. Williams, *Sidelights on Negro Soldiers,* p. 135. See also Miles Mark Fisher, "The Negro Church and the World-War," *The Journal of Religion* 5 (September, 1925): 483-99.

22. *Ibid.,* pp. 26-27.

23. Williams, "Resumé of Conditions Surrounding Negro Troops."

24. *Ibid.*

25. "Minutes of the Meeting of the Committee on the Welfare of Negro Troops," August 5, 1918, *Minutes of Committees.*

26. "The Negro Soldier," *The Christian Advocate* (New York), 93 (September 12, 1918): 1146-47.

27. "Subjects for Conference with War Department on Welfare of Negro Troops," September 25, 1918, *Minutes of Committees.*

28. "Minutes of a Conference with Assistant Secretary Keppel Concerning Matters Related to the Welfare of Negro Troops," September 25, 1918. Appended to "Minutes of the Meeting of the Committee on the Welfare of Negro Troops," November 4, 1918, *Minutes of Committees.*

29. Reported in "Proceedings of the Second Biennial Meeting of the Association for the Study of Negro Life and History," *The Journal of Negro History* 4 (October, 1919): 476-77.

30. *War Work by the Church for Negro Soldiers and Sailors,* December 31, 1918. A General War-Time Commission Pamphlet.

31. *A Race Crisis* (New York: Home Missions Council, 1919).

32. Quoted in Joseph Butsch, S.S.J., "Negro Catholics in the United States," *Catholic Historical Review* 3 (April, 1917): 45.

33. William A. Osborne, *The Segregated Covenant: Race Relations and American Catholics* (New York: Herder and Herder, 1967), p. 24.

34. John T. Gillard, S.S.J., *The Catholic Church and the American Negro* (Baltimore: St. Joseph's Society Press, 1929. Reprinted by Johnson Reprint Company, 1968), pp. 45, 288.

35. Egan and Kennedy, *The Knights of Columbus in Peace and War* 1:241.

36. *Pastoral Letter* (Washington, D.C.: The National Catholic Welfare Council, 1920), p. 16.

37. John Tracy Ellis, "Contemporary American Catholicism in the Light of History," *The Critic* 24 (June–July, 1966): 15–16. See also Tom Froncek, "American Catholics and the American Negro," *The Catholic Mind* 64 (January, 1966): 4–11.

IX

The Churches Face the Peace

The churches faced the peace very differently from the way they had faced the war. When the war began, they were largely unprepared for wartime ministry, and spent some months mobilizing. They had to gather leaders, organize new committees, and in the case of the Roman Catholics, create entirely new coordinating agencies. The churchmen who organized and presided over the wartime ministries did not wait until the Armistice to plan for peace. They first faced the idea of it in their wartime policies. Acknowledging peace as their main goal, in the broadest sense at least, they had accepted the war as necessary and just in order to regain it. The Hierarchy hoped that "an enduring and blessed peace" would crown the war and the Federal Council pledged to join the fight "to safeguard the right of all the people, great and small alike, to live their lives in freedom and peace."[1] The Council also agreed to apply the lessons learned in the war when "that just and sacred peace for which we pray" arrives.[2]

Churchmen in positions of leadership understood that their commitment to peace carried with it the responsibility of reconstruction. The link between peace and reconstruction may appear both obvious and inconsequential, but it was neither during the war, attracting its share of hostility. They based their conviction on the fundamental idea that peace, not war, remained the normal way of life. While war might temporarily interrupt that life, it should never be allowed to damage or dominate it. Insofar as it did either to people, values, or possessions, plans had to be made to rebuild and reconstruct them. The spirit of unleashed patriotism, espoused by the militants, provoked calls for citizens to put peace and reconstruction from their minds. Speer warned about this mentality when he told the Special Meeting of the

Council that some people were advocating diminishing and narrowing the churches' ministry. Catholics felt the pressure when they tried to support the Pope's peace initiatives. Father Ryan encouraged continued discussion of peace despite Wilson's gracious but firm rejection of the Holy Father's proposals. Frederick Lynch, associated with the Federal Council and the Church Peace Union, suggested in the fall of 1917 an appropriate slogan for wartime: "In times of war, prepare for peace."[3] He urged discussion of the principles of peace before it arrived, including the possibility of a league of nations, so that adequate time would be available for a careful analysis of the issues. Moreover, the church, itself an international community, could "with peculiar right, be teaching the people to talk in terms of the world, of the kingdom, of the commonwealth of nations, of the republic of God, while the nation may have to be confining itself to its own problems."[4] Although his views did not attract wide public support, some people were listening. When the War Council organized a Committee on Reconstruction, its chairman wrote: "If it is true that in time of peace we should prepare for war, it is equally certain that in time of war we should prepare for peace."[5]

Reconstruction meant more than planning, even if the plans were for worthy things like a community of nations or a new scheme of industrial relations or replacing blasted brick and mortar in war ravaged nations. Churchmen in general and Protestants in particular related their practical efforts to their theological understanding of the Kingdom of God. Many of them shared Walter Rauschenbusch's twofold version of the Kingdom: (1) "The Kingdom of God is divine in its origin, progress and consummation"; and (2) "The Kingdom is for each of us the supreme task and the supreme gift of God. By accepting it as a task, we experience it as a gift. By laboring for it we enter into the joy and peace of the Kingdom as our divine fatherland and habitation."[6] They saw through the clouds of war the remote, but potentially reachable shores of the Kingdom. It could come—the very spirit of the times cried out that it could come—if they could disperse the clouds and help share a clearer vision. Henry Churchill King put the goal in the somewhat mundane terms of "a better civilization"; the collective leadership of the Council looked farther into the future and sought to join hands "with all men of good-will of every land and race, to rebuild on this war-ridden and desolated earth the commonwealth of mankind, and to make the kingdoms of the world the kingdom of Christ."[7]

The churches sought various ways to actualize this vision. They enlisted in a number of projects shortly after the war began in Europe, including relief appeals for the peoples of Belgium and France. Some of these were oriented to particular religious groups, like the collection on behalf of Huguenot Churches; others were more general, like those sponsored by the Red Cross. American entry into the war spurred existing efforts and stimulated new ones. Protestant appeals became so numerous that the Federal Council persuaded a number of programs to join in January, 1918, to form the United Committee on Christian Service for Relief in France and Belgium. In addition to relief, Protestants became involved in two projects for international Christian fellowship: Swedish Archbishop Nathan Soderblom's call for a conference of Christians, and the Committee on Interchange of Ministers between the Churches of America, Great Britain, and France. Neither of these propositions achieved its objectives during the war. Beyond these ventures Protestants and Catholics established special committees to develop reconstruction plans and begin working for peace. Their programs, heavily concentrated in the period September, 1918, to September, 1919, formed the heart of their reconstruction efforts, but not the final word. They also formulated new policies for their post-war ministries, and the Catholics, in particular, created a new agency to carry them out.

By late fall, 1917, the Federal Council and its newly formed General War-Time Commission were awash in reconstruction proposals. At the Council's Annual Meeting in December General Secretary Macfarland reported that the time had come to stimulate and unify "the education and work of the churches in reconstruction" and that the volume of work suggested some new group for the task.[8] Commission Secretary Brown supported this view and argued that when every community near a camp was mobilized, and every church member contributed to relief, the "church will still have left her greatest work undone . . . Besides the material reconstruction which must follow the war, there will be need of a reconstruction of spirit which is no less important and even more difficult. But for this even more than for the immediate tasks there is need of wisdom and unity."[9] The two leaders agreed that the kind of reconstruction they were talking about began at home, with American attitudes and social needs. After some study the Council created in March, 1918, the Committee on the War and the Religious Outlook as its agent for reconstruction and charged it "to consider the state of religion as affected by the war, with special reference to the duty and opportunity of the churches."[10]

Henry Churchill King convened the Committee and served as its Chairman until mid-1919 when he resigned and Brown took his place.

Secretaries were numerous, and included the Rev. Marion Bradshaw, the Rev. Charles W. Gilkey, the Rev. Samuel McCrea Cavert and the Rev. Angus Dun. Bradshaw joined it early after he was fired from his pastorate because of his "pacifist tendencies," and Cavert came on in February, 1919, after he returned from a tour of duty as a chaplain. Budgetary demands were minor. Financial resources came from individuals, from Oberlin College and Union Theological Seminary in New York in the form of stenographic assistance, from the sale of pamphlets and books, and from the Interchurch Emergency Campaign. Unlike many other Council groups, the Committee invited persons to membership because of their interest and potential contributions to the program, rather than in some representative capacity. Persons active in Council work dominated it at first and included in addition to Chairman King the following: North, Vance, Speer, Brown, Macfarland, Faunce, Mackenzie, and Mott. They were joined by others, including Mabel Cratty, Harry Emerson Fosdick, Dean Shailer Mathews, Bishop Walter R. Lambuth of the Methodist Episcopal Church, South, E. Y. Mullins of the Southern Baptist Convention, Bishop Francis J. McConnell of the Methodist Episcopal Church, and President Mary E. Woolley of Mount Holyoke College.[11] Although these people were drawn from many different groups, they reflected the Council's commitment to peace and reconstruction.

The Council projected a study committee and when the actual Committee met, it agreed to accept that role. The decision had far-reaching consequences. Ecumenical Protestant reconstruction took the form of research and publication, rather than action programs on behalf of specific social needs. The Committee set out to influence the nation's thinking and shape its attitudes on topics like industrial reform and the role of women in society, but did not institute programs to effect such changes. Some other Council agencies engaged in specific tasks, but most of the concrete work was carried on through denominational or non-denominational channels. The cooperative movement, as it looked to the future, chose the role of educator, convinced that its thought would fill a crucial gap in the thinking of the day.

The basic question of Committee research was the impact of the war on religion and the role of religion in the post-war world. The Committee organized as a working group and allowed the eventual shape of its finished work to evolve. Keeping in mind what North called "the progressive elements in the present programs of the churches, as seen in their social ministry and in the young people's organizations," it divided initial investigations into five fields: (1) the religious faith and life of individuals; (2) the degree of cooperation or lack of it among the churches; (3) the changes in theology and doctrine; (4) the new tasks of social reconstruction; and (5) the world-wide ecumenical movement.[12] It prepared a questionnaire on the first four topics and distributed it to church leaders, chaplains, soldiers and sailors, Y.M.C.A. and Y.W.C.A. workers, and other persons working for the religious and social welfare of the men in the armed forces. Marion Bradshaw began an annotated bibliography on the war and religion and had preliminary drafts of parts of it finished by the fall of 1918.[13]

As completed questionnaires began to accumulate and other research multiplied the data, ideas about what to do with all the material changed. One study had grown into many studies. But what kind? The Armistice interrupted this quandry and compelled some kind of action. The Committee decided to publish immediately a series of pamphlets or tracts for the times in order to bring fresh data to bear on a number of different areas needing reconstruction. At the same time intensive investigation continued so that larger, more comprehensive studies, could be made available as quickly as possible. The first pamphlet appeared in May, 1919, and others followed quickly, ten in all. Although they were issued under the by-lines of individuals, the Committee carefully edited them to represent its collective thought. They were for the most part creative, forward-looking documents, painting in bold, impressive strokes some of the less attractive features of the churches and the social order, both national and international. They also outlined the kinds of actions the churches could take to set their own houses in order and to minister to the disordered elements of society. They did not attempt to determine in every case the Christian answer to a problem, but only to present several alternative ones which had some basis in the Christian faith, since they sought to stimulate the thinking of churchmen on reconstruction tasks, not define a final world order. Pamphlet subjects included the religious outlook, the national outlook, the new world order, religious education, industrial reforms, home missions, economic reform, and the local church.[14] The Committee prepared the longer reports in the same collective way. They repeated some of the pamphlet topics, but in greater depth, and added the themes of Christian unity and the missionary outlook. Five volumes were published, beginning in early 1920.[15]

Speer prepared the first pamphlet on the religious outlook. He opened up the general theme of the effect of the war on religion and introduced most of the topics explored in later publications. He wrote that the early days of reconstruction revealed several negative influ-

ences the war had had on religion. Many of the men who had served
overseas were returning to America with European moral standards,
and that often meant a distinct lowering of moral tone in the life of the
men and of their home communities. Those who remained at home had
begun to show the effects of the emotional tensions built up by the war.
The nation's idealism had served it well, but had been and was still
being weakened by constant appeals to the passions of hatred and re-
venge. Many people were also criticizing the churches, first for failing
to prevent the war and second for being too much a part of it. Favorable
influences more than balanced these unfavorable ones. If the war had
shaken the personal moral life of many men, it had also magnified the
moral values of discipline and righteousness and lifted up for widespread examination such basic themes of Christianity as service and
vicarious sacrifice. The fact that criticisms levelled at the churches
were for the most part coming from within them told Speer that critics
were trying to fulfil their ministries rather than destroy them. The
war also demonstrated a new spirit of Christian cooperation which
promised even fuller unity in the future.

When Speer looked toward peace, he saw two important tasks for
the churches. In the first place, they must help build a Christian social
order at home. This meant becoming involved in the daily life of men in
the specific areas of industrial relations and race. They must seek to
democratize and Christianize industry and they must also solve the
race problem. Racial harmony went beyond toleration to respect, and
the Christian principle of brotherhood provided the only stable foundation for it.[16] In the second place, the churches must help reconstruct
international relations. He favored a league of nations, but he outlined
no specific plan, since the important thing about reconstruction was
not the plan, but the spirit of cooperation and goodwill which had to be
substituted for the spirit of selfishness. These two tasks could not be
accomplished without a substantial reorganization of the churches. If
they were to realize a full ministry in the future, they needed a more
effective and progressive program of Christian education; a fuller and
richer experience of life, which to Speer meant a more effective program of evangelism; and, a greater degree of Christian cooperation.
They could not preach unity to the world without practicing it themselves. Christian unity was the great lesson of the war, its possibilities
and its accomplishments. The churches, he concluded, "have actually
found themselves working together in great common tasks in a way
which they had not realized to be possible before. But the tasks that
now confront the Church are no less challenging than those that faced

it during the war. The Church cannot hope to deal with them adequately unless it approaches them in a spirit of common purpose and united endeavor."[17]

The Committee shared a longstanding Council conviction that reconstruction of the economic and industrial aspects of the social order held extremely high priority. Bishop Francis McConnell prepared the tract on this topic. He wrote that the churches' main goal should be "to introduce into the economic struggles of individuals and of groups the principles and spirit of the Gospel of Jesus."[18] Jesus taught the supreme value of human life, which meant, McConnell argued, that institutions were made for men, not men for institutions. An industrial system which treated men as "tools," "hands," or a "labor market" violated a basic Christian principle. Jesus also taught men to live together in a brotherhood of mutual service. Brotherhood did not dominate the industrial life of the day, but it should. An industrial democracy focused on brotherhood would treat workers justly, accept labor unions, include collective bargaining, and give labor a place on company boards of directors.

McConnell also applied these basic principles to the life of the churches. If they wanted to follow Jesus, they should encourage their prophetic leaders to attack social and economic forces which were obviously evil; to promote study and understanding of radical social groups; and to do their part in creating a social atmosphere in which change for the better could occur without resorting to violence. But studies were not enough. Churches were investors and employers, and through their missionaries they were influential in international affairs. He asked: "Has money gone into interest that should have gone into better tenements, or into better shop ventilation, . . . or into wages . . . ?" How good were labor conditions in denominational publishing houses, and did they practice collective bargaining in those businesses?[19] He did not spare the churches from his piercing inquiries for he believed, as did the other members of the Committee, that if they did not lead in practicing Christian principles in the economic aspects of their work, the rest of society could hardly be expected to follow. He acted in accord with his own directives when he accepted the position as Chairman of the Interchurch World Movement's Commission of Inquiry of the steel strike of 1919.[20]

The book-length reports were strongly critical of the past performance of the churches, especially in education and social action; however, they were more concerned with suggesting ways to reconstruct ministry for peacetime. The universal theme of these reports, their key idea for renewal of ministry, was Christian unity. The final section of the report on missions included an appeal for a more fully developed international missionary agency and said: "The present situation calls . . . for missionary statesmanship and missionary unity on a scale never realized in the past."[21] The report on religion in the army noted that soldiers paid little or no attention to denominational differences. If this did not prove "that our divisions and exclusions far outrun any living differences between our constituencies,"[22] at least it strongly indicated it. The cooperation among chaplains suggested the possibility of cooperation in local communities. The report concluded with this question: "Shall we not rather go forward, in the unity of the spirit of Christ, into an ever increasing cooperation and more effective achievement of our common tasks?"[23] The report on Christian unity concluded that the movement toward church union was "irresistible." It might suffer various delays, but it could not be permanently stopped, for the hope of union was inherent in the Christian faith. Moreover, the path to it lay through united action. Doing things together, in social work, in missions, in Christian education, removed the barriers of the past and built bridges for the future.[24] Wartime ministries, sacramental and social, had proved that ecumenical approaches worked. They could also, report after report concluded, work in peacetime ministries.

While the Committee was at work, but before its pamphlets and reports were issued, the Federal Council took steps to conclude its war work and establish a policy for peace and reconstruction. It decided to do this by convening a special meeting like the one it had held in May, 1917. Any policy adopted by such an assembly would officially represent the thinking of the entire Council. The call went out to constituents and the same cooperative agencies which had participated in the Special Meeting in Washington, and in addition to the Council of Church Boards of Education, the Sunday School Council of Evangelical Denominations, the Salvation Army, and the Executive Committee of the Interchurch World Movement of North America, to gather for a Special Meeting from May 6 to 8, 1919, at the Euclid Avenue Baptist Church in Cleveland, Ohio. They were to come prepared to reflect on the theme "From World War to World Brotherhood".

Over three hundred delegates journeyed to Cleveland. The procedures of the meeting were almost identical to those used two years earlier. The program consisted of a series of reports, discussions, and addresses on the war work of the churches and its results, which in turn became the basis for a new policy. Macfarland and Tippy spoke

for the Council. Brown made a final report for the General War-Time
Commission which had just concluded its work and disbanded. Chaplain John T. Axton reported on the attitudes of soldiers toward religion. The general atmosphere was electric. Participants shared a conviction that their wartime cooperative ventures had been successful
and felt challenged by post-war possibilities. Some of the reports
matched those of 1917 for insight and drama. The report of the Commission on the Church and Social Service attracted particularly close
attention since it outlined reconstruction tasks in many different
areas, but especially in industry and industrial communities. Speer's
speech also stood out. He declared that the Christian Church should
continue to witness to the nation her "deathless and impregnable hope
of a new and different world," and called for support for a league of
nations as one step toward a new world order.[25]

On May 8 the delegates turned to their most important business,
the formulation of a special ecumenical ministry for peace. They approved a series of resolutions in the fields of social service, national
and international affairs. They reaffirmed the Social Creed of the
Churches and added that "constructive democracy in industry is as
necessary as political democracy. . . ."[26] They endorsed the League of
Nations, but urged an amendment to the covenant to guarantee religious freedom. Following the meeting the Council launched a vigorous
campaign on behalf of the League.[27] Another resolution supported the
Interchurch World Movement. Leaders of that Movement, organized
in December, 1918, and of the Council had already reached an agreement and the resolution simply made it public. They pledged mutual
support, but retained their separate structures and programs. When
the Movement later collapsed, its fall affected the Council but did it no
long-term damage.

The resolutions formed the backdrop of the new policy, set forth in
general terms under the theme of the meeting. The churches faced
four "prime demands of the hour." First and foremost, they were
called to proclaim the basic elements of the Christian Gospel, renewing
their commitment to the primacy of religion in human life. Second,
they must gain and propagate a new sense of world responsibility by
increasing missions and supporting the proposed League. This involved taking a leading role in the ministry of reconciliation, not only
by requesting repentance by the enemies, but "by penitence on our
own part for those elements in our national life which the war has
revealed to be sinful." Third, they should seek to understand what a
Christian social order in America could mean and try to attain it. This

required nothing less than a serious attempt to secure on earth the Kingdom of God by a sincere application of the basic principles of the Social Creed. Finally, they were called to work for a swiftly increasing cooperation among themselves by joining the cooperative movement in ever more extensive ways. In a final summary the message acknowledged the difficulty of changing a world at war into a world "pervaded by the spirit of Christian brotherhood," for the task required the transformation of society itself. Audacious as that sounded, it was possible, for the war had revealed and made available hitherto unknown capacities of sacrifice and service. "We have begun to believe," the delegates concluded, "that God is calling for a generation of men fully consecrated to His purposes as revealed in Christ, through whom He can work adequately for the redemption of the world."[28] The Council published the message immediately and followed it with a variety of special reports, including those of the Committee on the War and the Religious Outlook, and one by the Commission on the Church and Social Service.[29]

The National Catholic War council organized its reconstruction work in the spring of 1918 in response to proposals similar to those made to the Federal Council. The Committee on Reconstruction and After-War Activities, later simply called the Committee on Reconstruction, immediately assumed attitudes toward its work markedly different from those of its Protestant counterpart. It adopted a two-pronged program, including action as well as education. Although it began to lay the basis of this program in May, it decided to delay any implementation until the war ended. At that point it stepped forward with well formed plans and took its place alongside the other churches and welfare agencies engaged in reconstruction work. Chairman M. J. Splaine and Secretary John F. O'Grady did most of the planning and coordination, joined, once the action began, by a small army of field secretaries and clerical assistants. It had no financial needs until the program started and then the budget soared to hundreds of thousands of dollars. The War Council financed it from United War Work Campaign funds.

Committee membership included prominent churchmen invited to serve because of their expertise. No more than a dozen persons were on the Committee at any one time. They contributed as advisers rather than as a working group and seemed primarily important in the early stages, helping to establish priorities. Charles Fenwick, Professor of Political Science at Bryn Mawr College, suggested the Committee make a study of the "underlying causes of the War, and of the eco-

nomic and political measures which must be taken to secure order."[30]
Rev. Frank O'Hara, Professor of Economics at Catholic University of
America expressed a particular concern for encouraging returning
soldiers and sailors to settle on the land. These two were joined by Dr.
James E. Haggerty, Professor of Economics at Ohio State University;
the Rev. Fred Siedenburg, Dean of the School of Theology at Loyola
University, Chicago; Dr. Charles Neill, former member of the Commission on Training Camp Activities; Robert Biggs of Baltimore and M. P.
Mooney of Cleveland, leaders in the Society of St. Vincent de Paul; the
Rev. C. Hubert LeBlond, Director of Diocesan Charities in Cleveland;
the Rev. Edwin O'Hara of Portland, Oregon, and a leader in Catholic
education in his archdiocese; and the Rev. J. Elliot Ross, C.S.P., of Austin, Texas. Neill and Biggs had helped found the War Council.

Secretary O'Grady began to put things together in the fall of 1918.
He divided the general categories of education and action into departments. Education constituted a separate department, whereas the action programs were further divided into the areas of employment, hospital social service, rehabilitation, and Americanization. The Committee later added a library and a department of land colonization. The
land scheme survived only long enough for a field agent to investigate
the possibilities of creating a Catholic colony in a rural section of Pennsylvania or Maryland. O'Grady set guidelines for the action programs,
projected ideas for the educational component of the work, scouted
about for potential workers and authors, and formulated tentative
budgets. Only a few weeks after the Armistice his plans had become
programs, albeit very modest ones. They grew considerably through
December and by mid-January, 1919, they were in full operation.[31]

Several principles governed all the practical work. Spiritual help
accompanied all material work. Cooperation with and through established Catholic agencies marked every program, except where no
agencies existed or where they declined to share the work. Coordination with government bureaus and agencies which had similar programs often directed but was not allowed to dictate the nature and
practical content of the programs. These principles created some problems. O'Grady noted in January that War Council committees needed
to consult so as to avoid overlapping effort. Both the Men's and
Women's Committees gave vital support to reconstruction programs.
Coordination with the Knights of Columbus did not start well and
never seemed to reach an entirely satisfactory level. The problems
seemed to be located in the Knights' national office, although various
local Committee offices ran into uncooperative attitudes. Most K. of C.

groups did cooperate and in the difficult cases the Committee withdrew its work rather than provoke a confrontation. The Comittee's religious orientation led to a few problems in the employment program. Some large cities, particularly in the West, centralized that program in municipal offices and refused cooperation with sectarian agencies. None of the problems ever grew to proportions to seriously threaten any of the programs.

The employment work blossomed first. The Committee worked closely with the United States Employment Bureau of the Department of Labor. The need was vast. Millions of men were being mustered out of the armed forces, and some 4,000,000 workers lost jobs in the various war industries like the munitions plants. The government opened as many employment offices as it could to handle the flood of people. The offices were points of contact between employers and potential employees. Their staffs counselled with the unemployed and solicited employers for job listings. The Committee had forty-seven offices at one time in April, 1919, employing about the same number of field secretaries. They were in K. of C. halls, War Council Service Clubs, and various other buildings as available. The peak demand passed in midsummer. Congress declined to continue to fund the work once the army had largely demobilized. The Committee shut down most of its offices by September and closed out the entire program by the end of the year.

The able-bodied soldiers in search of work were accompanied by their less fortunate disabled buddies. Veterans had certain legal rights, including vocational training and a year's medical care for themselves and their families. Several agencies had programs for them, including the Red Cross, the Bureau of War Risk Insurance, and the Federal Board for Vocational Education. They too needed outlets staffed by adequate personnel. The Committee moved into a more general program first, developing a Hospital Social Service in Catholic hospitals across the country. Many of the hospitals already had clinics and outpatient facilities. The idea was to expand them in the major urban centers and to tie them to a social service office which would give counsel and advice on insurance, educational opportunities, compensation claims, and other war related matters. The Committee contacted the hospitals, helped work out specific plans, and spent considerable money refitting rooms, purchasing equipment, and hiring counselling staff. In some cases it provided money for additional medical personnel as well. Carney Hospital, Boston; Misericordia Hospital, Philadelphia; St. Vincent Charity Hospital, Cleveland: and twelve others joined the program. This work proved to have lasting value, and like many of the Community Houses survived long after formal reconstruction work ended.

Hospitals and clinics provided care for the injured and partially disabled, but no adequate facilities existed for the severely injured, especially for those who had other needs, like learning the English language. The Federal Board for Vocational Education worked to provide for them but many faced permanent unemployment or institutionalization. The source of the idea is not clear, but the Committee decided to create a special school for such persons, with support from the Federal Board. The Men's Committee lent Secretary John Greer for the work. His investigations showed that existing government vocational programs trained bodies, not minds, and he proposed a school for the whole person.[32] The Committee's Rehabilitation School opened on the campus of Catholic University of America on May 1, 1919, and projected a complete experience for the men, spiritual as well as material. The School began in a rented University building, with lent equipment and a small staff. The curriculum included reading, writing and civics, and various skills like carpentry and automobile repair. The skill studies were oriented to uncover aptitudes. If a man could learn English and had some aptitude commensurate with his disability, he was sent on to one of a number of vocational or educational training centers, many of them attached to colleges. The program was unique and served as a model for others. The Committee soon built a new facility for the School at the University and opened a second one for rural vocations in Leonardtown, Maryland.

Americanization had a pre-war history and became reconstruction work because the war highlighted the needs of those persons who shared neither the language nor the experience in democracy of their adopted country. O'Grady considered several ideas, including both publications and programs, but from the outset he wanted John A. Lapp to run the department. Lapp, formerly a member of the Federal Commission on Vocational Education and the author of a widely used civics textbook, joined the Committee in January and launched an ambitious program. He wrote pamphlets, organized educational programs, and wrote for Americanization courses a textbook which was subsequently translated into a number of languages. He highlighted the cultural resources of the immigrants as gifts to American culture, and repudiated the jingoism associated with some Americanization efforts.[33] The programs were often offered through Catholic organizations, including the Service Clubs, Community Houses, and parish groups, and included lectures, text book work, films and entertainments.[34] They were also presented in cooperation with the War Civics Committee, a joint venture of the War and Interior Departments. During the summer the War Council separated Americanization from the reconstruction work and turned it into a large Civic Education Program. It soon became an important part of the program of the Welfare Council, which retained Lapp to direct it.

The Committee generated much activity through these departments, but it also had an education department, charged to stimulate thinking. To this end it developed and published a series of small tracts, designated Reconstruction Pamphlets. They began to appear in February and came off the press almost monthly until late in the year. The major ones, nine in all by 1920, fell into two broad groups: specific reconstruction needs like land colonization, unemployment, and girls' welfare; and civic education.[35] They provided interesting reading and some creative ideas, but in general they did not match those produced by the Protestants in depth of thought or breadth of vision. This was true only in general, because one of the pamphlets presented the creative power of Catholic thought at its best. That document was Reconstruction Pamphlet No. 1, issued in February, and titled: "Social Reconstruction: A General Review of the Problems and Survey of Remedies." In fact, it was never just a Committee pamphlet. Father John Ryan wrote it as a speech for a Knights of Columbus meeting in Louisville but felt it was too long for public presentation and put it aside. Father O'Grady learned about it, secured it, and submitted it to the bishops who sat as the Administrative Committee of the War Council for consideration as their official reconstruction program.[36] They made a few minor changes and endorsed it. When it was published, it came from the bishops as well as from the Committee. People received it as the official position of the Hierarchy of the Church and dubbed it the Bishops' Program.

The Program joined many others already issued. They had begun to appear several years earlier and at least forty or fifty were already vying for public attention.[37] The small tract surfaced immediately and became a popular favorite with working men, churchmen, and leaders of reform opinion alike. Many readers found it brought clarity in a time of confusion. It marked out general principles in plain language and provided highly specific examples of how the principles could be realized. Others were attracted by the moderate character of its proposals. Citing radical reform options of some European schemes, the bishops affirmed that such ideas were neither desirable nor useful in America.

Private ownership of capital did not need to be scrapped, just reformed. They repudiated socialism, which they said would introduce "bureaucracy, political tyranny, the helplessness of the individual. . . , and in general social inefficiency and decadence."[38] Some people were drawn to it by its open espousal of Christian ethics in an economic context. Raymond Fosdick told Bishop Muldoon it thrilled him to see the Church, so often the seeming tool of economic interests, take such a position of leadership. To him it marked "a new emphasis, a new inspiration and a new leadership."[39] In fact, the degree to which some people were surprised chastened Church leaders. To critics, both friendly and hostile, they responded that the underlying principles of the Program were a basic part of traditional Catholic social thought or, as Muldoon put it, "the immutable principles of justice and charity which the Church holds, has ever held, and will ever hold."[40] Cardinal Gibbons admitted to the bishops, however, that perhaps "our principles, the principles of the Gospel, have lain hidden in our theologies, so much so that the recent pamphlet on Social Reconstruction appeared to many a complete novelty."[41]

The tract provided a quick review of some of the most prominent reconstruction proposals, providing judgments on the value of them. The British Labor Party's "Social Reconstruction Program" contained a number of radical reforms which appeared to lead to socialism. Prominent labor groups in the United States had not gone so far, although the "Fourteen Points" of the Chicago Federation of Labor seemed to approach the same goal. The bishops were most encouraged by the views of the British Quaker employers and most disappointed by those of American businessmen. Twenty Quaker employers took a position in favor of labor and suggested the restriction of employer income until all employee needs were met. The program issued by a recent Convention of the National Chamber of Commerce simply perpetuated the problems of class division. Apparently, the bishops concluded, the businessmen were "not yet ready to concede the right of labor to be represented in determining its relations with capital."[42]

The Bishop's Program, which they defined as "practical and moderate," did not propose a comprehensive solution to all the social problems. Instead, it focused only on economic and industrial reforms and particularly on those which "seem to be desirable and also obtainable within a reasonable time. . . ."[43] The plan was premised on three main defects in the current social system: it created great inefficiency and waste in the production and distribution of commodities; it failed to provide adequate incomes for the vast majority of wage earners;

and, it rewarded a small minority of privileged owners excessively.[44] These were serious problems, but not fatal ones. The bishops divided their solution into two parts: first, the continuation of existing reforms; second, the introduction of some additional important changes.

Many of the existing reforms were in fact temporary wartime measures which the government had adopted in order to mobilize the nation. While some people saw them as coercive, most admitted that they were necessary for the duration of the war. The bishops' point was that these measures, war inspired or not, were vitally needed reforms and abolishing them, as seemed likely, would destroy gains already made. Begin reform, they advised, by keeping the measures and building on them. The United States Employment Bureau had rendered good service and could give more, not only to returning members of the armed forces but to unemployed civilians. It provided a national coordination of labor needs important for the society. The National War Labor Board guaranteed a family living wage, recognized the right of labor to organize, and protected non-union workers from union coercion. It served the public well and should be continued, or at least those things it guaranteed should continue. In particular, they urged national support of the living wage. "After all," they said, "a living wage is not necessarily the full measure of justice." Workers should have funds for leisure and the future as well as for life.[45] Other government agencies had improved housing, even built some, and checked the rise in prices. If the agencies did not survive, their goals of decent housing for all Americans and the reduction of the cost of living should.

These changes would help create a better society, but genuine reform should also include some other innovations, such as a legal minimum wage, social insurance for all workers, employee participation in management, vocational training, and the abolition of child labor. The state should provide for insurance needs, with help from employers. Workers should be protected against loss of income from illness, unemployment and old age. Somewhat naively, they hoped that few employers would ever again seriously question the right of labor to organize. The next obvious step was provision for labor to share in management, perhaps through shop committees. Although the first bill to end child labor failed its constitutional test, they hoped another would succeed or that the states would enact their own laws. The reforms were all important and could help create a new society, but they were not, in themselves, enough. The bishops announced that all the proposals put together would fail "without a reform in the spirit of both labor and capital."[46] A laborer must learn he owes his employer an honest day's work in return for a fair wage. The capitalist must learn that wealth is stewardship. The owner must above all "cultivate and strengthen within his mind the truth which many of his class have begun to grasp for the first time during the war; that the laborer is a human being, not merely an instrument of production; and that the laborer's right to a decent livelihood is the first moral charge upon industry. The employer has the right to get a reasonable living out of his business, but he has no right to interest on investment until his employees have obtained at least living wages. This is the human and Christian, in contrast to the purely commercial and pagan, ethics of industry."[47] The bishops and their Church soon realized that the Program constituted an important part of their peacetime policy. Perfectly congruent with pre-war and wartime goals, it also pointed them toward the future. The Program became an important part of the Welfare Council's agenda.

The end of the war intersected with the golden jubilee of Cardinal Gibbons. Several people already had the idea of a peacetime version of the War Council, but the jubilee celebration became the occasion for the birth of a specific mechanism to create such an agency. The meeting had been postponed twice, once because of the Cardinal's heavy schedule and once by the influenza epidemic. When it assembled on February 20, 1919, in the Divinity Hall Chapel of Catholic University of America, it turned out to be an impressive gathering. Almost seventy of the archbishops and bishops attended and although present at an informal gathering, they constituted the most widely representative meeting of the Hierarchy since 1884. Pope Benedict's delegate, Archbishop Bonaventura Cerretti, Secretary of the Congregation for Extraordinary Ecclesiastical Affairs, brought official greetings and praise of Gibbons for his long and faithful ministry, and the Holy Father's request that the archbishops join him "in his efforts for a just and lasting peace and for the adjustment along the lines of Christian ethics of the many difficulties in the world of education and labor."[48]

Gibbons responded immediately. He appointed a committee to determine how to implement the Pope's wishes. It reported the following day to a meeting of the archbishops that the answer lay in an annual meeting of the entire Hierarchy, with a standing committee of bishops to represent them in matters of Catholic concern. The Cardinal promptly designated himself and the bishops of the Administrative Committee of the War Council as a General Committee on Catholic Interests and Affairs, and charged it to spell out the details of organization for presentation to the first annual meeting which he called for the coming September. Bishop Joseph Glass of Salt Lake City replaced Bishop Hayes when the latter became Archbishop of New York in early March. The Pope wrote the bishops through Cardinal Gibbons in April reviewing these actions and declared: "This is truly a worthy resolve, and with the utmost satisfaction We bestow upon it Our approval."[49] The lines of authority were now absolutely clear. Some bishops opposed this General Committee and resented it as a challenge to their autonomy, but the Cardinal said he regarded it "as a divine call to summon our best thought and maximum energy in order to organize and direct them for the kindling of religion in the hearts of the American people. Coming at this time it is providential; the formation of this Committee begins, I believe, a new era in our Church."[50]

The General Committee met several times during the late spring and summer, including one long meeting at the University of Notre Dame in July, where it was joined by representatives of the Catholic press, social work groups, and domestic and foreign missions. It worked from experiences with the War Council and pressures from its leaders to provide for continuation of its work and from an outline of concerns provided by the Cardinal, and it worked against the September deadline. Gibbons divided the study into eleven sections, including these: The Holy See, Home Missions, Foreign Missions, Social and Charitable Work, the Catholic University, Catholic Education in General, Catholic Literature, Catholic Press, Legislation, A Catholic Bureau, and Finances. The scope, even compared with the War Council's widespread concerns, was breathtaking. Under Home Missions he noted this: "Every bishop in his own diocese will try to reap the harvest which was sown during the War. But is it not possible for us to make larger plans?" American Catholics were almost invisible in Foreign Missions. Something must be done to correct the attitude that "American is synonymous with Protestant. The wonderful strength of the Church in this country is almost unknown to foreign lands." Social ideals must become living ideals. How, he asked, can the Church "inspire a more general impulse to put our social principles and methods into action?"[51]

Trenchant as these reflections were, key Council leaders believed the heart of the matter lay in his rather brief comments on the creation of a Catholic Bureau. Annual Meetings of the bishops without a national action agency would simply move the entire situation back to pre-war circumstances. Father Burke's vision never faded. He advised Kerby in June to lay stress when talking with bishops, and anyone else in authority, on the "advantages of a national committee actually at work here at the Capitol," and that such a committee "even with the appointment of a permanent Bishop's committee, is an essential."[52] Burke wrote again after the Notre Dame meeting that the General Committee had decided on a national bureau at Washington, but it remained for the total Hierarchy to decide. "Our offices," he said, "are commodious. The work is growing: the possibilities are wonderful, if what we have built were made permanent."[53] At a final preparatory meeting the General Committee on motion of Bishop Glass recommended the new organization be named the National Catholic Welfare Council.[54]

The largest gathering of bishops in the history of the American Church met at Catholic University on September 24, 1919. Cardinal Gibbons presided, with Bishop Muldoon close by his side, and 92 of the 101 bishops present. The carefully prepared report of the General Committee met some initial resistance over the issue of episcopal autonomy, but found positive support from the vast majority. Bishop J. Regis Canevin of Pittsburgh proposed and Archbishop Keane of Dubuque seconded the successful motion that created the new national agency. Archbishop Edward Hanna of San Francisco became the Chairman, with Bishops Muldoon, Schrembs, and Russell among those elected to the new Administrative Committee. At its first meeting it designated the offices of the War Council as the headquarters of the new Welfare Council and elected Father Burke Executive Secretary with power to preside at meetings in the absence of members of the Administrative Committee. Early in 1920 Cardinal Gibbons sought and won from the Paulists his release from other duties for full-time commitment to this new task. The Welfare Council moved quickly to take over War Council tasks and to develop a program commensurate with the rich variety of Catholic life and ministry.

Protestants in the Federal Council and Catholics through the Hierarchy arrived at the end of their wartime ministries with a sense of satisfaction in the work accomplished and with clear commitments to new ministries for the time of peace and reconstruction. They had accepted the war as a solemn necessity and had worked to provide an adequate ministry of Word and sacraments to those in the armed forces as well as those at home. Wartime psychology had made some inroads on the imperatives of repentance and loving one's enemies, but had not succeeded in silencing them. The war spirit had occasionally led them to adopt government programs uncritically, but when that spirit had challenged what they believed to be their basic ministry, they had joined to protect it and maintain their prerogatives. Initial patriotic sentiments had quickly moderated in the face of repeated government limitations on the number of chaplains, their fair recognition and treatment. The culturally powerful Protestants had discovered that opportunities for ministry would not simply be granted by a willing government, but would have to be fought for by personal consultation, public lobbying and legislative action. They generally achieved their goals but only after they learned the usefulness and power of ecumenical action. They were particularly disturbed by the camp pastor situation, when the government seemed to restrict the traditional individuality of Protestant ministry and to present a clear limit on the rights of the churches. The Catholics had always had to prove themselves to the culture and were less surprised by the situation, but they were also less prepared to engage in the consultation, lobbying and public confrontations. The War Council gave them a new vehicle for national action and they moved toward their goals in the chaplaincy and in matters related to social hygiene, despite possible reaction and attacks by nativists.

The war did not seriously alter the substance of the churches' understanding of the nation's social problems or their ministry to them, but it broadened that ministry immensely. Post-war statements, while somewhat stronger and more comprehensive than pre-war ones, retained the basic conviction that the nation needed greater democracy in many areas of its life, especially in its economic life. Bishop McConnell's Protestant version used the more urgent language and the Catholic's Bishops' Program painted the more detailed picture, but the essential reform proposals remained the same as before the war. The major exception to this was the Protestant discovery of racism as a national issue in which they were implicated and their decision to add racial brotherhood to their social goals.

If the war did not greatly change the substance of these social policies, it certainly worked a major revolution in the strategy used to implement them. The policies were representative and cooperative in the pre-war period, but they were that largely at the top, among the leaders in the inter-denominational agencies and in the denominations, and among the members of the Hierarchy. The war challenged that dramatically. The leaders were awakened to the power of the laity. Catholic leaders in particular discovered in the laity a slumbering giant, ready when alerted to bring new vitality and strength to the Church and its ministry. The leaders awakened others to the idea of a national, united ministry. As they worked for effective social ministries in the camps, in industrial centers, and in immigrant communities, they saw that their goals could be achieved only by the stimulus of national direction and funds. They argued with those in their fellowships who did not grasp this vital lesson. North and Speer worked for a united financial campaign against those who feared centralization. The Men's Committee worked for national programs against those local groups which could not see beyond their own areas. Burke and Muldoon worked against those bishops who could not see the ministry of the chaplains beyond the limits of their own dioceses. Protestants had already begun to move in this direction, but they were surprised by the degree of centralization and cooperation demanded by the situation. Catholics were startled. Father Burke caught the vision, saw that is was perfectly congruent with Catholic thought, but then found it very difficult to persuade others in his Church of the changes that needed to be made. He persisted and succeeded. The experience of the war and the cooperation the War Council generated taught the lesson permanently. The Church could not return to pre-war levels of insularity and disorganization. It could not surrender the expanded social ministry. The Hierarchy acted to perpetuate the War Council in a Welfare Council. It also sent its first "Pastoral Letter" since 1884 to the Church. In this long and detailed communication, the bishops announced their determination to maintain "for the ends of peace, the spirit of union and the coordination of our forces."[55] Two years later when they approached Pope Pius XI, appealing for a reversal of his decision to abolish the Welfare Council, they invoked this lesson of the war again when they argued: "The Catholic Church of this country needs a central organization to promote and defend the interests of the whole Church of America; if it did not already exist, it would be necessary to create an organization along the lines of the National Catholic Welfare Council."[56]

The war did not shake the basic convictions of the churches about the Kingdom of God. They continued to believe that it could come with their assistance, the Protestants expressing anticipation more frequently than the Catholics. They both saw it in somewhat national terms, but never identified it with the nation. Protestants after the war looked to a worldwide Kingdom and proposed to work for it in terms of a league of nations and a new spirit of world brotherhood. The aspect of the Kingdom most enhanced by the war was unity. The leaders grasped this first and most fully. The unity was organizational, in terms of their churches, for the war had shown that internal divisions could be overcome. The unity was theological in terms of ecumenicity, for the war had shown how practical projects could cross old barriers and break new ground. The Committee of Six and the work for the chaplains marked a very small, but real, beginning. The reality did not match the vision but at least the war started the churches in the direction of fuller unity. The leaders were encouraged enough to continue to seek it. Speer became President of the Federal Council in 1920, even as Father Burke became Executive Secretary of the Welfare Council. Each sought to perpetuate in his own version of the Christian faith the lessons of cooperation and national ministry which he had learned and used so well during the war.

1. See the Hierarchy's statement of April, 1917, and Macfarland, *The Churches of Christ in Time of War*, p. 131.

2. *Ibid.*, p. 132.

3. Frederick Lynch, "In Time of War, Prepare for Peace," *The Christian Work* 103 (September 29, 1917): 367.

4. *Ibid.*, p. 368.

5. Williams, *American Catholics and the War*, p. 302.

6. Walter Rauschenbusch, *A Theology for the Social Gospel* (New York: The Macmillan Company, 1917), pp. 139, 141.

7. Macfarland, *The Churches of Christ in Time of War*, pp. 47, 133.

8. *Annual Reports of the Federal Council*, 1917, p. 59.

9. *Ibid.*, p. 246.

10. *Annual Reports of the Federal Council, 1918*, p. 39.

11. See Renton, *War-Time Agencies of the Church*, p. 223, for the complete membership of the Committee.

12. "Report of the First Meeting of the Committee on the War and the Religious Outlook," April 2, 1918, *Minutes of Committees*.

13. See Marion J. Bradshaw, comp., *The War and Religion* (New York: Association Press, 1919).

14. Robert E. Speer, *The War and the Religious Outlook* (New York: Association Press, 1919); Harry Emerson Fosdick, *The Church's Message to the Nation* (New York: Association Press, 1919); William H. P. Faunce, *Christian Principles Essential to a New World Order* (New York: Association Press, 1919); William Douglas Mackenzie, *The Church and Religious Education* (New York: Association Press, 1919); Francis J. McConnell, *Christian Principles and Industrial Reconstruction* (New York: Association Press, 1919); William P. Shriver, *The New Home Mission of the Church* (New York: Association Press, 1919); Herbert N. Shenton, *Christian Aspects of Economic Reconstruction* (New York: Association Press, 1920); Charles W. Gilkey, *The Local Church After the War* (New York: Association Press, 1920); Rhoda E. McCulloch, *The War and the Woman Point of View* (New York: Association Press, 1920); and, William Adams Brown, *The Church Facing the Future* (New York: Federal Council of Churches, 1921).

15. The Committee reports were these: *Religion Among American Men* (New York: Association Press, 1920); *The Missionary Outlook in the Light of the War* (New York: Association Press, 1920); *The Church and Industrial Reconstruction* (New York: Association Press, 1921); *Christian Unity: Its Principles and Possibilities*; and *The Teaching Work of the Church* (New York: Association Press, 1923).

16. Speer, *The War and the Religious Outlook*, p. 24.

17. *Ibid.*, p. 27.

18. McConnell, *Christian Principles and Industrial Reconstruction*, p. 3.

19. *Ibid.*, p. 20. See also Francis J. McConnell, *Democratic Christianity* (New York: The Macmillan Company, 1919), p. 57.

20. See Eldon G. Ernst, "The Interchurch World Movement and the Great Steel Strike of 1919-1920," *Church History* 39 (June, 1970): 212-23.

21. Committee on the War and the Religious Outlook, *The Missionary Outlook in the Light of the War*, p. 301.

22. Committee on the War and the Religious Outlook, *Religion Among American Men*, p. 153.

23. Ibid., p. 155.

24. Committee on the War and the Religious Outlook, *Christian Unity: Its Principles and Possibilities*, pp. 327, 340.

25. Robert E. Speer, "The Witness Bearing of the Church to the Nation," *FC Bulletin* 2 (June, 1919): 100-1.

26. "Resolutions Adopted by the Federal Council of the Churches of Christ in America in Special Session in Cleveland, Ohio, May 6-8, 1919," *FC Bulletin* 2 (June, 1919): 94.

27. See James L. Lancaster, "The Protestant Churches and the Fight for Ratification of the Versailles Treaty," *Public Opinion Quarterly* 21 (1967): 597-619.

28. *From World War to World Brotherhood*, May 6-8, 1919. A Federal Council Pamphlet.

29. *The Church and Social Reconstruction*, July 1, 1919 (New York: Commission on the Church and Social Service).

30. Quoted in "Report of the Committee on Reconstruction and After War Activities," May, 1918, NCWC Archives.

31. "Report of the Committee on Reconstruction," January 22, 1919, NCWC Archives.

32. John J. Greer, "Recommendations for Cooperating with Federal Board of Vocational Education, Rehabilitation Division," March 28, 1919, NCWC Archives.

33. Abell, *American Catholicism and Social Action*, pp. 196-97.

34. John A. Lapp, "The Campaign for Civic Instruction," NCWC *Bulletin* 1 (July, 1919): 11-12.

35. The Pamphlets were as follows: *Land Colonization; Unemployment; For Soldiers and Sailors and Those Dependent on Them; Scouting Under Catholic Leadership; Fundamentals of Citizenship; Outlines of a Social Service Pro-*

gram for Catholic Agencies; A Program for Citizenship; A Plan of Civics Education Through Motion Pictures; and *Girls' Welfare.*

36. John A. Ryan, *Social Doctrine in Action: A Personal History* (New York and London: Harper and Brothers, 1941).

37. Estella T. Weeks, *Reconstruction Programs* (New York: The Womans Press, 1919).

38. *Social Reconstruction: A General Review of the Problems and Survey of Remedies* (Washington: National Catholic War Council, 1919), p. 21.

39. Raymond Fosdick to Bishop Muldoon, June 9, 1919, NCWC Archives.

40. To the Editor of *The Nation* from Peter J. Muldoon, *The Nation* 108 (April 19, 1919): 608.

41. James Cardinal Gibbons to The Committee on General Catholic Interests and Affairs, May 5, 1919.

42. *Social Reconstruction*, p. 9.

43. *Ibid.*, p. 11.

44. *Ibid.*, p. 22.

45. *Ibid.*, p. 14.

46. *Ibid.*, p. 24.

47. Ibid.

48. Ellis, *The Life of James Cardinal Gibbons*, 2:298. For an account of the creation of the Welfare Council see McKeown, "The National Bishops' Conference: An Analysis of Its Origins," pp. 565–83.

49. Pope Benedict XV to the American Episcopate, April, 1919. Quoted in *The Catholic World* 109 (July, 1919): 440.

50. James Cardinal Gibbons to The Committee on General Catholic Interests and Affairs, May 5, 1919.

51. *Ibid.*

52. John J. Burke to William Kerby, June 15, 1919, Kerby Papers.

53. John J. Burke to William Kerby, August 15, 1919, Kerby Papers.

54. Ellis, *The Life of James Cardinal Gibbons* 2:302.

55. *Pastoral Letter*, p. 21.

56. The Petition of the Seven Bishops of the Administrative Council of the National Catholic Welfare Council to His Holiness, Pope Pius XI, April 22, 1922, quoted by Elizabeth McKeown, "Apologia for an American Catholicism: The Petition and Report of the National Catholic Welfare Council to Pius XI, April 25, 1922," *Church History*, 43 (December, 1974): 520.

Bibliography

This selected bibiography is divided into four major sections. The manuscript collections cited in the first section are those which were used extensively. Other archival materials were used to a lesser degree, including the Papers of Josephus Daniels, Newton D. Baker, and Bishop Charles Brent in the Library of Congress, the Papers of Shailer Mathews in the Archives of the library of the University of Chicago, and the Papers of William Douglas Mackenzie in the Case Memorial Library of the Hartford Seminary Foundation, Hartford, Connecticut. The reports and pamphlets listed in the second section include only those cited in the text. The library of Union Theological Seminary in New York has a complete collection of the pamphlets issued by the Federal Council of Churches and its related agencies, and the library of the Catholic University of America in Washington, D.C., has an extensive collection of the pamphlets issued by the National Catholic War Council and its various committees. The third section includes some volumes not cited in the footnotes; however these were important for the development of the book. The list of periodicals and newspapers in the fourth section includes those in which appear the unsigned articles cited in the footnotes. The dates indicate the years in which the articles cited were published. Most of these same periodicals were examined for pertinent material for the years 1917 to 1919.

I. Manuscript Collections

Archives of the Diocese of Rockford, Rockford, Illinois

Archives of the National Catholic War Council, library of the Catholic University of America, Washington, D.C.

Minutes of the General Committee on Army and Navy Chaplains, library of the General Commission on Chaplains and Armed Forces Personnel, Washington, D.C.

Papers of William Adams Brown, library of Union Theological Seminary, New York, New York

Papers of William J. Kerby, Archives of the Catholic University of America, Washington, D.C.

Papers of Eric M. North, in the possession of Eric M. North

Papers of Frank Mason North, in the possession of Eric M. North

Papers of Robert E. Speer, Speer Library of Princeton Theological Seminary, Princeton, New Jersey

Papers of Woodrow Wilson, Library of Congress, Washington, D.C.

Records and Papers in the Office of the Chief of Chaplains of the United States Army, Washington, D.C.

Records of the Adjutant General's Office, Record Group 94, Army and Air Corps Branch of the National Archives, Washington, D.C.

Records of the A.E.F., Chaplains' Office, Record Group 120, Army and Air Corps Branch of the National Archives, Washington, D.C.

Records of the Bureau of Naval Personnel, Record Group 24, Navy and Military Service Branch of the National Archives, Washington, D.C.

Records of the Federal Council of the Churches of Christ in America, 1894–1952, Record Group 18, Records of the National Council of Churches of Christ, in the Presbyterian Historical Society, Philadelphia, Pennsylvania

World War I Organization Records, Commission on Training Camp Activities, Record Group 120, Army and Air Corps Branch of the National Archives, Washington, D.C.

II. Official Reports and Publications

A. The Chaplains' Aid Association
Bulletin, 1918.
Schiavone, Francis P. *The Honor Legion.* 1917.

B. The Federal Council of Churches

1. Official Reports
Annual Reports of the Federal Council of the Churches of Christ in America, 1913. New York: National Offices, 1913.
Annual Reports of the Federal Council of the Churches of Christ in America, 1915. New York: n.p., 1915.
Annual Reports of the Federal Council of the Churches of Christ in America, 1917. New York: Missionary Education Movement, 1917.
Annual Reports of the Federal Council of the Churches of Christ in America, 1918. New York: Missionary Education Movement, 1918.
Federal Council of the Churches of Christ in America: Report of Special Meeting. Washington, D.C. May 7–9, 1917. New York: Federal Council of Churches, 1917.
Macfarland, Charles S. ed. *The Churches of Christ in Council.* ("Library of Christian Cooperation," vol 1.) New York: Missionary Education Movement, 1917.

2. Pamphlets

a. Federal Council
The Duty of the Church in This Hour of National Need. May, 1917.
From World War to World Brotherhood. May 6–8, 1919.

b. General War-Time Commission
Brent, Bishop Charles. *Soldiers of the Wooden Cross.* January 5, 1919.

Brown, William Adams. *The Record of a Year.* September, 1918.

A Call to Prayer. November 12, 1918.

The Country Church and the City Boy. (1918).

General War-Time Commission of the Churches: Survey of National Army Cantonments and National Guard Camps, November 20, 1917.

Moral and Religious Forces in the Military and Naval Hospitals in the United States. August 1, 1918.

Survey of the Moral and Religious Forces in the Military Camps and Naval Stations in the United States. May 1, 1918.

A Wartime Program for Country Churches. (1917).

A Wartime Program for Local Churches with Emphasis upon Churches Distant from Training Camps. (1917, 1918).

War Work by the Church for Negro Soldiers and Sailors. December 31, 1918.

c. Commission on the Church and Social Service

The Church and Social Reconstruction. July 1, 1919.

d. Joint Committee on War Production Communities

Bouher, Elmer J. *100% American: The War Story of a Country Church.* 1918.

A Reconstruction Program for Country Churches. 1919.

Tippy, Worth. *Documentary Report on the Logging Camps of the Pacific North West, With Recommendations.* 1919.

e. Committee on the War and the Religious Outlook

Bradshaw, Marion J., comp. *The War and Religion.* New York: Association Press, 1919.

Committee on the War and the Religious Outlook. *Christian Unity: Its Principles and Possibilities.* New York: Association Press, 1921.

————. *The Church and Industrial Reconstruction.* New York: Association Press, 1921.

————. *The Missionary Outlook in the Light of the War.* New York: Association Press, 1920.

————. *Religion Among American Men.* New York: Association Press, 1920.

————. *The Teaching Work of the Church.* New York: Association Press, 1923.

Faunce, William H.P. *Christian Principles Essential to a New World Order.* New York: Association Press, 1919.

Fosdick, Harry Emerson. *The Church's Message to the Nation.* New York: Association Press, 1919.

Gilkey, Charles W. *The Local Church After the War.* New York: Association Press, 1920.

Mackenzie, William Douglas. *The Church and Religious Education.* New York: Association Press, 1919.

McConnell, Francis J. *Christian Principles and Industrial Reconstruction.* New York: Association Press, 1919.

McCulloch, Rhoda E. *The War and the Woman Point of View.* New York: Association Press, 1920.

Shenton, Herbert N. *Christian Aspects of Economic Reconstruction.* New York: Association Press, 1920.

Shriver, William P. *The New Home Mission of the Church.* New York: Association Press, 1919.

Speer, Robert E. *The War and the Religious Outlook.* New York: Association Press, 1919.

C. The Home Mission Council
Home Missions Council. Eleventh Annual Meeting. New York: Home Missions Council, 1918.

Home Missions Council. Twelfth Annual Meeting. New York: Home Missions Council, 1919.

A Race Crisis. 1919.

D. The National Catholic War Council
The Catholic Soldier In Camp and Out of Camp. Handbook of the National Catholic War Council of America. Executive Committee, National Catholic War Council, n.d.

Fight and Pray.

"Fit to Win." 1919.

Handbook of the National Catholic War Council. Washington, D.C.: National Headquarters, 1918.

Manual National Catholic War Council. New York: Special Campaign Headquarters, 1918.

The Promise Fulfilled. January, 1920.

Reconstruction Pamphlets
  For Soldiers and Sailors and Those Dependent Upon Them.
  Fundamentals of Citizenship.
  Girls' Welfare.
  Land Colonization.
  Outlines of a Social Service Program for Catholic Agencies.
  A Plan for Civics Education Through Motion Pictures.
  A Program for Citizenship.
  Scouting Under Catholic Leadership.
  Social Reconstruction: A General Review of the Problem and Survey of Remedies.
  Unemployment.

E. The National Catholic Welfare Council
Address of Rev. John J. Burke, C.S.P., at The National Conference Catholic Women. 1920.

Pastoral Letter. 1920.

F. The National Civil Liberties Bureau
Conscription and the Conscientious Objector. New York: The Civil Liberties Bureau of the American Union Against Militarism, 1917.

The Facts About Conscientious Objectors in the United States. New York: National Civil Liberties Bureau, 1918.

Report of Treatment of Conscientious Objectors at the Camp Funston Guard House. New York: Relatives and Friends of Conscientious Objectors, 1918.

G. Protestant Denomination Reports.

The Acts and Proceedings of The General Synod of The Reformed Church in America, 1917. New York: The Board of Publication and Bible-School Work, 1917.

Annual of the Northern Baptist Convention, 1917. American Baptist Publication Society, 1917.

Minutes of the General Assembly of the Presbyterian Church in the United States, 1917. Richmond: Presbyterian Committee of Publication, 1917.

Minutes of the General Assembly of the Presbyterian Church in the United States of America, 1918. Philadelphia: Office of the General Assembly, 1918.

The National Council of the Congregational Churches of the United States, Minutes, 1917. Boston: Office of the National Council, 1917.

H. United States Government Reports

U.S. Congress, Senate. *Army Chaplains - Veto Message.* Document No. 216, 65th Congress, 2nd Session, 1918.

U.S. Congress, Senate, Committee on Military Affairs. *Increasing the Number of Chaplains in the Army.* Hearing on S. 2917, 65th Congress, 1st Session, 1917.

III. Books

Abbott, Lyman. *The Twentieth Century Crusade.* New York: The Macmillan Company, 1918.

Abell, Aaron I. *American Catholicism and Social Action.* Notre Dame, Indiana: University of Notre Dame Press, 1960.

_____. *The Urban Impact on American Protestantism, 1865-1900.* ("Harvard Historical Studies," vol. 54) Cambridge: Harvard University Press, 1943.

Abrams, Ray H. *Preachers Present Arms.* New York: Round Table Press, Inc., 1933.

Ahlstrom, Sydney E. *A Religious History of the American People.* New Haven and London: Yale University Press, 1972.

Alumni Catalogue of the Union Theological Seminary, 1836-1936. New York: Union Theological Seminary, 1937.

The Army and Religion. New York: Association Press, 1920.

Atkins, Glenn Gaius. *Religion in Our Times.* New York: Round Table Press, Inc., 1932.

Bainton, Roland, E. *Christian Attitudes Toward War and Peace.* New York: Abingdon Press, 1960.

Baker, Ray Stannard. *The New Industrial Unrest.* Garden City, New York: Doubleday, Page and Company, 1920.

————. *Woodrow Wilson: Life and Letters.* 8 vols. New York: Doubleday, Doran and Company, 1939.

Baron, Salo Wittmayer. *Modern Nationalism and Religion.* New York: Harper and Brothers Publishers, 1947.

Batten, Samuel Z., ed. *The Moral Meaning of the War.* Philadelphia: American Baptist Publication Society, (1918).

————. *The New World Order.* Philadelphia: American Baptist Publication Society, 1919.

Bennett, John C., and others. *The Church Through Half a Century.* New York: Charles Scribner's Sons, 1936.

Bennett, Lerone Jr. *Before the Mayflower: A History of the Negro in America, 1619-1964.* rev. ed., Baltimore, Maryland: Penguin Books, 1968.

Bodein, Vernon Parker. *The Social Gospel of Walter Rauschenbusch and its Relation to Religious Education.* ("Yale Studies in Religious Education," vol. 16) New Haven: Yale University Press, 1944.

Bowman, Rufus D. *The Church of the Brethren and War, 1708-1941.* Elgin, Illinois: Brethren Publishing House, 1944.

Braeman, John, Robert H. Bremer and Everett Walters, eds. *Change and Continuity in Twentieth-Century America.* Columbus: Ohio State University Press, 1964.

Brauer, Jerald C. *Protestantism in America.* Philadelphia: The Westminster Press, 1953.

Broderick, Francis L. *Right Reverend New Dealer: John A. Ryan.* New York: The Macmillan Company, 1963.

Brown, William Adams. *Christian Theology in Outline.* New York: Charles Scribner's Sons, 1906.

————. *Church and State in Contemporary America.* New York: Charles Scribner's Sons, 1936.

————. *The Church in America.* New York: The Macmillan Company, 1922.

————. *A Teacher and His Times.* New York: Charles Scribner's Sons, 1940.

Burr, Nelson R. *A Critical Bibliography of Religion in America.* In collaboration with eds. James Ward Smith and A. Leland Jamison. ("Religion in American Life," vol. 4, pts. 1, 2; pts. 3, 4, 5.) Princeton: Princeton University Press, 1961.

Carroll, Henry K., ed. *Federal Council Year Book.* New York: Missionary Education Movement of the United States and Canada, 1917.

Carter, Paul A. *The Decline and Revival of the Social Gospel.* Ithaca, New York: Cornell University Press, 1956.

Cauthen, Kenneth. *The Impact of American Religious Liberalism.* New York and Evanston: Harper and Row, Publishers, 1962.

Cavert, Samuel McCrea. *The American Churches in the Ecumenical Movement: 1900-1968.* New York: Association Press, 1968.

Chambers, Frank P. *The War Behind the War, 1914-1918.* New York: Harcourt, Brace and Company. 1939.

Coffin, Henry Sloane. *A Half Century of Union Theological Seminary, 1896-1945.* New York: Charles Scribner's Sons, 1954.

Commager, Henry Steele. *The American Mind.* New Haven: Yale University Press, 1950.

Cramer, Clarence H. *Newton D. Baker: A Biography.* Cleveland and New York: The World Publishing Company, 1961.

Creel, George. *How We Advertised America.* New York and London: Harper and Brothers Publishers, 1920.

Curti, Merle E. *Peace or War: The American Struggle, 1636-1936.* New York: W.W. Norton and Company, 1936.

Daniels, Josephus. *The Wilson Era: Years of War and After, 1917-1923.* Chapel Hill: The University of North Carolina Press, 1946.

Dohen, Dorothy. *Nationalism and American Catholicism.* New York: Sheed and Ward, 1967.

Douglass, Harlan Paul. *Church Unity Movements in the United States.* New York: Institute of Social and Religious Research, 1934.

Douglass, Harlan Paul, and Edmund deS. Brunner. *The Protestant Church as a Social Institution.* New York and London: Harper and Brothers, 1935.

Drury, Clifford M. *The History of the Chaplains Corps, United States Navy.* 3 vols. Washington: U.S. Government Printing Office, 1949.

Dulles, Foster Rhea. *The American Red Cross: A History.* New York: Harper and Brothers, 1950.

————. *America's Rise to World Power, 1898-1954.* New York: Harper and Brothers, 1954.

Eddy, George Sherwood. *The Right to Fight: The Moral Grounds of War.* New York: Association Press, 1918.

Egan, Maurice Francis, and John B. Kennedy. *The Knights of Columbus in Peace and War.* New Haven, Connecticut: The Knights of Columbus, 1920.

Ellis, John Tracy. *American Catholicism.* Chicago: The University of Chicago Press, 1956.

————. *The Life of James Cardinal Gibbons.* 2 vols. Milwaukee: Bruce Publishing Company, 1952.

Ellis, John Tracy, and Robert Trisco. *A Guide to American Catholic History.* Second Edition. Santa Barbara, California: ABC-Clio, 1982.

Faunce, William H.P. *The New Horizon of State and Church.* New York: The Macmillan Company, 1918.

————. *Religion and War.* New York: The Abingdon Press, 1918.

Fosdick, Harry Emerson. *The Challenge of the Present Crisis.* Philadelphia: American Baptist Publishing Society, 1917.

————. *Finishing the War.* New York: Association Press, 1919.

————. *The Living of These Days.* New York: Harper and Brothers, 1956.

Fosdick, Raymond B. *Chronicle of a Generation, An Autobiography.* New York: Harper and Brothers Publishers, 1958.

Fosdick, Raymond, and Edward F. Allen. *Keeping Our Fighters Fit.* New York: The Century Company, 1918.

Frank, Emma L. comp. *The Chaplaincy in the Armed Services.* (A Preliminary Bibliography) Oberlin, Ohio: The Library, Oberlin Graduate School of Theology, 1945.

Franklin, John Hope. *From Slavery to Freedom: A History of American Negroes.* Third Edition. New York: Alfred A. Knopf, 1967.

Gibbons, James Cardinal. *Catholic Loyalty.* New York: The Paulist Press, 1917.

Gill, Charles O., and Gifford Pinchot. *The Country Church.* New York: The Macmillan Company, 1913.

Gillard, John T., S.S.J. *The Catholic Church and the American Negro.* Baltimore: St. Joseph's Society Press, 1929. Reprinted by Johnson Reprint Company, 1968.

Guild, Roy B. ed. *The Manual of Inter-Church Work.* New York: The Federal Council of the Churches of Christ in America, 1917.

Harris, Frederick ed. *Service With Fighting Men.* 2 vols. New York: Association Press, 1922.

Hartzler, Jonas S. *Mennonites in the World War.* Scottdale, Pennsylvania: Mennonite Publishing House, 1922.

Heaton, John L., comp. *Cobb of "The World."* New York: E.P. Dutton and Company, 1924.

Herberg, Will, and others. *Religious Perspectives in American Culture.* Edited by James Ward Smith and A. Leland Jamison. ("Religion in American Life," vol. 2.) Princeton: Princeton University Press, 1961.

Hershberger, Guy F. *War, Peace, and Nonresistance.* Scottdale, Pennsylvania: The Herald Press, 1944.

Hillis, Newell Dwight. *German Atrocities.* New York: Fleming H. Revell Company, 1918.

Hofstadter, Richard. *The Age of Reform: From Bryan to F.D.R.* New York: Vintage Books, 1960.

Honeywell, Roy J. *Chaplains of the United States Army.* Washington, D.C.: United States Government Printing Office, 1958.

Hopkins, C. Howard. *History of the Y.M.C.A. in North America.* New York: Association Press, 1951.

_____. *John R. Mott: 1865-1955.* Grand Rapids: William B. Eerdmans Publishing Company, 1979.

_____. *The Rise of the Social Gospel in American Protestantism, 1865-1915.* ("Yale Studies in Religious Education," vol. 14.) New Haven: Yale University Press, 1940.

Hudson, Winthrop S. *American Protestantism.* Chicago: The University of Chicago Press, 1961.

_____. *Religion in America.* New York: Charles Scribner's Sons, 1965.

Hutchison, John A. *We Are Not Divided.* New York: Round Table Press, Inc., 1941.

Johnson, Donald. *The Challenge to American Freedoms: World War I and the Rise of the American Civil Liberties Union.* Lexington, Kentucky: University of Kentucky Press, 1963.

Jorgensen, Daniel B. *The Service of Chaplains to Army Air Units,*

1917-1946. ("Air Force Chaplains," vol 1.) Washington, D.C.: U.S. Government Printing Office, 1961.

Keppel, David. *FPK: An Intimate Biography of Frederick Paul Keppel.* Washington: Privately Printed, 1950.

Keppel, Frederick P. *Some War-Time Lessons.* New York: Columbia University Press, 1920.

Lacy, Creighton. *Frank Mason North.* Nashville: Abingdon Press, 1967.

Lawler, Loretta. *Full Circle.* Washington, D.C.: Catholic University of America Press, 1951.

Lawrence, William. *Memories of a Happy Life.* Boston and New York: Houghton, Mifflin Company, 1926.

Lee, Robert. *The Social Sources of Church Unity.* New York: Abingdon Press, 1960.

Link, Arthur S., ed. *The Impact of World War I.* New York, Evanston, and London: Harper and Row Publishers, 1969.

_____. *Wilson: Campaigns for Progressivism and Peace, 1916-1917.* Princeton: Princeton University Press, 1965.

_____. *Wilson: The New Freedom.* Princeton: Princeton University Press, 1956.

Lynch, Frederick. *The Christian Unity Movement in America*: London: James Clark and Co., Limited, 1922.

_____. *President Wilson and the Moral Aims of the War.* New York: Fleming H. Revell Company, 1918.

Macfarland, Charles S. *Across the Years.* New York: The Macmillan Company, 1936.

_____. *Christian Unity in the Making.* New York: The Federal Council of the Churches of Christ in America, 1948.

_____, ed. *The Churches of Christ in Council.* ("Library of Christian Cooperation," vol 1.) New York: Missionary Education Movement, 1917.

_____, ed. *The Churches of Christ in Time of War.* New York: Missionary Education Movement of the United States and Canada, 1917.

Mackenzie, William Douglas. *Christian Ethics in the World War.* New York: Association Press, 1918.

Maritain, Jacques. *Man and the State.* Chicago: The University of Chicago Press, 1951.

Mathews, Basil. *John R. Mott: World Citizen.* New York and London: Harper and Brothers Publishers, 1934.

Mathews, Shailer. *Patriotism and Religion.* New York: The Macmillan Company, 1918.

May, Henry F. *Protestant Churches and Industrial America.* New York: Harper and Brothers Publishers, 1949.

Mayo, Katherine. *That Damn "Y".* Boston: Houghton Mifflin Company, 1920.

McConnell, Francis J. *By the Way.* New York: Abingdon-Cokesbury Press, 1952.

_____. *Democratic Christianity*. New York: The Macmillan Company, 1919.

McLoughlin, William G., Jr. *Billy Sunday Was His Real Name*. Chicago: The University of Chicago Press, 1955.

Mead, Sidney E. *The Lively Experiment: The Shaping of Christianity in America*. New York: Harper and Row, 1963.

Meyer, Donald B. *The Protestant Search for Political Realism, 1919-1941*. Berkeley: University of California Press, 1960.

Miller, Albert R.H. *The Church and War*. St. Louis, Missouri: The Bethany Press, 1931.

Miller, Robert Moats. *American Protestantism and Social Issues, 1919-1939*. Chapel Hill: The University of North Carolina Press, 1958.

Moellering, Ralph L. *Modern War and the American Churches*. New York: The American Press, 1956.

Moton, Robert R. *Finding a Way Out*. Garden City, New York: Doubleday, Page, and Company, 1921.

Mott, John R. *The Young Men's Christian Association*. ("The Addresses and Papers of John R. Mott," vol. 4.) New York: Association Press, 1947.

Muelder, Walter G. *Methodism and Society in the Twentieth Century*. ("Methodism and Society," vol. 2.) New York: Abingdon Press, 1961.

Myrdal, Gunnar. *An American Dilemma: The Negro Problem and American Democracy*. New York and Evanston: Harper and Row, 1944, 1962.

Nichols, James Hastings. *Democracy and the Churches*. Philadelphia: The Westminster Press, 1951.

Niebuhr, H. Richard. *The Kingdom of God in America*. New York: Harper and Brothers, 1959.

Niebuhr, H. Richard, and others. *The Shaping of American Religion*. James Ward Smith and A. Leland Jamison, eds. ("Religion in American Life," vol. 1.) Princeton: Princeton University Press, 1961.

Niebuhr, Reinhold. *Leaves from the Notebook of a Tamed Cynic*. New York: Meridian Books, 1957.

O'Grady, John. *Catholic Charities in the United States*. Washington, D.C.: National Conference of Catholic Charities, 1930.

Olmstead, Clifton E. *History of Religion in the United States*. Englewood Cliffs, New Jersey: Prentice-Hall, Inc., 1960.

Osborne, William A. *The Segregated Covenant: Race Relations and American Catholics*. New York: Herder and Herder, 1967.

Page, Kirby. *The Sword or the Cross*. Chicago: The Christian Century Press, 1921.

Palmer, Frederick. *Newton D. Baker: America at War*. New York: Dodd, Mead and Company, 1931.

Paxson, Frederick L. *America at War, 1917-1918*. Boston: Houghton, Mifflin Company, 1939.

Pershing, John J. *My Experiences in the World War*. 2 vols. New York: Frederick A. Stokes Company, 1931.

Peterson, Horace C., and Gilbert C. Fite. *Opponents of War, 1917-1918.* Madison, Wisconsin: The University of Wisconsin Press, 1957.

Poling, Daniel A. *Huts in Hell.* Boston: Christian Endeavor World, 1918.

Rauschenbusch, Walter. *A Theology for the Social Gospel.* New York: The Macmillan Company, 1917.

Renton, Margaret, ed. *War-Time Agencies of the Churches: Directory and Handbook.* New York: General War-Time Commission of the Churches, 1919.

Rihbany, Abraham M. *Militant America and Jesus Christ.* Boston: Houghton Mifflin Company, 1917.

Roth, Jack J., ed. *World War I: A Turning Point in Modern History.* New York: Alfred A. Knopf, 1967.

Rouse, Ruth, and Stephen C. Neill, eds. *A History of the Ecumenical Movement, 1517-1948.* Philadelphia: The Westminster Press, 1954.

Rowe, Henry K. *The History of Religion in the United States.* New York: The Macmillan Company, 1924.

Rudwick, Elliott M. *Race Riot at East St. Louis, July 2, 1917.* Cleveland and New York: The World Publishing Company, 1964.

Ryan, John A. *Social Doctrine in Action: A Personal History.* New York and London: Harper and Brothers Publishers, 1941.

Scheiber, Harry N. *The Wilson Administration and Civil Liberties, 1917-1921.* Ithaca, New York: Cornell University Press, 1960.

Schneider, Herbert W. *Religion in 20th Century America.* Cambridge: Harvard University Press, 1952.

Scott, Emmett J. *Negro Migration During the War.* ("Preliminary Economic Studies of the War," no. 16.) New York: Oxford University Press, 1920.

_____. *Scott's Official History of the American Negro in the World War.* Chicago: Homewood Press, 1919.

Seidler, Murray B. *Norman Thomas, Respectable Rebel.* Syracuse, New York: Syracuse University Press, 1961.

Sharpe, Dores R. *Walter Rauschenbusch.* New York: The Macmillan Company, 1942.

Sheerin, John B., C.S.P. *Never Look Back: The Career and Concerns of John J. Burke.* New York: Paulist Press, 1975.

Slosson, Preston W. *The Great Crusade and After, 1914-1928.* ("A History of American Life," vol. 12.) New York: The Macmillan Company, 1939.

Smith, Daniel M. *The Great Departure.* New York: John Wiley and Sons, Inc., 1965.

Smith, Fred B. *I Remember.* New York: Fleming H. Revell Company, 1936.

Sneath, E. Hershey, ed. *Religion and the War.* New Haven: Yale University Press, 1918.

Speer, Robert E. *The Christian Man, the Church and the War.* New York: The Macmillan Company, 1918.

_____. *The New Opportunity of the Church.* New York: The Macmillan Company, 1919.

Sperry, Willard L. *Religion in America.* New York: The Macmillan Company, 1946.

Stokes, Anson Phelps. *Church and State in the United States.* 3 vols. New York: Harper and Brothers, 1950.

Sweet, William Warren. *The American Churches, An Interpretation.* New York: Abingdon-Cokesbury Press, 1948.

———. *The Story of Religion in America.* rev. ed. New York: Harper and Brothers, 1950.

Thomas, Norman. *The Conscientious Objector in America.* New York: B.W. Huebsch, Inc., 1923.

Tippy, Worth M. *The Church and the Great War.* New York: Fleming H. Revell Company, 1918.

The Union Theological Seminary: Alumni Directory, 1836-1958. New York: Union Theological Seminary, 1958.

Weeks, Estella T. *Reconstruction Programs.* New York: The Womans Press, 1919.

Wheeler, W. Reginald. *A Man Sent From God.* Westwood, New Jersey: Fleming H. Revell, 1956.

White, William Allen. *The Autobiography of William Allen White.* New York: The Macmillan Company, 1946.

Wiley, S. Wirt. *History of Y.M.C.A.—Church Relations in the United States.* New York: Association Press, 1944.

Williams, Charles H. *Sidelights on Negro Soldiers.* Boston: B.J. Brimmer Company, 1923.

Williams, Michael. *American Catholics and the War.* New York: The Macmillan Company, 1921.

Willoughby, William F. *Government Organization in War Time and After.* New York: D. Appleton and Company, 1919.

Wilson, Woodrow. *The Public Papers of Woodrow Wilson.* Ray Stannard Baker and William E. Dodd, eds. 6 vols. New York: Harper and Brothers Publishers, 1925-1927.

Work, Monroe N., ed. *Negro Year Book, 1918-1919.* Tuskegee Institute, Alabama: The Negro Year Book Publishing Company, 1919.

Zabriskie, Alexander C. *Bishop Brent: Crusader for Christian Unity.* Philadelphia: The Westminster Press, 1948.

IV. Articles

A. Signed

Abell, Aaron I. "The Catholic Church and Social Problems in the World War I Era," *Mid-America* 30 (July, 1948), 139-51.

Abrams, Ray H. "The Churches and the Clergy in World War II," *The Annals of the American Academy of Political and Social Science* 256 (March, 1948), 110-19.

Althomar. "American Protestantism Faces the War Task," *Zion's Herald* 96 (October 2, 1918), 1262.

Anthony, Alfred Williams. "Some Compensations of War," *The Missionary Review of the World* 41 (November, 1918), 811–17.

———. "A War Task for Industrial Workers," *The Missionary Review of the World* 41 (November, 1918), 836–39.

Armitage, Clyde. "Chaplains Get Results," *The Homiletic Review* 76 (August, 1918), 100–101.

———. "What to Preach to Soldiers," *The Methodist Review* (New York) 101 (November, 1918), 962–65.

Atkinson, Henry A. "Christian Unity at Work," *The Congregationalist and Christian World* 102 (October 18, 1917), 518.

Auerbach, Jerold S. "Woodrow Wilson's 'Predictions' to Frank Cobb: Words Historians Should Doubt Ever Got Spoken," *The Journal of American History* 54 (December, 1967), 608–17.

Bainton, Roland H. "The Churches and War: Historic Attitudes Toward Christian Participation," *Social Action* 11 (January 15, 1945), 5–71.

Bridgman, Howard A. "Putting the Church Behind the Nation," *The Congregationalist and Christian World*, 102 (May 17, 1917), 630–31, 638.

Brown, William Adams. "The Church's Message for the Coming Time," *The Homiletic Review*, 75 (April, 1918), 272–73.

———. "The Contribution of the Church to the Democracy of the Future," *Religious Education* 13 (October, 1918), 343–48.

———. "The Place of Repentance in a Nation at War," *The North American Student* 6 (May, 1918), 365–66.

———. "The Service of the General War-Time Commission," *Federal Council Bulletin* 2 (June, 1919), 110–13.

———. "The Work of the War-Time Commission of the Church," *The Christian Work* 105 (November 9, 1918), 543–45.

———. "The Work of the War-Time Commission of the Church," *The Christian Work* 105 (November 16, 1918), 575–76.

Brunner, Edmund deS. "A Year of Cooperative Work in the Rural Church Field," *Federal Council Bulletin* 2 (February, 1919), 30–31.

Burke, John J. "The Catholic Federation Convention," *The Outlook* 113 (August 30, 1916), 1030–32.

———. "The Historical Attitude of the Church Toward Nationalism," *Catholic Historical Review* 14 (April, 1928), 69–80.

———. "Special Catholic Activities in War Service," *The Annals of the American Academy of Political and Social Science* 79 (September, 1918), 213–20.

Butsch, Joseph, S.S.J. "Negro Catholics in the United States," *Catholic Historical Review* 3 (April, 1917), 33–51.

Clark, Kenneth B. "Morale of the Negro on the Home Front: World War I and II," *The Journal of Negro Education* 12 (Summer, 1943), 417–28.

Craiger, Captain Sherman M. "Emergency Housing for War-Time Industrial Workers," *The American Review of Reviews* 57 (January, 1918), 68–72.

Cramer, W. Stuart, "National Service Headquarters," *Reformed Church Messenger* 87 (September 19, 1918), 14–15.

_____. "National Service Headquarters," *Reformed Church Messenger* 87 (November 28, 1918), 19.

Cross, George. "Federation of the Christian Churches in America—An Interpretation," *The American Journal of Theology* 23 (April, 1919), 129–45.

Cuddy, Edward. "Pro-Germanism and American Catholicism, 1914–1917," *Catholicism in America*, Philip Gleason, ed. New York, Evanston, and London: Harper and Row Publishers, 1970, pp. 92–100.

Davis, Allen F. "Welfare, Reform and World War I," *American Quarterly* 19 (Fall, 1967), 516–33.

Donald, Henderson H. "The Negro Migration of 1916–1918," *The Journal of Negro History* 6 (October, 1921), 383–498.

Ellis, John Tracy. "Contemporary American Catholicism in the Light of History," *The Critic* 24 (June-July, 1966), 8–19.

_____. "The Spirit of Cardinal Gibbons," *Records of the American Catholic Historical Society of Philadelphia* 76 (1965), 14–20.

Ernst, Eldon G. "The Interchurch World Movement and the Great Steel Strike of 1919–1920," *Church History* 39 (June, 1970), 212–23.

Faunce, William H.P. "The Clear and Urgent Duty of the Church in the Present World Crisis," *The Homiletic Review* 73 (January, 1917), 20.

Fisher, Miles Mark. "The Negro Church and the World-War," *The Journal of Religion* 5 (September, 1925), 483–99.

Fosdick, Raymond B. "The War and Navy Departments Commission on Training Camp Activities," *The Annals of the American Academy of Political and Social Science* 79 (September, 1918), 130–42.

Frazier, John B. "The Kind of Chaplains the Navy Wants," *Federal Council Bulletin* 1 (November, 1918), 18–19.

Froncek, Tom. "American Catholics and the American Negro," *Catholic Mind* 64 (January, 1966), 4–11.

Fulton, Hugh K. "Training Army Chaplains," *The Outlook* 120 (October 2, 1918), 167–68.

Gibbons, James Cardinal. "Patriotism and Politics," *The North American Review* 154 (April, 1892), 385–400.

Guilday, Peter. "American Catholics and the War," *The Historical Outlook* 9 (1918), 431–32.

Hicks, Granville. "The Parsons and the War," *The American Mercury* 10 (February, 1927), 129–42.

Hirschfeld, Charles. "The Transformation of American Life," *World War I: A Turning Point in Modern History*, Jack J. Roth, ed. New York: Alfred A. Knopf, 1967, pp. 63–81.

Holmes, John Haynes. "Belated Aid for Objectors," *The New Republic* 18 (March 15, 1919), 217–18.

Keppel, Frederick P. "The War Department and the Chaplains," *Federal Council Bulletin* 1 (November, 1918), 21–22.

Kerby, William J. "Re-Education by War," *The Catholic World* 106 (January, 1918), 451–61.

Lancaster, James L. "The Protestant Churches and the Fight for Ratification of the Versailles Treaty," *Public Opinion Quarterly* 21 (1967), 597-619.

Lapp, John A. "The Campaign for Civic Instruction," *National Catholic War Council Bulletin* 1 (July, 1919), 11-12.

Leete, W.W. "The Church and the Camp," *The Congregationalist and Advance* 103 (April 11, 1918), 462.

Leuchtenburg, William E. "The New Deal and the Analogue of War," *Change and Continuity in Twentieth-Century America*, John Braeman, Robert H. Bremner, and Everett Walters, eds. Columbus: Ohio State University Press, 1964, pp. 81-143.

Lowrie, Stephen. "The Church on the Eve of the Great Settlement," *The Nation* 107 (December 21, 1918), 771-72.

Lynch, Frederick. "In Time of War, Prepare for Peace," *The Christian Work* 103 (September 29, 1917), 367-68.

Macfarland, Charles S. "The Churches and the Conscientious Objectors," *The New Republic* 18 (April 12, 1919), 351.

_____. "The Clear and Urgent Duty of the Church in the Present World Crisis," *The Homiletic Review* 73 (January, 1917), 24-25.

_____. "Shoulder to Shoulder in Christian Service," *The Congregationalist and Advance* 103 (November 21, 1918), 541-42.

_____. "Spiritual Unity Through Sacrificial Suffering," *The Survey* 39 (December 29, 1917), 357-59.

Macfarland, Charles S., and Herbert Croly. "American Protestant Churches During the War," *The New Republic* 30 (March 29, 1922), 140-43.

Mackenzie, William Douglas. "Shall Ministers Become Soldiers?" *The Congregationalist and Advance* 103 (July 4, 1918), 23.

Mathews, Shailer. "Can We Love Our Enemies?" *The Biblical World* 51 (June, 1918), 321-22.

_____. "Christianizing Patriotism," *The Biblical World* 50 (July, 1917), 1-2.

_____. "The Church and the War," *The Biblical World* 49 (June, 1917), 329-30.

_____. "The Conscientious Objector," *The Biblical World* 50 (December, 1917), 329-30.

McDowell, William F. "The Church in a World at War," *The Methodist Review* 101 (July, 1918), 507-23.

McKeown, Elizabeth. "Apologia for an American Catholicism: The Petition and Report of the National Catholic Welfare Council to Pius XI, April 25, 1922," *Church History* 43 (December, 1974), 514-28.

_____. "The National Bishops' Conference: An Analysis of Its Origins," *The Catholic Historical Review* 66 (October, 1980), 565-83.

Mecklin, John E. "The War and the Dilemma of the Christian Ethic," *The American Journal of Theology* 23 (January, 1919), 14-40.

Moody, Paul D. "The Precedent of the First World War," *Religion of Soldier and Sailor*, Willard L. Sperry, ed. Cambridge: Harvard University Press, 1945, pp. 3-20.

Morris, George P. "The War-Time Commission of the Churches at Washington," *The Christian Work* 105 (October 12, 1918), 427ff.

Murphy, May M. "The National Service School for Women," *National Catholic War Council Bulletin* 1 (June, 1919), 12.

Murphy, Sara P. "Lending a Hand to the Chaplains," *National Catholic War Council Bulletin* 1 (June-July, 1920), 3.

North, Eric. "Training Chaplains for the Army," *The Homiletic Review* 76 (August, 1918), 107-8.

Piper, John F., Jr. "The American Churches in World War I," *Journal of the American Academy of Religion* 38 (June, 1970), 147-55.

_____. "Father John J. Burke, C.S.P., and the Turning Point in American Catholic History," *Records of the American Catholic Historical Society of Philadelphia* 92 (March-December, 1981), 101-13.

_____. "Robert E. Speer: Christian Statesman in War and Peace," *Journal of Presbyterian History* 47 (September, 1969), 201-25.

Radcliffe, Wallace. "Presbyterian Chaplains," *The Christian Work* 105 (November 16, 1918), 580-81.

Rupp, Paul B. "The Making of an Army Padre," *Reformed Church Messenger* 87 (August 8, 1918), 6-7.

Ryan, John A. "Freedom of Speech in Wartime," *The Catholic World* 106 (February, 1918), 577-88.

Seabrook, John H. "Bishop Manning and World War I," *Historical Magazine of the Protestant Episcopal Church* 36 (December, 1967), 301-21.

Smith, Frank W. "Work With Drafted Men Before They Leave for Camp," *The Christian Advocate* (New York) 93 (January 31, 1918), 156.

Speer, Robert E. "The Church and the World Today," *The Missionary Review of the World* 40 (September, 1917), 667-73.

_____. "Looking Through the War Clouds," *The Missionary Review of the World* 41 (January, 1918), 11-15.

_____. "The Witness Bearing of the Church to the Nation," *Federal Council Bulletin* 2 (June, 1919), 100-101.

Spencer, Claudius B. "American Protestantism Takes Action As to the War," *Central Christian Advocate* 30 (May 23, 1917), 5-7.

Sweets, Henry H. "A Government School for Chaplains," *The Presbyterian* 88 (October 3, 1918), 22.

Tamblyn, George O. "The Inter-Church Emergency Campaign," *Federal Council Bulletin* 2 (January, 1919), 24.

Tawney, Richard H. "The Church and Industry," *The New Republic* 26 (April 27, 1921), 255-57.

Thirkield, Wilbur P. "No Longer 'Nigger,' But American Negro," *The Christian Advocate* (New York) 93 (October 31, 1918), 1386.

Thomas, Norman. "Conscientious Objector Replies," *The New Republic* 11 (July 7, 1917), 274-75.

_____. "Justice to War's Heretics," *The Nation* 107 (November 9, 1918), 547-49.

_____. "War's Heretics," *The Survey* 41 (December 7, 1918), 319–23.

Thomas, Norman, and others. "The Religion of Free Men," *The New Republic* 11 (May 26, 1917), 109–11.

Tippy, Worth. "Conditions in the Reserve Officers' Training Camp, Plattsburg," *The Christian Advocate* (New York) 92 (July 12, 1917), 702.

_____. "The Latest Concerning Army and Navy Chaplains," *The Homiletic Review* 75 (March, 1918), 197–98.

_____. "Logging Camps of the Pacific Northwest," *Federal Council Bulletin* 2 (April, 1919), 64–65.

_____. "The New Chaplains at Work," *The Homiletic Review* 75 (February, 1918), 99–102.

_____. "What Army and Navy Chaplains Are Doing and May Do," *The Homiletic Review* 75 (January, 1918), 9–14.

Tobias, Channing H. "Shall America Be Made Safe for Black Men?" *The North American Student* 6 (March 1918), 266–67.

Tyson, Levering. "Frederick P. Keppel of Columbia," *The American Review of Reviews* 57 (May, 1918), 497–98.

Washburn, Henry B. "The Army Chaplains," *Papers of the American Society of Church History*, Series 2, 7 (1923), 1–23.

Wilhelm, Donald. "Dean Keppel in the War Department," *The American Review of Reviews* 57 (May, 1918), 498–99.

Wolgemuth, Kathleen L. "Woodrow Wilson and Federal Segregation," *The Journal of Negro History* 44 (April, 1959), 158–73.

Young, Theodore B. "'Camp Upton,' National Army Cantonment," *The Christian Advocate* (New York) 93 (February 14, 1918), 208–9.

B. Unsigned.
Catholic Mind, 1917.
The Catholic World, 1917, 1918, 1919.
The Christian Advocate (New York), 1917, 1918.
The Congregationalist and Advance, 1918.
The Congregationalist and Christian World, 1917.
Evangelical Weekly Letter, 1919.
Federal Council Bulletin, 1918, 1919, 1941.
The Homiletic Review, 1918.
The Journal of Negro History, 1919.
The Lutheran, 1917.
National Catholic War Council Bulletin, 1919, 1920.
The Nation, 1918.
The New York *Times*, 1918.
The Presbyterian, 1917, 1918.
The Survey, 1918.

Index